Virginia and
the Great War

Virginia and the Great War

Mobilization, Supply and Combat, 1914–1919

LYNN RAINVILLE

McFarland & Company, Inc., Publishers
Jefferson, North Carolina

ISBN (print) 978-1-4766-7192-5
ISBN (ebook) 978-1-4766-3147-9

Library of Congress cataloguing data are available

British Library cataloguing data are available

© 2018 Lynn Rainville. All rights reserved

No part of this book may be reproduced or transmitted in any form or by any means, electronic or mechanical, including photocopying or recording, or by any information storage and retrieval system, without permission in writing from the publisher.

Front cover photograph of World War I Memorial Carillon in Richmond, Virginia © 2018 traveler1116/iStock

Printed in the United States of America

*McFarland & Company, Inc., Publishers
Box 611, Jefferson, North Carolina 28640
www.mcfarlandpub.com*

To the Virginians of 1917–1918 who served
in the Great War and the Virginians
of 2017–2018 who planned exhibitions,
lectures and online commemorations
to remember the sacrifices of a century ago.

Table of Contents

Acknowledgments   viii
Preface   1

1. Provisions   5
2. Participants   39
3. Vestiges   82
4. Remains   115
5. Homecomings   152
6. Commemorations   177

Epilogue   210
Chapter Notes   215
Bibliography   233
Index   241

Acknowledgments

Half of this book derives from the research that I uncovered about Virginia's role in the Great War. The other half comes from the hundreds of conversations, thousands of emails, and countless chance encounters that I've had over the past three years. My interest in the "war to end all wars" began in an American graveyard along the Western Front in rural France. I owe a debt of thanks to the organizers and funders of that trip: Andrew Mink, University of North Carolina, Chapel Hill, and the American Battle Monuments Commission, especially Tim Nosal. While on that two-week trip in 2014 to study the graves and memorials to the American Expeditionary Force at the Meuse-Argonne American Cemetery, I was fortunate to cross paths with and learn from the cemetery's superintendent, Dave Bedford, and from a dozen Virginia and North Carolina high school teachers who were researching elements of the site's history to integrate into their classrooms back home.

After I returned to my home in Charlottesville, I began a project to document World War I memorials in Virginia. Given the Old Dominion's prominent role in the American Civil War, I didn't expect to find that many statues or plaques to the Great War. To my surprise, and with the help of colleagues at the University of Richmond, the Virginia Foundation for the Humanities (VFH), the Department of Historic Resources (DHR), Old Dominion University, and the Library of Virginia, I located over two hundred memorials. Dozens of Virginians submitted photographs of and historic background about these memorials. I especially want to thank Steve Miller, Bert Dunkerly, Brian Groban, and Nancy Sorrells for their help with images that appear in this book. The process of photographing and recording information from dozens of towns and cities was the catalyst behind this book: to document the experiences of thousands of Virginians who played a role in the conflict, at home and abroad.

Other people who contributed photographs, letters, or locations of the Virginia memorials are thanked on the project website: www.lynn rainville.org/ww1-memorials. Special thanks are due to Sweet Briar College, which supported an early version of the website and provided support for the project via the Tusculum Institute for Public History, where I have served as the director for eight years. I received funding for the website from the VFH and intellectual support from several colleagues, most notably Eric Yellin (associate professor of history, University of Richmond) and his student Matt Digan; Steve Miller (for his comprehensive photo albums of war-related sites); Gene Shultz (for his work on Winchester memorials); J. Jefferson Looney (for his archival research into the War Commission); Alexander F. Barnes (chief warrant officer 4, retired); Marc Holma (architectural historian, DHR); Maura Hametz (professor of history, Old Dominion University) and two of her student researchers, Elijah Palmer and Justin Hall; and Warren Hofstra (professor of history, Shenandoah University) and the students in his World War I class.

Other individuals took me on much-appreciated tours of the remnants of World War I places and events: Kate Christen (graduate and professional training manager, Smithsonian Conservation Biology Institute) and her research intern, Meredith Bowhers, who took me on a tour of the old Front Royal Remount Depot; Patty Conte (cultural resource manager, Regional Archaeological Curation Facility, Fort Lee) and her colleagues who took me on a tour of the World War I–era trenches at Fort Lee; Sue Woodward (who shared her knowledge of historic Suffolk); and Jesse Smith (curator, Virginia War Memorial). Other colleagues answered queries and shared their research about the war or relatives who served: Chris Garcia (Virginia War Museum), Heather Sutton (education coordinator, Woodrow Wilson Presidential Library and Museum), Amanda Williams (education manager, MacArthur Memorial), Terry Sharrer (curator of Health Sciences, Smithsonian Institution), Gordon Morse (freelance speech writer and newspaper contributor), Beth O'Leary (retired curator, Virginia Museum of Fine Arts), Peter Broadbent (an attorney who helped to establish the Virginia World War I Commemoration Foundation, where I serve as one of the founding directors), Roger Christman (senior state records archivist, Library of Virginia), Barbara C. Batson (exhibitions coordinator, Library of Virginia), Tom Kapsidelis (fellow, VFH), Elaine Taylor (director, Louisa County Historical Society), Evelyn Edson (president, Scottsville Museum), Douglas K. Harvey (museum director, Lynchburg Museum System), and Marc Marsocci (director of digital services, Mariners' Museum).

Acknowledgments

In the fall of 2014, upon my return from France, I was welcomed into an all-volunteer group of enthusiasts in a Richmond-based "World War I Committee." Headed by Betsy Carr, we plotted ways to increase awareness about the upcoming centennial of America's entry into the war. I was honored to join the many passionate individuals who worked to host lectures, conferences, and events in their communities. Many of these committee members provided me with invaluable leads as I was writing this book, especially Beth O'Leary, Peter Broadbent, Edwin Fountain, Al Barnes, Brian Groban (who deserves kudos for creating a popular page on Facebook titled "Virginia in the Great War"), Marc Holma, John Metz, Andrew Talkov, and Parker Agelasto, among others. In 2016, the General Assembly of Virginia combined this volunteer effort with an existing commission and created the Virginia World War I and World War II Commemoration Commission. Thanks to Cheryl Jackson (executive director), Rusty Nix (communications manager), and Lily Jones (research assistant) for their support of this book.

In the fall of 2016 I was honored to be named a fellow at the Virginia Foundation for the Humanities. I am very grateful for the one-year residency that enabled me to finish this book. I especially indebted to Jeanne Siler, Carolyn Cades, David Bearinger, Trey Mitchell, Sarah McConnell, and Rob Vaughan for their support of my research while I was in residence.

Research into Virginia's war years would have been much harder without Arthur Kyle Davis's seven-volume series from the Virginia War History Commission (published in the 1920s). The archival documentation for those books has been curated by the Library of Virginia for almost a century. In addition, the Virginia Historical Society (VHS) and its archivists have done a wonderful job preserving the papers and artifacts from this period. I am very grateful for the staff at both institutions for helping me with my research requests and for serving as stewards for these irreplaceable materials. Thanks to Kathleen Placidi (grants officer, Sweet Briar College) for her help in writing a successful application for an Andrew W. Mellon Research Fellowship at the VHS, where I conducted archival research for this book. I appreciate the invaluable help from the VHS staff, especially John McClure (reference department manager of the library), Frances Pollard (chief librarian), and Graham Dozier (editor, *Virginia Magazine of History and Biography*).

I am indebted to the individuals who took the time to read through early drafts of the manuscript and provide insightful and valuable comments. I take responsibility for the remaining errors while recognizing that their contributions improved the final product immeasurably. These talented editors and content experts include Marc Holma, David Bearinger, Alexander F. Barnes, Minal Hajratwala, Thomas Wells, and Roger H. Rainville. I am especially grateful to George Roupe for editing help.

Preface

One Sunday afternoon the heir to the Austro-Hungarian throne and, mistakenly, his wife were assassinated by a teenage Bosnian-Serb nationalist. The next day, after the news was disseminated via telegram across the globe, the *Richmond Times-Dispatch* published a touching family portrait of the murdered Archduke Franz Ferdinand posing with his daughter, one arm clutching her securely to his side. The article related the chronology of the "tragedy," which included a failed attempt to bomb the archduke and his motorcade before the successful shooting by Gavrilo Princip. Richmonders read about how the sad events of June 28, 1914, were the latest in a series of deaths, executions, and suicides within the Hapsburg family.[1] For decades, Virginia papers had been keeping their readers abreast of the drama associated with Franz Joseph I's reign as emperor of Austria and king of Hungary, Croatia, and Bohemia. Up until the summer of 1914, these stories were often relegated to the back pages of Sunday papers or the "News and Gossip from Foreign Courts and Capitals" section and seemed of little relevance to the everyday lives of families in the Old Dominion. Most of these stories framed the ups and downs of the Austro-Hungarian family as part of a "curse," although the German-language paper in the Shenandoah Valley reported on the Austrian royal family in greater detail and with more reverence.[2]

Despite the early 20th-century instability of the Balkans—the "bloodlands where the empires of Russia, Turkey and Austro-Hungary met and clashed in tectonic plates of rivalry"—and its role as a lynchpin of international relations among the Russian Empire and its partners in the Entente Alliance of 1907 (France and Great Britain), no one could have predicted the extent of collateral carnage caused by those shots fired from a Browning pistol.[3] Accordingly, the announcement of Franz Ferdinand's and his wife's deaths in the Monday edition of Virginia newspapers was accompanied by more locally relevant headlines about two girls who drowned in Alexandria, the discovery of a body in Hanover County, and the successful fund-raising campaign for a new hospital. In the Tuesday edition, Virginia newspapers began to include articles published in Vienna and Britain, outlining the flow of condolences and mourners expected to attend the funeral for the archduke and his wife on July 3, 1914.[4] In the end, the guests at the funeral were restricted, but the diverse array of cabinet ministers, diplomats, and military officials who sent expressions of grief and consolation to the Austrian kaiser provides a clue as to the complex web of international marriages and alliances that were impacted by the killings. As the dominos began to fall throughout the summer of 1914—Austria-Hungary declared war on Serbia (July 28), allies of each side began to mobilize their troops thereby increasing global tensions, Germany declared war on Russia (August 1) and shortly thereafter France (August 3), and in response, Great Britain declared war on Germany (August 4), the Austro-Hungarian Empire declared war on Russia (August 6), and German troops besieged the Belgian city of Liège (August 4–16)—the United States declared its neutrality (August 4).

An important consequence of America's neutrality was its ability to continue to trade with the belligerents. By 1915, American factories and agricultural fields were providing the Allies (Great Britain, France, Russia, Belgium, Italy, Serbia, Japan, and several other countries) and the Central Powers (Germany, Austria-Hungary, Bulgaria, and the Ottoman Empire) with billions of dollars' worth of equipment, munitions, foodstuffs, and loans. Because of Virginia's geographic diversity, the state played a large role in supplying the combatants starting in 1915 and continuing after the cessation of hostilities on November 11, 1918. The commonwealth and its citizens repaired ships, built planes, grew crops, bred and transported horses, and loaned or donated money to the war effort long before President Wilson proclaimed that "the world must be made safe for democracy" on April 2, 1917, and, a few days later, Congress voted in favor of the United States entering into the war as an "associated power."

This book explores the involvement of Virginia and Virginians in the Great War from its beginning in 1914 through the end of American neutrality in 1917 and the experience of the American Expeditionary Forces (AEF) on the bloody fields of France in 1918 and concludes in 1919 when the majority of American troops finally returned home. The actions of a wide range of civilians are analyzed, illustrating the surprisingly important roles played by African American citizens, women, and children in the national war effort. In each of these roles one must be careful to separate wartime government propaganda from the real-life experiences of Virginia communities. In many instances the latter are far stranger, and more interesting, than the former.

The initial catalyst for this book was a visit that I took to an American cemetery in eastern France where more than 14,000 Americans lie six feet under the idyllic countryside. To me, this scene resembled a vintage postcard vista more so than the killing grounds it was in 1918 where many of these men died. The sea of white crosses and stars of David was overwhelming; how could I know so little about the causes and legacy of this global catastrophe? After studying the mortuary practices of the Allies and Central Powers through their military graveyards, I returned to my home state of Virginia and decided to locate and compile information about memorials to the Great War within the commonwealth. I was surprised by the numbers; after one year of searching and the help of colleagues and members of the public, I had compiled photographs of over two hundred statues, plaques, honorific namesakes (like a "memorial" bridge), and symbolic sculptures (like an archway).

Each memorial commemorated the service and, oftentimes, the violent deaths of Virginians who served during the war. Given the prevalence of these mostly forgotten memorials, how could we as a culture have so thoroughly expunged our understanding of the First World War from our thoughts? And there were more surprises to come, such as the way the conflict permeated every household, affecting Virginians from every socioeconomic stratum, racial and ethnic community, gender, and age. When I began the research for this book, I didn't think that I would find evidence of trenches, unexploded ordnance, or grieving towns in Virginia. But indeed I found each of these and more in the Old Dominion. My challenge was figuring out how to find the records of these wartime events and to locate their remnants today and to discover the roles of tens of thousands of Virginia's sons who fought in the trenches, while recognizing the crucial contributions that civilians made in the war effort and the hard-fought Allied victory. To frame it quantitatively, while over 93,000 Virginia men served in the military during the Great War, many of them never made it overseas. In contrast, of the 2.2 million residents living in Virginia as of 1917, a majority of the adults and a surprisingly large number of children worked on war-related projects and crusades. Thus, this book borrows from the historical concept of "total war," where both civilian and military assets were mobilized; with the implementation of total war, the home front became the foundation for Virginia's surprisingly large contribution to the Great War.[5]

1

Provisions

> It should be well understood that this country is for many years to come to be the supply center of the world. We have not only to feed our own people, but every principle of humanity will prompt us to make this country the granary of the entente powers of Europe.
> —General E. W. Nichols, chairman of the Virginia Defense Council, 1917[1]

In the three years of global fighting before the United States entered the "Great War" on April 6, 1917, Virginia played a surprisingly large role as a breadbasket for the European soldiers. One of the state's earliest contributions to the worldwide conflict was to feed the Allied troops. First, the Old Dominion supplied grain and meat to the Allied forces from 1915 to 1917. These food exports turned the United States into a creditor rather than a debtor nation for the first time in its history.[2] Virginia farmers were a key part of this nationwide agricultural assistance. Second, Virginians were fundamental in devising new techniques to increase agricultural yields.

The Northern Virginia county of Loudoun contributed more than its share of agrarian products and revolutionary agrarian techniques. A week after Austria-Hungary declared war on Serbia, the local Loudoun newspaper tried to make sense of the ensuing political domino effect for its readers. On August 7, 1914, its headlines read, "All Europe Now in Ferment, Nationals All Prepare for War," "German Kaiser Rushing Subjects to Death," "America Would Benefit from Great War," and "People of Paris Mad to Fight Germany." But it also contained an important local observation: Isaac Ballinger had more than doubled the previous wheat output on his 19-acre farm, located in the small town of Hamilton, seven miles west of the county seat.[3]

In his 1914 harvest, Ballinger produced 36.5 bushels of wheat per acre. This was newsworthy because the average output for U.S. farms in pre–World War I America was half of that, around 16 bushels per acre.[4] Ballinger was one of many Loudoun farmers who had begun experimenting with new approaches that improved the annual yield from their fields. Decades earlier, the pioneering agricultural bacteriologist Edwin Broun Fred was born nearby in Middleburg, Virginia. He received his Ph.D. in bacteriology at the University of Göttingen (in Germany) but returned to Virginia to teach, briefly, at Virginia Polytechnic Institute, better known today as Virginia Tech.[5] Dr. Fred was one of the first bacteriologists in America to study nitrogen-fixing bacteria to better understand the nutritional and soil requirements of plants. His work formed the basis for ensilage (preserving fodder in silos), vaccines, and seed inoculations—all necessary foundations for increasing agricultural productivity. Virginia farmers implemented Dr. Fred's groundbreaking techniques throughout the war years to increase their output.

To further improve their agricultural yields, Loudoun and other Virginia counties established cooperative extensions and vocational agricultural classes under the Smith-Lever Act of 1914. This legislation created a national Cooperative Extension Service that offered classes in agricultural practices and technology at land-grant universities throughout the country. Professional farmers and specialists taught rural Americans about agricultural advances that could help them improve their yields. In 1917, Virginia schools contributed to this effort by offering courses in agricultural and domestic sciences. All over the South, the "horsepower revolution" enabled farmers to transition to mechanized farm tools such as sulky plows (which enabled a farmer to ride instead of walk), grain drills, self-binders for twine, automatic twine cutters, feeders, weighers, and blowers.[6]

By combining these educational and technological advances, Loudoun County aided the Virginia war effort more than most other counties. Loudoun's annual wheat production in 1917 was 1,040,000 bushels. The local paper recognized that the key to "winning the war is now one of bread and bullets, and every bushel and every pound of Loudoun County wheat is necessary for victory."[7] Farmers across the country endorsed this sentiment and, in the end, the largest acreage of record in the United States was harvested in 1917 to meet the wartime demand.[8]

Farmers also worked to improve their breeds of cattle, horses, hogs, and sheep. Merchants assisted with this effort; for example, the owner of a local Purcellville hardware store, J. V. Nichols, served as the president of the Loudoun County Breeders Association. Other local citizens joined the Loudoun Heavy Draft Association, the Loudoun Valley Cow Testing

Association, the Catoctin and Lovettsville Farmers Clubs, or the Loudoun County Farm Loan Association.⁹

At home, female heads of households led food conservation and canning efforts. Loudoun County women packaged 1.2 million containers of "home produce," some of which was sent to Camp Lee (25 miles south of Richmond), including two large barrels of jelly.¹⁰ To ensure that all Virginians were properly preparing their canned produce, the government hired Anne E. Sale, from Georgia, to teach safe canning practices at the Newport News Cannery. Over the next four months, she helped four hundred local residents prepare 8,932 containers of food.¹¹ These efforts provided crucial food supplies that were sent to troops abroad. One wartime propaganda poster summed up the goal: "Can vegetables, fruit, and the Kaiser too!" The accompanying illustration depicted a sad-looking German emperor, Wilhelm II, imprisoned in a glass jar, wearing an ill-fitting *pickelhaube* or "hun helmet." The propaganda artists used some of their best puns for this effort with slogans like "Can all you can" and "Of course I can."

Virginia women preserving food at the Charlottesville Canning Factory, 1916 (Holsinger Studio Collection, X04542DB, Special Collections, University of Virginia Library, Charlottesville).

The statewide support network required for these agricultural contributions was complex. Rural roads had to be improved in order to move products from fields to markets. On July 11, 1916, the Federal Aid Road Act legislated new highway construction. Later, after the United States entered the war and large army trucks were tearing up the Virginia roads, the state asked for federal assistance to repair and maintain its busy highways.[12]

The banking industry was a second national infrastructure that helped rural Americans contribute to the war effort. Some Virginia farmers required loans before they could successfully improve their agricultural output. The Federal Farm Loan Act of July 1917 established a dozen banks that allowed farmers to negotiate long-term loans at low interest rates and repay them in installments. These federal initiatives complemented state and local efforts.

As important as agricultural production was between 1917 and 1918, the hearts and minds of Loudoun County citizens were on a different matter. Two local residents, Asa and Werner Janney, noticed an inscription on an outhouse wall behind Hirst's lumberyard in Purcellville:

> Here's to the Kaiser, you son of a bitch,
> I hope he'll have always the seven year itch.
> May his thumbs be hammered with a heavy trip hammer
> Till his nostril will whistle the Star Spangled Banner.[13]

Hundreds of Loudoun County men served their country during the war (590 were drafted); 11 were cited for conspicuous bravery; 30 never returned. The Loudoun County War memorial, a bronze plaque mounted on a three-foot-wide rectangular pillar adorned with Corinthian pilasters, attests, "Their Bodies are Buried in Peace but their Name Liveth for Evermore."

Unfortunately, in other parts of the Old Dominion many names, dates, places, and events from Virginia's role in the Great War have been forgotten.

Food Rationing

> I hereby pledge myself to do my bit as follows: I will use only those amounts of food required for adequate nourishment. I will endeavor to control the waste in all kinds of materials in the household and to live simply. I will begin now.
>
> —Pledge made by members of
> Richmond's Women's Clubs, ca. 1917[14]

In 1917, before radio and television news sources became available, most Americans relied on a combination of newspapers, community gossip, and locally posted announcements for their daily updates. Billboards and other large-scale printed media were rare, but smaller posters could be pasted onto the inside or outside of buildings, placed in windows, or reprinted in the local newspaper. Between America's formal entry into the war on April 6, 1917, and the first draft two months later, the U.S. government had an important task on its hands: increase domestic support for intervention in a war that President Wilson had promised to keep America out of. To turn the tide of public opinion, Wilson created the Committee on Public Information just days after the official declaration of war. Known for his pointed style, journalist George Creel took charge of this effort. He recruited writers and artists to help publicize the cause. One of his most successful programs was the production of propaganda posters. Despite America's involvement in the war for less than a quarter of the time that other nations fought, it produced more posters than any of its allies (or enemies). Charlottesville followed this trend, as evidenced by a series of photographs taken of Charlottesville businesses between 1915 and 1919 that reveal war posters in storefronts, like the army recruiting poster in the window of the Cooperative Drug Company.[15]

In the case of messages encouraging food production, these hand-colored posters often featured patriotic elements like cowboys (or possibly Rough Riders) carrying American flags or red, white, and blue rainbows arching over the Statue of Liberty, with baskets conspicuously added to the scene, overflowing with food. Sometimes the artist stretched a pun or a reference a little too far. In one poster, a hat-wearing gardener is pictured chasing after a crop of anthropomorphized root crops (the pumpkin carries an American flag). This flight is described by the title at the top of the poster: "War Gardens Over the Top." As the vegetables run from the gardener's hoe, the slogan at the bottom admonishes the viewer, "The seeds of victory insure the fruits of peace." A companion poster shows the same gardener, but this time he is followed by happy rows of potatoes, carrots, turnips, and two excessively joyous jack-o'-lanterns (again carrying an American flag). The optimistic captions on this poster proclaim: "War Gardens Victorious" and "Every War Garden A Peace Plant." Both posters were commissioned and paid for by the National War Garden Commission based in Washington, D.C. Across the commonwealth of Virginia residents viewed a more direct poster produced by the U.S. Food Administration that summed up the government's message: "Food is Ammunition—Don't Waste It!"

Wartime poster promoting domestic food production in "war gardens." Created by Maginel W. Barney, ca. 1919 (Library of Congress Prints and Photographs Division, Washington, D.C. Call number POS–US .B383, no. 5).

Victory Gardens

> We are having an abundance of snaps now also peas and corn but not tomatoes.
>
> —Lucy Ashton Faulkner on her Mecklenburg County garden, April 1918[16]

In wartime rationing, backyard gardeners had an important role to play in food production and conservation. The term "Victory Garden" conjures up the lean World War II years when the federal government encouraged American householders to plant fruit and vegetables in their backyards to supplement their grocery-store purchases. But the governmental initiative to support this practice began earlier, in World War I. President Wilson himself assured Americans that gardening "is just as real and patriotic an effort as the building of ships or the firing of cannons."[17] But as any failed gardener can attest, it wasn't as simple as throwing seeds into the dirt. Instead, the National Emergency Food Garden Commission urged, "it is of the utmost importance that expert advice and supervision be provided for this garden work."[18] This plan included teaming up with more experienced gardeners, purchasing labor-saving garden tools (wheel hoes or spray pumps), and enlisting the help of a volunteer manager to organize the overall efforts. In just one month, July 1917, the Women's Committee of the Virginia Council of Defense rallied 105,505 "housewives" to pledge their support for the strategies endorsed by the Food Administration.[19]

Wilson and his advisors included children in their plans and created a program called the United States School Garden Army. In the spring of 1918, Richmond students were scheduled to learn "the significance of four letters as applied to the gardening activities of the schools. The four letters are 'U.S.S.G.'"[20] The U.S. commissioner of education made no secret of the ulterior motive behind these efforts: "to prepare [students] for intelligent, virtuous living, for economic production, and for the duties and responsibilities of citizenship after the war."[21] Gardening was also used as part of the government's propaganda campaign to establish daylight saving time. The government argued that "setting the clock ahead at once one hour from now until November 1 would permit thousands of workmen, who have planted food gardens to spend one more hour each day in the cultivation of their garden."[22] In the summer of 1918, the National War Garden Commission reported that "springing forward" an hour resulted in an additional 546 million hours of garden work across the country, the equivalent of six months' worth of supplies for an army of a million men.[23]

In addition to encouraging citizens to plant gardens, the federal government issued a series of food-related restrictions. On January 26, 1918, the newly appointed food administrator, Herbert Hoover, called for voluntary "wheatless Mondays and Wednesdays, meatless Tuesdays, porkless Thursdays and Saturdays and the use of 'victory bread.'" That last item was bread baked with less than 50 percent white or wheat flour, relying instead on government-endorsed substitutes like corn, barley, oats, or rye flour. Lucy Faulkner mentioned that her daughter Alice had "gone to the canning demonstration to learn how to make and take various 'war breads'" during the winter of 1918.[24]

By eating less wheat, meat, sugar, and fats, citizens could save these more calorically and nutritionally dense foods for the soldiers and for export abroad where these items were in short supply. Meals in Virginia households between 1917 and 1919 were supposed to contain corn, oats, and rye (instead of wheat); fish and poultry (instead of red meat); little to no added sugar; and plenty of domestically available fruits, vegetables, and potatoes. One poster from the U.S. Department of Agriculture asked, "Have you eaten your pound of potatoes today?"[25] In 21st-century buzz words, the campaign boiled down to "buy local" and "eat healthy foods."

World War I–era food ration posters may convey the false impression that Americans were eating healthy meals consisting of non-red meats, vegetables, home-cooked breads, and fresh greens, but this was not actually the case. They enjoyed their sweets and desserts as much as we do today. As a result, Virginia newspapers encouraged residents to consider "General Sugar Conservation." More to the point, an advertisement in the Tazewell paper encouraged local families to stop eating sugar and instead use honey or fruit to sweeten their meals. To drive the point home, one government-sponsored publicity campaign chided, "The American people last year spent enough money on candy to feed all Belgium for two years." In case that argument didn't convince the audience, another smaller notice read, "Save Sugar. Sugar means Ships—Ships mean Soldiers—Soldiers mean Victory."[26] In a more honest recollection, two Virginians in Purcellville noted, "While all the youngsters were drilling with broomsticks, and all the gabbers were talking about slackers, no one so far as we know ever turned down an opportunity to buy an extra pound of sugar at Cornwell's—or in any other store."[27]

Virginia women were encouraged to cook "foods from corn" because it was so plentiful in American fields. A poster meant to be informative during wartime shortages showed a box or can each of corn starch, corn oil, and corn syrup alongside the "wholesome—nutritious" food products made from these ingredients: canned peaches, cornbread, bagels (although they might be donuts), a cream pie of some sort, an even more amorphous image of a bowl with floating objects in it, and an unappetizing plate of corn-filled apples. Wartime meals might help America win the war, but they weren't appetizing.

Promotional poster encouraging American families to substitute corn for wheat in their recipes. Created by Lloyd Harrison, ca. 1918 (Library of Congress Prints and Photographs Division, Washington, D.C. Call number POS–World War I–US, no. 176).

Another propaganda poster encouraged "little Americans" to do their bit by eating "oatmeal-corn meal mush—Hominy—other corn cereals—and Rice with milk." The wheat-based cereals should be "saved for our soldiers." The poster, featuring a cherubic, smiling blonde child saluting his cereal bowl, concluded with the admonition, penned in red ink, "Leave nothing on your plate."[28]

One of the more optimistic pieces of World War I food conservation advice was to eat more cottage cheese. On first consideration, why not? It's nutritious and pretty tasty. But in reading the promotional material more closely, it specified that one pound of cottage cheese contained more protein than a pound of lamb or even beef.[29] But who sits down to eat an entire pound of cottage cheese? That's the equivalent of eating a tub of sour curds. And according to modern-day nutritional guides, beef and most other meats contain double or triple the amount of protein found in a comparable amount of cottage cheese. The only seemingly accurate part of the poster was the closing query: "Cottage Cheese or Meat? Ask Your Pocketbook!" That part, at least, made sense.

Recipes, or "receipts" as they were then called, illustrated what types of meals could be made with all of these food restrictions in place. The "Berkshire Muffin" recipe in a Warrenton cookbook substituted corn meal, rice, and barley for the rationed wheat, and suggested reducing the sugar to one tablespoon. Another recipe from this cookbook was an "English Meat Substitute Dish."[30] Intrigued by the reference to Britain, hardly renowned for its culinary temptations, I looked at the ingredients: lentils, water, onions, and a "little" salt and butter, along with a "full teaspoon" of curry powder. Not a bad recipe for curried lentils, but probably not a satisfying "meat substitute" for a Virginia family in 1917. Indeed, these sustenance modifications caused a backlash among some Virginians. As one sardonic writer joked, "Hooverizing" was "when the wise housewife studies up on how to make chicken croquettes out of the left-over mashed potatoes."[31] A *Richmond Times-Dispatch* headline announced, "Meatless Meal Plan Has Disadvantages."[32] These restrictions inconvenienced Lucy Faulkner, despite her backyard garden. In February 1918, she complained to her daughter that she was "scared about supper—everything scarce and high—eggs 40 and 45 cents a dozen."[33] Meanwhile, the Defense Council's Women's Committee continued registering women in Virginia who pledged to abide by the appropriate bread and meat substitutes and fruit and vegetable preservation methods. In the end, over 285,000 Virginia women enrolled.[34]

Railside Canteens

> So many collations of sandwiches, coffee &c. have been served to trainloads of hungry troops passing through Lynchburg, Va., by the patriotic women of that Southern city that the army, out of a sense of gratitude, has dubbed the place "Lunchburg."
> —*Evening World*, August 29, 1918[35]

Much of the food produced by Virginians was shipped overseas to the troops, but some was given to the soldiers directly as they passed through Virginia towns in railcars. In the early 20th century, Lynchburg was one of the crucial hubs on the Virginia railroad. The city's tracks collected trains from every direction and sent them off in radiating spokes to the larger cities of Richmond, Danville, Lexington, and Newport News. In September 1917, local women began to serve sandwiches and coffee to the large numbers of troops who passed through the city on transport trains. The need was so great that more than 150 men and

Volunteers handing out food and refreshments to troops on their way to Virginia training camps in Lynchburg, ca. 1917. Lynchburg was nicknamed "Lunchburg" during the war because of the extensive canteen service (Lynchburg Museum System).

women contributed to the refreshment effort. After a few months the U.S. Army recognized their service and assigned the stop as an official "canteen" or temporary mess hall. The American Red Cross stepped in to assist with the food purchases and distribution.[36]

Handing out food and drinks may sound like a trivial contribution, but organizing the canteen took as much coordination as organizing a mess camp located in the middle of a battlefield. First, the arrival and even existence of the transport trains was a closely guarded secret. During the first few months of the unofficial effort to serve refreshments, the volunteers were unable to obtain any advance information about troop travel, resulting in long and often unfruitful waits. Second, in an era when ice was still obtained by cutting blocks from frozen ponds during the winter and storing them in straw for as long as possible during the summer, it was a logistical challenge to set up a temporary railside kitchen. Instead, the Red Cross organized the construction of a "substantial hut" at the Southern Railway Station on Kemper Street in Lynchburg. This crude workplace included a poorly functioning wood stove whose wood had to be gathered from two blocks away.

After several months, the volunteers solicited additional donations and upgraded their equipment to a gas range, coffee percolator, tables and shelves, a sink, an ice box (literally a box for storing ice, not an electric refrigerator), and a bread slicer.[37] The last item is not described in any detail, but unlike a modern version, an electrified knife with a cord, it was almost certainly a hand-operated, much larger piece of equipment that included a guillotine-like blade housed in an iron frame, which was manually raised and lowered for each of the hundreds of thousands of pieces of bread that these women sliced between September 25, 1917, and the summer of 1919 (troops continued to stream through the city long after the war ended as they were gradually demobilized).

The canteen workers were organized into a military hierarchy, headed by the commandant (who alone had the authority to request the train schedules) and supported by an elaborate team of assistants, a treasurer, secretary, and subcommittees headed by captains (with lieutenants at their service, seven a piece, one for each day of the week). Then there were the prosaic yet time consuming, tasks of boiling water, preparing and pouring coffee, making meals and packing them, and passing out the bags and milk cans (filled with coffee) to thousands of soldiers as their trains passed through town on brief layovers.

The efforts of the canteen workers did not end with these duties. Because they were the main source of interactions for the troops during these stops, the workers were sometimes called upon to carry men who had fallen ill to local hospitals or send messages, via telegram or letters, to the families of sick or dying men. Later, a "hospital room" was added to the canteen hut to handle the sick until they could be transported to military hospitals. Lynchburg citizens also contributed cigarettes, magazines, ice, cakes, candies, and even postcards that bore a photograph of the canteen itself and the volunteer workers.[38]

Sometimes a troop commander would wire ahead to request a special favor. These requests ranged from drinking water during a heat spell to baths for 150 men. To fulfill the latter, 50 automobiles met the train and carried off three men each to the local YMCA for showers. Another time the Lynchburg Municipal Band hosted an impromptu concert. This canteen was one of several throughout Virginia, most of which operated without any paid workers.[39]

The Lynchburg effort to maintain a canteen service for 24 months was duplicated in towns across the commonwealth and represented just one of the dozens of ways that Virginia cities contributed to the war effort. Residents also contributed to the Belgian relief fund, knitted items, purchased war bonds and stamps, organized fund drives, and harvested produce from the fields of "farmerettes" (a World War I–era term for female farmers). Sometimes the contributions were more unusual and specific, like the sateen dresses made by college women to give to French orphans, financial contributions to educate two Serbian students, or the sewing of 145 "helpless case shirts." The last item was a special design for military patients who injured or lost one of their arms. Unfortunately, for many veterans the long-lasting damage from their wartime service was psychological and not sufficiently understood or treated. But in the first several months of recruitment in Virginia, these tragic repercussions were still in the future, and communities were instead focused on how they could help defeat the Huns.

Remount Depots

> The experts of the United States government have declared Warren to be the best county in the whole country in which to raise good horses.... After investigating soils and grasses in all the States ... the experts settled upon this county.
> —*Richmond Times-Dispatch,* March 11, 1917[40]

While Virginia's civilian contributions were extensive, it also hosted dozens of military installations and training camps, including sites to train nonhuman participants. In the case of horses, the idea of a remount station dated to the Civil War, when military leaders realized that they could not rely on soldiers to furnish their own mounts, even in rural areas like Virginia. Instead, the army established a series of receiving stations to supply the cavalry and artillery with horses and mules.

In the decades after the Civil War, as inventors from around the world began to apply for patents for the new "horseless carriages," American remount stations were closed. As a result, during the 1898 Spanish American War, military leaders were caught unprepared and lacked sufficient horses to carry out their time-honored equine strategies. The responsibility for managing the governmental stables switched from the cavalry to the Army Quartermaster Corps, the branch tasked with supplying the army.

During World War I, tens of thousands of horses and mules from all over the country passed through Virginia Remount Depots on their way to the front lines in Europe. At the depots, breeders and trainers worked to raise and train the finest equids.[41] After they were properly seasoned to work under adverse conditions and to endure loud noises, their handlers loaded these four-legged soldiers onto railroad cars and sent them to Newport News, where they boarded ships for Europe.

In Europe, the horses served two main duties: as mounts for cavalry officers and, more commonly, as beasts of burden to haul wagons and artillery pieces. These transports moved vital supplies to and from the front and carried the dead and wounded back to the hospitals in the rear. To put their service in perspective, a single five-ton Whitworth cannon required a team of a dozen mules to haul it through the mud-filled tracks found along the western front. Thousands of these artillery pieces were placed along the trenches.[42]

Given the number of horses and mules required for this work and Virginia's important role in their breeding and distribution, I thought it would be easy to find the old stables, presumably still standing in some rural Virginia county. Instead, my search for military equestrian sites led me to Civil War locations such as the final resting place of Traveller, Robert E. Lee's beloved horse, now buried near him on the campus of Washington and Lee University in Lexington.

But then I received a more specific lead: a reference to a World War I Remount Station in Front Royal, Virginia. I found it disguised within its modern-day function as the Smithsonian Conservation Biology Institute, one of the off-site campuses associated with the National Zoo. It no longer focused on horses; its current priority is veterinary and reproductive

The 111th Field Artillery leading their horses off railroad cars in Norfolk (Virginia War Museum, Newport News, VA).

research among endangered species. Nearby, a newer Transportation Security Administration station trains another four-legged military aid, dogs.

In the early 20th century, the federal government decided to run a stable in Front Royal where it could obtain, breed, train, and provide horses for military use. Between 1908 and 1913, the government purchased five thousand acres of land in this rural Shenandoah Valley community.

Here it erected stables, planted hay fields, and built silos for storing fodder.

Front Royal sat at the junction of two railroads and along a major highway, increasing the ease of obtaining horses from a wide area and, in turn, of sending them off to service after their training. Originally called the Federal Government Remount Station and Cavalry Horse Training and Breeding Station, these stables housed a valuable weapon in an era when "horseless carriages" were still unreliable.

The Front Royal Remount (Quartermaster) Depot was commissioned on March 13, 1911, but the official dedication was postponed to a more auspicious date: July 4, 1913.[43] Not only did this tie the opening to Independence Day, it was the 50th anniversary of the surrender of the southern town of Vicksburg, Mississippi, to the northern forces under Major General Ulysses S. Grant (and a day earlier, July 3, 1913, was the half-century anniversary of the end of the Battle of Gettysburg).

The military planners organized the depot into a central post, with a handful of structures, surrounded by 11 barn complexes. There was a hospital for horses and another for men, a dispensary, a granary, a grain elevator, hay sheds, a fire station, stables, a drinking-water source, a sewage disposal plant, barracks, and officer quarters.

Miles and miles of split-rail fences were built to divide the land into individual pastures, create quarantine spaces for new arrivals, provide training rings, and create a corridor from the remount station to the nearby railhead on Luray Avenue in Front Royal. This system of obtaining, training, and distributing equids was put to the test in 1916 when it provided horses for Major General John J. Pershing's expedition to locate Pancho Villa, a Mexican Revolutionary leader, who led a raid against a town along the U.S.–Mexican border. Pershing was recalled from the "Punitive Expedition, U.S. Army" (now referred to as the "Mexican Expedition") to fight in the Great War before he could complete his mission.

The federal veterinarians and trainers made every effort to obtain quality horses. In this era before genetic testing, "quality" was determined by visible traits and/or competitions. Thus, one of the first donated horses was Henry of Navarre, born in 1891 to a Preakness Stakes winner and a race champion in his own right, earning the title of "horse of the year" in 1894. In 1897, he suffered a career-ending injury during a race, and his owners put him out to stud. In 1911, he was given to the Remount Station to begin the national breeding program at the depot.[44] The remount station solicited high-quality mares and studs from farms, fairs, and livestock shows to create a breed that would "be second to none anywhere."[45]

These high-quality horses caught the attention of British military planners. They had established their own stables in eastern Virginia to take advantage of the transatlantic ports for easy shipments abroad. They searched all over North America for equestrian soldiers. As early as 1915, the British were purchasing horses from the Front Royal Remount Station and shipping them to the European battlefields via Newport News. That winter, a Charlottesville resident observed 49 railroad cars filled with horses en route from the Front Royal Remount Station to the British Remount Station in Newport News and, from there, across the ocean to Liverpool. To get a sense of the scale of this transport, each individual train car could hold 20 horses or 22 mules per car; most trains contained 30 cars each. Thus, each train trip was transporting about six hundred animals, and there were countless train trips back and forth on the Southern Railroad.

The Charlottesville reporter noticed that the horses on the trains that day were a uniform dark color and sadly concluded, "When we think of the probable fate of these poor beasts, it somehow brings the meaning of this war nearer home to us."[46] The life expectancy of these exceptional equids could often be counted in days after they reached their military destinations.[47] Only a quarter of the World War I horses died in combat. The rest drowned in the mud after collapsing from exhaustion, died from exposure or sickness, or starved to death.[48] In the American depots, preventing equine illnesses, such as "shipping fever" which included diseases like glanders, a deadly bacterial infection of the lungs, was a priority.

I have been studying historic American graveyards for two decades but I had never considered the cultural significance of an equid burial ground until I visited the one at the Front Royal Remount Station. Located on the site of an old racetrack, the marble headstones parallel an old stone fence and command an impressive view of the rolling Blue Ridge foothills. Henry of Navarre is here, as well as another racehorse named Octagon. They lie together under a tablet-style marble stone, a curved shape more commonly used to signal the graves of American soldiers, with the inscription "both famous racehorses and breeding stallions." Two of General Pershing's horses, Jeff and Kidron, are buried here but their gravestones were removed to a midwestern museum.[49] When I visited the site, my guide explained that they were given "full body" burials, a rarity for horses. Most war horses rest where they died, their weight of 1,000 to 2,000 pounds making it impractical to transport them. For those rare beasts deemed worthy of graves, gravediggers usually bury just the head, while soldiers dispose of the bulky and heavy body near the site of death.[50]

But those combat deaths were in the future; first the horses had to travel from the western mountains of Virginia to ships docked in eastern harbors. In Newport News, pens and stables were erected near the piers to house the horses while they awaited their transatlantic journey. With typical military efficiency, these sites were given unimaginative names, like Embarkation Depot 301. Similar to the western supply point, the dockside stables required a large support staff including veterinarians, farriers, stablemen, loaders, and wranglers. There was also the initial labor required to obtain lumber and construct the pens and carrying cages.[51] In 1915 alone, 170,000 horses and mules were shipped abroad to assist in the war effort; today this cargo would be worth almost $1 billion dollars.[52]

One military officer estimated that two-thirds of the horses and all of the mules used by the British army came from the British Remount Commission that shipped its American-born equids from Newport News ports.[53] These mules were so valuable that Germany devised a plot to poison them. In 1915 two African American stevedores working on Breeze Point Wharf in Newport News slipped into the animal pens and injected the mules with a pneumonia-like bacterium.[54] This deadly plot can be traced back to an American citizen, Anton Dilger, who grew up on a farm named Greenfield, located only a few miles away from the future site of the Front Royal Remount Station.

Dilger was born in the Blue Ridge Mountains in 1884 to a German father who had immigrated to America and served in the Union Army. Growing up on a Virginia stock farm under the tutelage of his father, an expert horseman, Anton was well versed in equestrian care. His parents dreamed of a more expansive education for their son; in 1894, they sent him to Germany with his newly married sister. He earned a degree in medicine at the University of Heidelberg, where he wrote a thesis titled "Concerning In Vitro Cultures: With Special Consideration of the Tissues of Adult Animals."[55] That same year, 1911, Anton's family homestead, Dilger Field, was incorporated into the new U.S. Army Depot at Front Royal. Four years later Anton's tissue research and his equestrian knowledge would take on an ominous significance. In 1915, disgusted by the carnage in Europe, Anton moved back to America and rented a house in Washington, D.C., located just six miles from the White House. His most important possession was a small case containing four glass cylinders.[56] These vials contained germ cultures, including one that caused glanders in horses and mules and another that contained the anthrax bacterium.

The mules that the two dock workers injected in May 1915 were some of the 457,000 equids that were shipped from the British Remount Service Depot in Newport News to Allied forces in Europe. Ironically, this scheme was not very successful, in large part because of a test for glanders, the mallein test, that the Germans had developed before the war.[57] Some of the other poisoned animals died when their ship transports were hit by German torpedoes, before they could effectively spread the infection throughout the Allied herds.[58] After this limited success, Dilger packed up his basement laboratory and traveled back and forth between American and Germany, participating in other espionage and anti–American plots. In the fall of 1917, fearing capture, he fled to Mexico. In a final twist of poetic justice, Dilger traveled to Spain, continuing his work for the German government. There he contracted the "Spanish flu," dying of complications from pneumonia at age 34 on October 17, 1918.[59] Although there had been earlier efforts to infect enemies with diseases, such as the smallpox-infected blankets given to Native Americans during the French and Indian War, Dr. Dilger's sabotage campaign was the first use of "germs" by a bacteriologist who had deliberately grown cultures to be used as a tool of modern warfare.

Weaponry

> You know, perhaps, that I have discovered a very simple method of transforming ordinary cotton into a material possessing all the necessary properties as a propellant.
> —Christian F. Schönbein, chemist, 1847[60]

If you had to name an important agricultural product in the South, two crops would top the list: tobacco and cotton. In surveying wartime products, I expected to see tobacco, recognizing that pipes and their more convenient cousins, cigarettes, became highly valued rations for troops. But I did not expect to find the more innocuous-sounding "cotton" in the long list of military products that Virginia produced during the war. Cotton turned out to be a convenient material with the appropriate absorptive properties. In the mid–19th century, German-Swiss chemist Christian Friedrich Schönbein inadvertently created a highly flammable material by soaking cotton in an equal blend of sulfuric and nitric acids. After reaching out to other scientists and modifying the production process (in an early effort a factory exploded, killing dozens of people), this smokeless and residueless substance became known as "guncotton" and replaced gunpowder as a propellant in various explosives. In Virginia, the E. I. DuPont company capitalized on the importance of this commodity and built a large guncotton plant in Hopewell, just south of the capitol.

Like many of wartime construction efforts, the huge Hopewell plant was built very quickly. It required 175 million board feet of lumber, 13 million bricks, 210,000 barrels of cement, 4.5 million square feet of roofing material, 6.5 million square feet of sheet iron, and 600 miles of wrought iron and steel pipe. The complex required similarly large quantities of cast-iron pipe, terra-cotta, and wooden stave pipe. Quantifying some of the construction materials used to construct the plant provides a window into the large support communities that were required to create these industrial sites. And, as with many of the production plants in Virginia, railcars were needed to move supplies to and within the plant. At Hopewell, 55 miles of narrow- and broad-gauge tracks were laid within the plant itself.[61]

The end result was a methodical process whereby the cotton was purified (through boiling) and dried; nitric acid was produced, mixed, and weighed; and then the two were combined with sulfuric acid, soda ash, and caustic soda and packaged for shipment down the James River to the transatlantic ports. The plant opened in 1915 and over the next four years produced over 1.1 billion pounds of guncotton, thereby satisfying the wartime demands of both the Allied and U.S. forces. Contemporaries called it the greatest guncotton plant in the world; at its peak, in 1917, it employed more than 28,000 workers.[62] A more observant contemporary eyewitness described Hopewell as "a lawless tar-paper town of 40,000 workers, wives, kids, merchants, gamblers, saloon-keepers, and prostitutes."[63]

DuPont's second-largest strategically crucial factory in Virginia was the Penniman plant. This facility was located roughly 40 miles east of Hopewell on the south shore of the York River, which runs parallel to and just north of its more famous cousin, the James. The factory, and eventual town, was named in honor of Russell Sylvanus Penniman, the inventor of ammonia dynamite. And while it sounds oxymoronic to talk about "safer" explosives, Penniman's invention improved upon the original nitroglycerin-based product created by Alfred Nobel. The Penniman plant was originally created to produce TNT.

Then came the bait and switch. Despite the company's own publicity campaign and the sudden interest of land speculators, the initial plant hired only two hundred workers instead of the expected thousands. On the eve of America's entry into the war, a DuPont executive wrote a letter to the local paper stating, "This plant is for purely commercial purposes and has nothing whatever to do with the manufacture of any type of munitions of war."[64] It was a startling announcement from an explosives plant

Advertisement for work at one of two Du Pont plants: Penniman (near Williamsburg) or Hopewell (along the James River). *Richmond Times-Dispatch* September 22, 1918, 9 (image provided by the Library of Virginia, Richmond, to the *Chronicling America: Historic American Newspapers* project at the Library of Congress).

as the United States rapidly prepared to enter a conflict that would become renowned for the number of explosives detonated on both sides. DuPont failed to explain that it had outfitted Penniman to produce dynamite from the less-expensive nitrostarch to avoid paying top dollar for the more effective nitroglycerine. The market for the cheaper dynamite evaporated, leaving the plant "a loafing vagrant."[65] The factory grew, only after 1916, when it secured a government contract to assemble artillery shells.

The plant became one of the largest in the country, producing more than 27,000 large-caliber artillery shells a day. In its reformulated blueprint, it was designed for 10,000 employees, with a surrounding community of up to 15,000 (to include about five thousand people serving as support staff). The rapid boom in real estate attracted land speculators and planners who mapped out no fewer than 18 housing developments. Foiling the speculators again, DuPont decided instead to create its own 250-home "Pullman Village," which became the community of Penniman. It provided a wide array of amenities, from temporary dormitories to a store, post office, bank, police station, church, and social outlets like the Young Women's Christian Association (YWCA), Young Men's Christian Association (YMCA), and dance halls. Despite the millions of dollars invested in the plant and the thousands of artillery shells assembled there, only a handful even reached the front before the war ended.[66]

The Penniman factory was one of many that turned to women to fill the labor shortages that developed after the draft. At the DuPont factory they were paid 45 cents an hour, and the ideal employees were "women who do not have to work, but who are willing to share the sacrifice their brothers are making … women who are working for patriotic reasons."[67] To fulfill this optimistic expectation, female employees were recruited from distant towns, such as Wilmington, Delaware, where more than 90 women left for Penniman to "stuff one for the Kaiser." But when they arrived they found few socially acceptable places for women to rest when there were off duty. Onerous social norms required proper chaperones and limited the type of diversions that women could enjoy in their free time. The president of the Richmond YWCA spoke up on behalf of these female workers and called for "war service centers, or clubs for girls working munitions plants … offering them rest and diversion required to facilitate work." Women workers even requested, and eventually received, a "shampoo parlor" in the town.[68]

DuPont was able to outfit the town with hundreds of homes almost overnight by using kits available through a burgeoning mail-order catalog company called Sears & Roebuck.[69] The piecemeal homes were shipped via railroad cars and assembled in place. Sears offered several styles including "The Cumberland," a popular choice in the Penniman community.[70] An advertisement touted the house's composition shingles, interior "beaverboard" (a type of fiberboard), four bedrooms (including a closet for clothes, a relatively new domestic feature replacing earlier, stand-alone wardrobes), upstairs bath, and "entrance hall." After the war ended, these types of modern improvements were touted by state officials as part of a "Home Beautiful" movement intended to entice more residents to come to or remain in Virginia cities.[71]

American soldiers had to be trained how to use the artillery shells produced at Penniman. The army spent over half a million dollars to purchase land in Newport News and built Camp Abraham Eustis not far from Penniman. Named in honor of a brigadier general who had been the first commanding officer of nearby Fort Monroe, the camp was located on Mulberry Island. Three hundred years earlier, a British ship had met deserting Jamestown colonists here, bringing crucial supplies to the struggling residents. Later, the Confederate army fortified this strategic location in an attempt to block the Union Navy from sneaking up the river toward the Confederate capital of Richmond.[72] During World War I, Camp Eustis became a coast artillery replacement center for the larger and older Fort Monroe and provided soldiers instruction in balloon observation techniques. After the war, Camp Eustis was converted to a permanent military installation and was named Fort Eustis.

The town of Penniman was not as lucky. Four days after the Armistice, an early-morning explosion killed four men and injured four others. The town was rapidly abandoned after the Armistice and became known as the "only ghost town in Virginia." Clever entrepreneurs swooped in and purchased the kit homes and arranged to move them into more densely populated cities where they could be resold at a profit. In a remarkable photograph, two Sears homes from Penniman are shown loaded back to back on a barge, on their way 40 miles downstream to Norfolk.[73]

In addition to the homes, the bricks of the iconic 250-foot Penniman smokestack were salvaged. After the war, they were used to build the segregated James City County Training School down the road in the historically African American community of Pottstown. The Williamsburg School Board chairman, W. L. Jones, purchased the *in situ* feature to salvage the bricks. It took 35 sticks of dynamite to topple the smokestack to access the bricks.[74] A remarkably astute and patient modern-day researcher used old photos to calculate that the smokestack contained at least 150,000 bricks while the training school would have required only about 40,000; Jones's recycling ingenuity resulted in a significant savings, which enabled him to follow through on his promise to build the black community a brick school house.[75]

As for the rest of the abandoned Penniman plant, in 1926 a businessman purchased the 2600-acre site along with all its tenements and appurtenances.

But he never capitalized on his purchase, and nothing further was ever built on or refurbished at the site. In 1938, a newspaper reporter described the "herd of peaceful cows [that] graze over the fields once covered with fifty miles of railroad" and where "wild flowers turn tender heads from broken vats where TNT once took form."[76]

In addition producing artillery and explosive cotton balls, Virginia also trained and sent men to serve in artillery regiments. For example, on August 3, 1917, the War Department organized the 313th Field Artillery of the 155th Brigade of the 80th Division at Camp Lee. Colonel Charles D. Herron led this unit and selected officers for the regiment from the First Training Battery at Fort Myer. He received enlisted men from the regular army and drafted men, mostly from West Virginia, to fill the rest of his quota. One former solider in this unit described the officers as "the men whose indignation over the deviltry of the Hun first came to white heat."[77]

These chomping-at-the-bit officers trained men to fire cannons. The challenge was finding sufficient artillery for training purposes when the majority of the weapons were sent directly to the front. In one case, cannoneer trainees used "antiquated 2.9 inch relics of the Spanish War."[78] The same was true of horses; a "dummy animal made of several lengths of timber and a barrel" was substituted during instructional exercises. The 313th trained at Camp Lee six months before they had sufficient horses and harnesses to move the four three-inch guns out to a nearby target range.[79] Finally, in late May 1918, nearly nine months after arriving at Camp Lee, the 313th was sent to France. The 1st Battalion and Headquarters Company were joined by the 305th Ammunition Train and part of the 305th Sanitary Train. They were loaded onto the USS *Siboney* that formed part of a ten-transport convoy that sailed east, protected by a naval cruiser for only part of their journey because of the high demand for such safety escorts.[80]

Coincidentally, one of the practice ranges for the 313th was at Dutch Gap, along the James River, about 12 miles away from crowded and dusty Camp Lee. During the Civil War, this site was called Parker's Battery; the defensive earthworks from that conflict were still extant in 1917. While practicing at the site, World War I trainees hunted for souvenirs from the 19th-century battles. A Great War–era photograph of officers observing their soldiers was captioned "Colonel Herron and other officers observing fire from Old Federal Positions."[81] As I would soon learn, the shadow of the 19th-century conflict touched many aspects of the Great War in Virginia.

Pilots and Aeroplanes

> [Eugene R.] Wheatley's machine caught fire in the air; by wonderful skill he was able to effect a landing, something that is almost impossible in the circumstances; but he was unfortunate enough to have to land on a railway track, and before he could extricate himself from his machine, he was run down by a train.
> —Account of the death of a University of Virginia alumnus, 1918[82]

Most Americans are introduced to World War I heroes (or antiheroes) as young children, even if they don't realize it. For example, many know who the famous German fighter pilot Manfred Albrecht Freiherr von Richthofen is, even if they only recognize him by his nickname, the Red Baron. Peanuts cartoonist Charles Schultz never depicted grown-ups in his comic strip, but a goggle-wearing, soft-helmeted Snoopy "flew" his doghouse into battle many times. In 1966, the Royal Guardsman immortalized these fictional encounters in their song "Snoopy and the Red Baron." More recently, you might recall the Red Baron pizza brand, which features the mustached World War I flying ace wearing a blood-red scarf billowing in the wind. And while the names of Virginia pilots, like Eugene Wheatley, James Rogers McConnell, or Kiffin Rockwell, may not be as engrained in our consciousness, they deserve to be remembered for their exceptional courage in flying into danger.

Virginia has ties to the very first flights, including an early visit and airborne trial at Fort Myer in 1908 by Orville Wright. Unfortunately, this demonstration ended tragically. Just after takeoff, the propeller disintegrated and the plane crashed, killing the sole passenger, Army Signal Corps lieutenant Thomas Selfridge. Orville was badly injured, while Lieutenant Selfridge had the dubious distinction of being the first aviation fatality.[83] Two years later (on November 14, 1910) in the nearby Hampton Roads port, a warship, the USS *Birmingham*, made naval aviation history when a plane was launched from its deck for the first time.

Hundreds of Virginians contributed to the Division of Military Aeronautics (the precursor to the U.S. Air Force) and its fighter planes during World War I. One of the war's first Virginia fighter pilots, and possibly the first American to volunteer to fight in the European war, was Kiffin Yates Rockwell. He was born in Tennessee but attended classes at both the Virginia Military Institute (VMI) (in 1908) and Washington and Lee University (from 1910 to 1911). On the same day that Germany declared war on France, August 3, 1914, Rockwell wrote a letter to the French consul-general to offer his services to France. Without waiting for a response, he and his brother, Paul, boarded an ocean liner for Europe and, upon arrival enlisted in the French Foreign Legion. Nine months later, Rockwell was shot in the leg and, after he recovered, he requested a commission in the newly formed Lafayette Escadrille (originally referred to as simply "N 124" to downplay the role of the then neutral United States). On March 14, 1916, the French Air Department authorized American pilots to fight in an air squadron on behalf of the Allies. Rockwell and six other Americans initially flew 13-meter Nieuports with Lewis guns under the command of two French officers.

Because of the high demand to fly in the Escadrille, a second unit, the Lafayette Flying Corps, was formed and, when necessary, provided replacements for injured or killed members of the original squadron.[84] These early biplanes traveled at 110 miles per hour and required 11 ground personnel for each of the six pilots. One of Rockwell's colleagues, James Rogers McConnell, described encountering sun-dappled fog, silver-hued bullets, and red flames bursting from artillery below on a routine flight, comparing the latter scene to an illustration from Dante's Inferno.[85] Rockwell is credited as the first American to shoot down an enemy plane, on May 18, 1916. Unfortunately, on a later flight on a Nieuport 17 in September, he was shot in the chest by the wingman of a German pilot and died instantly. He was the second American pilot to die in combat during the Great War. He was buried at the Lafayette Escadrille's field at Luxeuil-les-Bains in eastern France. He was also honored on the wall of the Pantheon in Paris, the post office in his hometown of Newport, Tennessee, on a plaque that hangs in the Robert E. Lee Chapel on the campus of Washington and Lee University, at VMI, and on a marker in Asheville, North Carolina.[86]

Rockwell and his early comrades flew Nieuport biplanes, built in France. But his American successors usually trained on American-built planes. Virginia was home to one of the few training fields in the country: the Curtiss Flying School in Newport News. This school opened a little more than a decade after the Wright brothers' famous flight one hundred miles to the south. Over its seven short years of operation (1915–1922), the school attracted aerial daredevils from all over the world. These pilots included the father of the U.S. Air Force (then the Army Air Corps) airman William Mitchell (who served in Virginia), as well as hundreds of army, navy, and coast guard aviators.[87] In the fall of 1916, the Army selected Newport News as its main aviation training station, took over its operations, and changed the name to the Atlantic Coast Aeronautical Station.

Pilots who trained here and fought in the war returned afterwards and opened two new, and better known today, training centers: the Aviation Experimental Station and Proving Grounds (soon renamed Langley Field) and Naval Air Station Norfolk.

Pilots were not the only heroes in airborne fighting. The planes had to be fitted with guns and other complex equipment. To meet this need an aircraft assembly factory was opened in Alexandria in 1918. Its high ceilings contained scaffolding to hang wings and propellers, while men worked meticulously on the wooden frames below. Just a year earlier, the first air-to-ground radio transmitter was tested by AT&T at Langley Field.[88]

Virginia made two other airborne crafts for the war. Glenn Hammond Curtiss, the founder of the eponymous flying school, built dirigibles. Often known by the German term zeppelins, these hydrogen-filled airships could fly higher and further than the biplanes of the era and could carry heavy payloads, such as bombs. Curtiss received a contract to build a motor for a dirigible in 1904 and later built one of the first balloons ordered by the U.S. Army. Soon after this effort, Curtiss formed the Aerial Experiment Association (with Alexander Graham Bell) and began making airplanes, which led to the creation of his Virginia school.[89]

The U.S. Army also trained soldiers in the use of observation balloons. In Virginia, these crews trained at Camp Morrison in Warwick County or at the Army's balloon supply depot in downtown Richmond. Surprisingly, these pilots were the first to use parachutes, long before they were commonplace on airplanes. In a letter written to his mother, a supply officer at Camp Morrison stationed with the 19th Balloon Company, complained, "We came here equipped with absolutely nothing," a fact that created a huge amount of paperwork. The letter writer explained that "I had to make out requisitions for all that stuff ['articles of wearing apparel'] in addition to all the supplies that a company needs from a Balloon down to a paper clip," concluding that "it is quite a job."[90]

Ships

> We shall build good ships here; at a profit, if we can; at a loss, if we must; But always good ships.
> —Collis P. Huntington[91]

A Victorian-era railroad entrepreneur, Collis P. Huntington was one of the first people to recognize the strategic importance of Hampton

Roads. In the mid–19th century, Huntington teamed up with other businessmen and in 1869 they drove a golden railroad spike into the last piece of the rail line at Promontory Point, Utah, thereby completing the transcontinental railroad. Next, the savvy businessman turned his attention to eastern routes. As Huntington scouted out railroad lines he recognized the potential of the surprisingly deep Hampton harbor, a strategically important spot since the 17th century. He built the Chesapeake and Ohio Railway to connect multiple rail lines and bring products like West Virginia coal to transatlantic shipping ports. Huntington founded the Chesapeake Dry Dock and Construction Company in 1886 to repair and manufacture seaborne crafts that could take these products to overseas markets. He officially opened his new venture in 1889 with the docking of the Navy's warship *Puritan*, and several years later the company received a contract to build two battleships: the *Kearsarge* and the *Kentucky*.[92] The increased trade and shipbuilding in Hampton Roads led to an increase in population in nearby cities including Newport News, Norfolk, and Portsmouth. Huntington recognized another business opportunity in this growth and formed the Old Dominion Land Company, which produced houses of varying cost, resulting in the neighborhoods "Quality Row" and "Poverty Row."[93] All of these economic changes and social inequalities accelerated between 1915 and 1919, when Hampton Roads transformed into a nationally significant military aviation and naval base. Official American naval operations began on April 6, 1917, when Congress declared war on the "imperial German government." The declaration of war meant that the U.S. Coast Guard became part of the Department of the Navy for the duration.

The U.S. Navy is not one of the first lines of offense (or defense) that comes to mind during the First World War. The more familiar World War I naval narrative is of the Allied battleships blockading the German fleet while the German U-boats (*Unterseeboot*) slipped into international waters and torpedoed mercantile and military ships. Some U.S. naval ships were part of the effort to protect Allied shipping, although most of the fleet remained in American waters because of severe fuel oil shortages.[94] Rather than engage with the enemy, most of the navy's service during the war focused on two tasks: transporting American troops and supplies (and protecting their ships) across the Atlantic, and patrolling the coastal waters off the eastern seaboard. Virginia dock workers and sailors played a major role in these patrols.

To understand the role of Virginia ships during the Great War we have to search the naval inventories of the 1910s because it takes several years to build a ship. In fact, only a handful of American ships—all dreadnoughts (an early version of a battleship)—were begun and completed in time to be put into service during the war. Dreadnoughts, named after a British ship launched in 1906, featured heavy caliber armaments and steam-turbine propulsion. Huntington's Newport News shipyard played an important role in producing and repairing seaborne crafts because it was "equipped with a Simpson's Basin Dry Dock, capable of docking a vessel 600 feet long, drawing 25 feet of water, at any stage of the tide."[95] This remarkable engineering feature secured an important role for Hampton Roads during the war.

Several of the Newport News Shipyard and Dry Dock Construction Company's earlier commissions were used during World War I. It built the USS *Nashville* in 1894, and the navy launched it in 1895. After serving for years in the Spanish-American War in the Caribbean and the Boxer Rebellion in China, military strategists sent her to Gibraltar in August 1917 to patrol off the North African coast. The ship was decommissioned the next year and eventually sold to a private company. The USS *Wilmington* is from the same era and was also built in Newport News. When America entered the European war it was on a routine cruise off the coast of China. The Chinese government reacted to America's declaration of war by interning all belligerent ships. The *Wilmington* sped away within an internationally-agreed-upon 48-hour limit to avoid this fate and sailed to Manila in the Philippines. There she patrolled Manila Bay through the fall of 1917. After the war ended she returned to her Shanghai patrol.[96]

A word about naming conventions: Ships that are commissioned for the U.S. Navy receive the appellation "USS," which stands for "United States Ship." The inventory of American ships as of 1917 used the following conventions: naval cruisers were named after U.S. cities, often state names were used to christen battleships, people were honored with the naming of destroyers, and Native American tribal names were used to identify tugs.[97] So the USS *Delaware*, also built and launched by the Newport News Shipbuilding Company, was a dreadnought battleship. The USS *Delaware* was built in 1909, commissioned in 1910, and served as an escort ship during World War I.

Fittingly, the Newport News Shipbuilding Yard launched the USS *Virginia*. Like most of the American ships that actually saw action during the war, it was built years earlier, in 1904, and commissioned in 1906. When the war broke out, the ship was docked in Boston receiving a much-needed overhaul, having served as part of President Theodore Roosevelt's "Great White Fleet" to demonstrate American naval power on a worldwide tour. After the repairs were completed, she joined the Third Division of the Atlantic in August 1917 and served as a training vessel for American naval gunners. She was briefly used as an escort vessel for convoys crossing the U-boat-infested Atlantic. When the war ended, she sailed five times to bring American soldiers home from Europe. She was decommissioned in 1919 and used as target practice for bomber pilots off the coast of North Carolina.[98]

Other U.S. Navy ships were obtained through seizure; such was the case with the *Camilla Rickmers*, a German steamer that carried 5,130 gross tons and was seized by U.S. custom officials in 1917. The Newport News shipyard refitted her for use by the U.S. Navy, which renamed her the USS *Ticonderoga* and used her cargo holds to ship automobiles, trucks, and animals. As a cargo ship with only a one-by-six-inch gun mounted on the stern and a three-inch gun in the bow, she was escorted by warships and sailed in a convoy for protection until she had engine trouble on the night of September 29, 1918, and, slipping behind the convoy, was spotted by a German submarine early the next morning.[99] Her crew fought the losing gun battle for two hours before the *Ticonderoga* sank; only 24 of her 237 sailors survived and two were taken prisoner. This tragedy hit home in Virginia. One of the men who died on the ship was Norfolk native Jesse Mack Breedlove. He was a mess attendant third class on the ship and had enlisted just eight months earlier, in January 1918. Like many of the Virginia casualties, he was young, just 21 years old, and left behind close family to grieve a personal loss from the global conflict.[100] Unlike many of his contemporaries, he changed his racial status in order to "pass" as white in the navy and avoid a segregated unit. In the 1900 Federal Census he and his Norfolk relatives, including his sister Vashtie are listed as "Black," but his draft registration card lists him as "Caucasian."[101] The world war was producing surprising social changes alongside the expected military carnage.

The shipboard notes in a Virginia quartermaster's log reveal some sketchy details of daily life aboard the USS *Maui*, a commercial passenger ship commissioned to serve as a troop transport in 1918. After stevedores loaded the hulls, the troops came on board, and the ship set sail. The log continued, sometimes providing minute-by-minute accounts of powering the engines up and down, taking bearings, and conducting fire and safety drills. Only occasionally did this daily script deviate, such as when a man fell overboard at 1:20 a.m. and a lifeboat capsized four minutes later when they tried to rescue him.[102] The crew did see a destroyer one day and changed course to evade it.[103] After the war ended, the ship transported

Americans between Brest and New York. As early as December 17, 1918, a group of 64 officers and 2,161 men returned home on the USS *Maui*.[104] One of these men was Major Oliver M. White from Roanoke. He was wounded at Verdun and remarked that "the only thing that beat the Germans at Chateau Thierry was the doggoned determination of the Americans to go ahead."[105]

Before the United States entered the war, the Hampton Roads region was a place of refuge for foreign ships. In one tense situation, a German ship, the *Prinz Eitel*, eluded its British pursuers and anchored off 33rd Street in Newport News, seeking refuge in the port of the then neutral United States. Neutrality laws dictated that combatant ships had 24 hours to resupply and refuel. But the *Prinz Eitel* had suffered damages in its latest ocean forays so it was no longer seaworthy. This early in the war, there was little anti–German feeling in America, so when customs collector Norman Hamilton boarded the ship to discuss the situation, the German captain invited him to lunch and the ship's band provided entertainment. The ship held three hundred British prisoners, who were quickly liberated and eventually boarded horse freighters that would take them back home. The German ship was moved into Drydock 3 for repairs. While this work was in progress, the Germans were treated as guests of honor. The British Royal Navy, furious at the honorific treatment their enemy was receiving in the Newport News drydocks, threatened to attack the ship.[106]

A second German ship, the *Kronprinz Wilhelm*, was interred in the navy yard at Portsmouth. Before the war the *Kronprinz Wilhelm* was a passenger liner, but at the outbreak of hostilities the German Navy converted her into a commerce raider. She docked in the American port because she was rapidly running out of coal and many members of her crew were sick with pneumonia, pleurisy, rheumatism, and scurvy. She was unable to recover in time to set sail within the 48-hour window so she too was interred. Between April 1915 and America's declaration of war in 1917, her crew of about a thousand sailors lived onshore, near the ship, as "guests" of the American government. They occupied themselves by building a German "village" from scrap materials and named it the Eitel Wilhelm. More than ten thousand tourists came over the next eight months to see the daring raider in dock and the miniature German village nearby. Locals hosted parties for the German officers while they waited for their ship to be repaired. When the United States entered the war, President Wilson signed an executive order enabling the U.S. Navy to take possession of the enemy ship and begin the necessary repairs. Oddly enough, given the new state of hostilities, she was renamed the *Von Steuben*, in honor of the German hero of the American Revolution. The German sailors became prisoners of war and were transferred to Fort McPherson in Georgia.[107]

The declaration of war provided the catalyst for the creation of Naval Station Norfolk, an entity that eventually became the world's largest naval base. In 1907, the land for the future training site was being used to host the Jamestown Exposition, one of the many world's fairs that were popular during this period. During that event, held to commemorate the three hundredth anniversary of the founding of the Jamestown settlement, visiting naval officers agreed that it was an ideal spot for a maritime installation: located on Sewell's Point and roughly equidistant from the cities of Norfolk, Portsmouth, Newport News, and Hampton. A decade would pass before America's entry in World War I convinced the secretary of the navy to buy the property. Construction began during the summer of 1917, and by the fall several elements were completed: "piers, aviation facilities, a recruit training station, a submarine base, and recreation grounds for fleet personnel."[108]

Because of the assembly-line pressure during the war, most of the

A makeshift settlement, "Eitel Wilhelm," built by German sailors between the spring of 1915 and 1917 while their ship, *Kronprinz Wilhelm*, was interred at the Portsmouth navy yard (The Mariners' Museum, MS0189/01–01#094).

Hampton Roads ships were launched with little or no fanfare. But on the Fourth of July 1918, three boats were "sent gracefully down into the welcoming James [River]" at Newport News: the *Haraden, Abbot,* and *Thomas.* The Abbot contained a banner that proclaimed, "Off to Berlin—down with the Kaiser, and three cheers for freedom."[109] Each of the three destroyers were christened by women, most of whom were related to the namesakes of the ships, such as the widow of naval officer C. C. Thomas.[110] Government officials promoted this rare occasion as "Liberty Launching Day"; on July 4, 1918, 14 ships were launched across America, including the three in Virginia. These ships, and every ship of the Allied forces, were at risk from German submarines patrolling the Atlantic shipping lanes.

Sunken Ship

> The Lusitania, the greatest of all ocean steamers in the world ... has just carried 3,600 passengers across the Atlantic in five days! The Lusitania is the marvel of all ages. She is the most talked of ship that was ever built.
> —*Lexington Gazette,* October 23, 1907

For most Americans, the most infamous naval encounter of the war was between the *Lusitania* and a U-20, a German submarine. Dubbed the "Greyhound of the seas" for her then remarkable 25-knot average speed and her camouflage gray paint, in early May 1915 the *Lusitania* was on her 202nd Atlantic crossing. Although she was touted as a luxury liner, in the same Cunard line as the sunken Titanic, the British had secretly outfitted her for war service years earlier, with gun mounts concealed under the teak deck. On that spring day, the ship set sail from New York to return to its home harbor in Liverpool, England, with a secret cargo: munitions and contraband. The Germans were, most likely, aware of these items.[111]

Only hours from her final destination the *Lusitania* was spotted by a U-20. The German submarine fired a torpedo into the starboard hull around two o'clock in the afternoon on May 7. Passengers and crew had only 18 minutes to abandon ship before it sank. Of the almost 2,000 people aboard the ship, 58 percent died, including 124 Americans.

One of these deaths impacted Virginia directly: Albert L. Hopkins, the president of the Newport News Shipbuilding and Drydock Company. Appointed only a year earlier, Hopkins was a trained engineer, with a degree from Rensselaer Polytechnic Institute in New York. He lived in

New York City with his wife and daughter. He was sailing on the *Lusitania* that day with two other shipping executives in order to negotiate contracts with Britain, including armored plates for battleships. His body, labeled #194 in the wreckage, was returned to New York, and Homer L. Ferguson was appointed his successor.[112]

Unlike Hopkins, Ferguson had a military background; he graduated from the U.S. Naval Academy at Annapolis in 1892 and was "widely known in naval construction circles."[113] He had begun working at the shipyard in 1895, resigning from the navy to supervise hull construction. He was promoted to vice president of the company in 1912, and his 1915 appointment as president was unanimous. A year earlier Ferguson had been appointed by President Wilson to represent the United States at an international conference to recommend measures to promote safety at sea.[114] While his efforts had failed to protect the *Lusitania*, he served successfully as the shipyard president until 1946.

A second Virginian on the doomed *Lusitania* was Richmond native Charles T. Hill. In 1900, Hill had moved to England to work for the British-American Tobacco Company. He was on the ship returning to work after leaving behind his sick wife in America. Hill was on deck that afternoon and saw the submarine periscope and the torpedo slam into the side of the ship. He narrowly avoided death as he first went in search of his friends before getting into a lifeboat that was launched incorrectly and landed upside down. He stayed with the small boat until he was rescued by another ship. Two days later the *Richmond Times-Dispatch* reassured the public that "Hill is Safe," reporting on a cable that he sent from Queenstown (where he was recovering from minor injuries) to his father, C. Emmett Hill, in Richmond.[115]

Many other Virginians participated in or felt the impacts from the war. In the next chapter I present some of their stories.

2

Participants

> If you make good, they will forgive any mistake. If you do not make good, they will probably hang us both to the first lamp-post they can find.
>
> —Secretary of War Newton D. Baker
> to General Pershing, 1917[1]

Newton D. Baker, secretary of war from 1916 to 1921, penned these words after Congress made the controversial decision to enter the conflict. A graduate of Washington and Lee University's Law School, Secretary Baker recommended instituting military conscription when America formally entered the war. This was a paradoxical position for a secretary of war appointed by a president who initially pledged to keep America out of the world war and who had himself promised to "fight for peace." Instead, Baker presided over the registration of four million American men, about 465,000 of whom were living in Virginia.[2]

Two weeks before President Wilson called for America to join the war, a Virginia newspaper headline proclaimed "Virtual State of War with Germany Exists."[3] That same day the Richmond Light Infantry Blues, a Virginia National Guard unit, paraded through the Virginia capital, feted for its recent service on the Texas border. One week later, the same paper led above the fold with the news that the "Navy is Seeking 25,000 Recruits," explaining that the navy was "rushing at top speed" to prepare for war: speeding up ship construction, opening up bidding for several submarines chasers, meeting with steel executives to increase production, and even compensating private citizens for donating their small motor boats to the cause.[4] War was just around the corner and Virginians were about to be called upon to do more than just breed mules, repair ships, and produce a food surplus.

On Monday, April 2, 1917, Virginians woke up to newspaper headlines alerting them to the "momentous issue" that faced Congress. President Wilson had spent his weekend "put[ting] the final touches" on the speech that he planned to deliver to Congress in which he would request troops to send into battle against Germany.[5] The House and Senate debated the measure on Wednesday and Thursday. The Richmond headlines confidently predicted, "War Resolution Asked by Wilson Sure of Passage." Young men in Virginia were considering the implications of another headline, "Army Plan Based on Conscription."[6] On Thursday, April 5, the U.S. Senate voted for war, 82 to 6, with only a "little group of willful" senators voting against the measure; on Friday, April 6, the House voted 373 to 50 to go to war. All ten Virginia representatives voted in favor of it.[7] With support from Congress, President Wilson signed the war resolution and, as the Associated Press framed it, for only the "second time since 1814" America entered into war with a European power.[8]

Hundreds of miles away, in far southwestern Virginia, residents of a rural community admitted that there was a "deep seated aversion on the part of the majority of Scott County people to entering this war." They, along with the millions of Americans had elected President Wilson to power in 1916, in part, based on his promise to retain neutrality in "a war with which we have nothing to do, whose causes cannot touch us." But only a few months later, in the spring of 1917, the Germans mounted an extensive submarine campaign to sink all ships trading with the Allies, including those belonging to neutral nations like the United States. After America lost several ships, Wilson and his advisors reviewed two years of German belligerent acts (such as the sinking of the *Lusitania* in 1915, in which more than one hundred American lost their lives, and the interception of the Zimmerman telegram that demonstrated Germany's attempted interference with Mexican/American relations) and came to the conclusion that America could no longer sit on the sidelines. On February 3, 1917, the United States severed diplomatic relations with Germany, and Virginia communities that had once been pro–German or antiwar began to change their opinions. By early April, the tone of the Scott County newspaper editorials changed from pro-neutrality to "active and hearty co-operation in carrying it [war] on."[9] And the *Lynchburg News* stated unequivocally, "It is a war against mankind, against all nations" and thus they supported President's Wilson decision to "indict German submarine policy" and "call America to arms."[10] By the summer of 1917, most Virginians came to see the war as a humanitarian necessity. As the editors of the *Clinch Valley News* explained, the congressional resolution to declare a state of war between the United States and Germany gave President

Wilson the authority to "force Germany to an observance of laws of humanity."[11]

As President Wilson urged the United States to proceed with "aggressive military action" against Germany, he faced a severe troop shortage. In April 1917, the strength of the U.S. Army was about 200,000, which included 80,000 serving in National Guard units. Members of his cabinet and top military leaders disagreed on whether to implement a draft or to encourage volunteers. Some Virginians may have been wondering, why deal with soldiers who might be serving unwillingly if you had a supply of volunteers? But, as the British had learned firsthand after several years of voluntary military service, volunteers could come from any part of society, thereby possibly decimating certain industries. In contrast, a draft enabled the government to set rules on who would and would not be drafted. In February and March 1917 President Wilson and Secretary Baker hoped to raise a sufficient fighting force from the standing army, the National Guard, and roughly half a million volunteers.[12] As part of this plan, Virginia would have been expected to send 18,000 troops, a combined force of volunteers and National Guardsmen.[13] Many Virginia communities were optimistically predicting that they would be able to rally plenty of volunteers but as events unfolded that spring, it became clear that few municipalities would be able to meet their enrollment figures without turning to conscription.

The president signed the Selective Service Act on May 18, 1917, in an effort to quickly increase the size of the newly minted American Expeditionary Force (AEF). A few weeks later, on June 5, 1917, all men aged 21 to 31 were required to appear before their local draft board to register. Each county (or every 30,000 residents) operated a draft board. In the larger cities, like Richmond, there were dozens of draft agencies. The draft registration application included questions about the applicants' height, "build," and whether they claimed any physical exemptions. If they looked closely, they would have seen a handwritten number at the top of this card. Later that summer, on July 20, these men would find out if they were going to be called up when two blindfolded men picked capsules, containing numbered slips, in the Senate Office Building in Washington, D.C. The first number drawn was 258, and men across the country with that number were drafted into service; it took 22 hours to draw the rest of the numbers. The headline of the *Richmond Times-Dispatch* announced the net quota of each Virginia county and city. The city of Richmond had the largest obligation, 788 men, while Spotsylvania County had the smallest quota, only 19 men.[14] The final total, 181,526 registrants, represented one of the highest participation rates of all 48 states.[15] Many Virginia counties were able to meet their quotas by a combination of professional and civilian recruits. For example, the large city of Petersburg sent men from its National Guard Unit (Company G of the Second Virginia Infantry), the Petersburg Home Guard, two Virginia volunteer companies (the A. P. Hill Rifles and the Petersburg

A poster encouraging Americans to "enlist now" in the U.S. Army. Created by Vincent Aderente, ca. 1916 (Library of Congress Prints and Photographs Division, Washington, D.C. Call number POS–US .H348, no. 1).

Guard), and drafted the rest of its quota from civilians. Between Petersburg and Dinwiddie County, 11,442 men registered for the draft. A much smaller number, 1,396, were accepted into the armed forces to train in nearby camps. Dozens of these men died over the next two years.[16]

In the first American draft, men from "well-recognized" religious sects that prohibited participation in war were exempted, as was the vice president of the United States, legislative and judicial officers, and certain key military and civilian personnel, such as workers at domestic armories or arsenals.[17] The next two conscriptions refined the rules surrounding a man's eligibility. Exemptions were permitted in some cases, but draftees were not allowed to pay someone else to serve in their place, as had been the case in the Civil War, when $300 bought a stand-in.[18]

In the end, three separate registrations were necessary to furnish the AEF with sufficient manpower: they took place on June 5, 1917; June 5, 1918 (for men who had turned 21 since 1917); and September 12, 1918. By the third draft, the eligible ages were expanded to between 18 and 45. In the end, about 24 million men filled out registration cards; this accounts for over 90 percent of all men in the United States born between 1872 and 1900.[19] Through this process, 2.8 million men were asked to serve; an additional two million men volunteered; of course, no women were conscripted.

But not everyone answered the call to serve. Nationwide, about three million eligible men failed to register, while as many as 350,000 men deserted after they were drafted.[20] In Virginia, Isaiah Ashby of Loudoun County was arrested by the local sheriff in February 1918 for resisting the draft.[21] More surprising was the arrest of three hundred "slackers" who were taken into custody at a powder packing plant in Seven Pines, Henrico County. It took 13 trucks to take them into custody, and they were held until they could produce draft cards proving that they had registered.[22] Contemporary accounts blamed "radicals" for inspiring this resistance. Major General Crowder, judge advocate general of the United States during the war, described these "delinquents" as using their "fantastic dreams" to "enchant and seduce the ignorant and artless folk who came under their influence." In the final Virginia conscription report, the Adjutant General's Office emphasized that "it should remain always a source of pride to the State that on registration day no anti-registration elements ... marred the expression of patriotism of Virginians."[23] While this might be technically be true, that on that one day there were no "unpatriotic demonstrations," the hundreds of draft dodgers and, in some counties, 50 percent or more of the registrants claiming an exemption, illustrated that not all Virginians were willing to put their lives on the line to "halt the hun."

Virginia patriots in 1917 had another political issue to address: the status of the former Confederate states. America hoped to enter into the world war with a united national front. And yet in the 1910s, southerners still erected memorials to the "Lost Cause" and Confederate heroes, thereby emphasizing the continued socioeconomic chasm between the industrialized North and the agrarian South. The cultural sensitivity of Virginians being drafted and fighting for the federal government is illustrated by an incongruous article about the American flag which merited a spot on the front page of the April 7 issue of the *Richmond Times-Dispatch*. Sandwiched between headlines about imprisoning "German plotters" on American soil and the banner headline that President Wilson had signed the papers for America to go to war was the headline "American Flag Raised over Confederate Home." Understanding the cultural significance of the otherwise quotidian act of raising an American flag may require some explanation. More than 50 years after the end of the Civil War, former Confederate states had not yet readopted the American flag as their own. In this case, the North Carolina Home for Confederate Veterans raised the Stars and Stripes for the first time since the "war of northern aggression."[24] And in Richmond, this item merited placement next to an announcement of America's entry into World War I.

Most American men and their families assumed that drafted men would soon be fighting the "Huns" along the western front. But only a fraction of the 93,000 Virginians who served during World War I made it to those deadly trenches.

Troops Abroad

> I was in Battles muse argone and St mihiel Drive I was gassed I went throu Rain snow mud and Stade in Battle Field where ded People was piled up I stade in trenches in till my Feet was Swelled up so I Coulden hardly walk I will never For Get the 26 of September we went over the top it was the Greatest Site I ever See Shells and Bullets was thick as hall it was ... lieutenant Killed and Captin Gassed and Several men Killed and wounded I thought my time had come.
> —Accomack County resident Private George Grover Cleveland Isdell, Company 4, 318th Regiment, 80th Division[25]

A lot of Americans thought that they would miss the action abroad completely because the United States entered the conflict so late. The

French said publicly that they had "no particular interest in having American troops in France," preferring our money, food, and munitions.[26] And then there was a significant logistical hurdle: how to transport tens of thousands of troops across the Atlantic. General Pershing bartered with France and Britain for ships and support. In order to streamline this process, several points of embarkation in America were established, including ports in Boston, Philadelphia, and Baltimore. Much has been written about the largest one, New York City, but the crucial role of its Virginia parallel, the city of Newport News, is often overlooked in discussions of America's role in World War I.[27]

Newport News was strategically located near the mouth of the Chesapeake Bay, linked to other cities across the state and country via extensive railroad facilities and already equipped with outstanding port facilities. Nearby Norfolk would have also been a good choice except for the fact that its shipping lanes and docks were already overcrowded. More than 261,000 soldiers embarked from the piers of Newport News aboard 145 transports. In addition, more than four million tons of military supplies and hundreds of thousands of animals were shipped to Europe from its facilities. After the war's end, 441,146 soldiers returned to the United States via this vital Virginia port of embarkation.[28]

Who were the Virginians sent over on these ships? And what were their duties abroad? In this chapter I will limit my focus to the Virginians who fought in just one of the theaters of war, France; the complexities of their service in Italy, the Middle East, and even the far reaches of Russia will be fodder for future research. Most men heading to France stopped first in Britain as their transports refueled, took on additional supplies, and left behind any sick or deceased men from the voyage. Once they arrived in France the troops rode on freight cars and walked from rail stations to the battlefields. Private Isdell, quoted above, arrived in the summer of 1918 on the *Leviathan* at the western port of Brest, France, more than five hundred miles from the heart of the fighting in the northeastern trenches. From there he traveled by train to Dion and eventually arrived at the front, where he fought in the Battle of Saint-Mihiel and the Meuse-Argonne offensive. The western front was a line of parallel trenches and other defensive features more than four hundred miles long, which stretched from Belgium through France, extending from the North Sea to the Swiss border. In 1917 and 1918, the majority of American forces were carrying out missions in this region to help the Allies defeat the German army. One of first Virginia soldiers to die in action was Captain Lloyd W. Williams, who uttered the famous retort to a French officer who advised him to withdraw, "Retreat? Hell, we just got here!" Promoted posthumously, Major Williams was gassed and shot on June 1, 1918, at Belleau Wood and awarded the Distinguished Service Cross.[29]

Virginians joined other American troops in the tense battle to hold the line and prevent the Germans from occupying Paris. Corporal Walter L. Haskett, from Giles County, fought in the Meuse Argonne offensive. He was with the 317th Infantry Regiment, 80th Division, and was cited for distinguished bravery during the battle. His unit was "held up by an enemy machine gun nest and Corporal Haskett and two others crawled on their stomachs in the face of machine-fun fire to a point sufficiently near to be able to throw hand grenades into the nest, killing and wounding two, thereby permitting the regiment to advance."[30] Another Virginian, Captain Charles Riticor from Loudoun County served bravely but did not survive. He died from shrapnel and gas wounds about a month after he participated in the Aisne-Marne offensive in the summer of 1918.

Twenty-year-old Private McKnight Tingle Hudson, from Accomack County, was also wounded. He survived but he was embittered and when asked about the "impressions made upon him by his experience," he replied, "I thought the devil was ruling the universe and God Almighty has let out."[31] Private Hudson shipped out from Camp Lee and arrived at the French port of Brest in the summer of 1918. He participated in several crucial and carnage-filled battles: the Second Battle of the Marne (mid–July to early August 1918), the Battle of Saint-Mihiel (September 12–15, 1918), and the Meuse-Argonne offensive (September 26–November 11, 1918). During the first of these battles, the Virginia resident helped to "h[o]ld the bank of the Marne East of Chateau Thierry where large forse of German Infantry sought to forse a passage under support of powerful artillery consentration under cover of smoke screens." Private Hudson and his fellow infantry soldiers fired "in three directions" to counter the German attack and "susseeded in throwing two German Divisions into complete confusion, capturing 600 prisoners." During Private Hudson's last mission, he inhaled mustard gas and was shipped to an AEF base hospital on November 25. While he did not talk about his injuries directly, his answer to a series of queries on a questionnaire sponsored by the Virginia War History Commission conveyed his deep antipathy toward his experiences. While he stated that he was "glad to be of some service to suffering humanity," he lamented that his "health [was] ruined" and he left the service having "lost faith in my own country."[32]

Not everyone was fighting; some were helping to boost morale and organize troop movement by playing instruments. A Virginian served as the director of the famed 116th Infantry Band. William Howe Ruebush and his fellow musicians were sent abroad to boost morale and were required to take on additional duties. Ruebush came from a family of musicians, poets, and teachers. He graduated from the Shenandoah Institute in 1893, remained to teach music at his alma mater, and at the relatively late age of 41, he enlisted in the First Virginia Infantry Band of the Virginia Volunteers in 1914.[33] After a brief stint along the Texas-Mexico border in 1916, Ruebush's unit became part of the National Guard's new 29th Division on October 4, 1917. This unit was called the "Blue and Gray" because it included men from "Confederate" Virginia and Maryland (Gray) and "Union" New Jersey, Delaware, and Washington, D.C. (Blue).[34] After almost a year of training, they sailed to France on June 15, 1918, a trip which Ruebush recalled as "delightful" and one that would "linger always in my mind."[35] In his numerous letters home to his mother, wife, and six-year-old son, he described a rolling, grass-covered landscape similar to the one he left behind in the Shenandoah valley. One day he took a break from his military duties to help a French farmer and his wife cut their hay. Otherwise, he and his 50-member band were sent to towns where American troops were billeted to provide musical relief. On other occasions they partnered with French musicians and played concerts, including a patriotic performance on July 14, Bastille Day, the French independence day. Back home in Virginia, waiting family members consoled themselves with songs featuring patriotic titles like "Somewhere in France Is My Daddy," "Soldier Boys," and "Come Boys, the Bugles Are Calling."[36]

While Ruebush's band was never called upon to fight with weapons, they did do double duty as litter bearers during the Meuse Argonne offensive. During this crucial and bloody battle along the front in northeastern France, the band reported to the regimental surgeon. On October 8, 1918, as part of this service, they helped evacuate the wounded to an ambulance dressing station.[37] Back home in Harrisonburg, Ruebush's local paper reported that the band cared for 60 to 80 percent of the 116th's wounded soldiers. Band member William E. Whitesell (born in Rockingham County in 1854) recalled, "We were nearly worked to death during the first few days of the battle, carrying wounded, enemy and all over those old shell torn and muddy hills and hollows."[38] In a letter to his mother on October 20, Ruebush concluded, "None of you will ever know the true story of conditions here untill such as are fortunate enough to gather with you around the old home fireside." Ruebush ended his time in service attending a multiweek AEF-sponsored bandmasters and musicians class in Chaumont, France.

Sheet music produced in Roanoke, Virginia, titled "Somewhere in France Is My Daddy." It includes the lyrics "When Uncle Sammy called upon his nephews, My Daddy was among the first to go" (200500460.c1, Virginia Historical Society).

Ruebush remained in France for months after the Armistice, playing concerts and providing music for dances. His army band left France in late April 1919, and on May 29 they arrived back in Dayton at 4:00 a.m., greeted by honking car horns and church bells. The all-day celebration included banquets, parades, a baseball game (between a local team and the band), and music.³⁹ Ruebush returned to the classroom, teaching music at Shenandoah Collegiate Institute (now Shenandoah College) for 25 years. He also served as mayor of Dayton, one term in the Virginia House of Delegates (1920–21), and as the Dayton postmaster (12 years).⁴⁰ Unlike some of his military colleagues, Ruebush turned his wartime service into a foundation for a successful postbellum career.

A second Virginia musician was not as lucky. One of two Virginia band members who died in France was George Washington Webster. Webster died in France on October 28, 1918, when he was only 28 years old. He is buried in the Dayton town cemetery, Rockingham County, under an obelisk inscribed, "Killed in France Argonne Forest.... Headquarters Co. 116 Inf. / Beloved one farewell."⁴¹

Still other Virginians served as drivers for the trucks that lumbered through the ubiquitous mud to transport men and supplies from the ships to the front. Percy Holladay of Richmond trained as a driver at Camp Lee and drove for General Charles S. Farnsworth before being shipped abroad. In his position as a driver he traveled hundreds of miles across the French countryside, where he observed many things. He saw a young boy accidentally run over by a colleague's truck, lived through intense nighttime shelling, witnessed biplanes battling in the skies, and watched the Germans destroying their own ammunition and hot air observation balloons as they retreated. All the while he worked under harrowing conditions hauling ammunition and guns to the front, where he encountered mud and rain for days at a time, "sleeping anywhere [he] could but always managing to get wet."⁴²

Percy and his brother Phillip Clayton both fell ill in Lorraine, France, during the fall 1918, suffering from the diarrhea that often spread through the crowded trenches. Much of the work to move food and armaments fell to the labor battalions. These units were often made up of African American soldiers led by white officers. And while some American military leaders planned to keep black troops armed with spades and wagons instead of guns, these labor units were occasionally called to fight. For example, the 92nd Division, originally organized as an engineering regiment, fought along Baulny Ridge during the Meuse Argonne offensive.⁴³ Eugene W. Ragland of Charlottesville served in a "Pioneer Unit" that took part in this deadly battle that helped change the course of the war. Despite his bravery and sacrifice, when Ragland died in the Veterans Administration Hospital in 1958 his obituary made no mention of his World War I heroics. That service is preserved, instead, on his marble headstone in the St. John's Baptist Church Cemetery in Cobham, which lists his company

(H) and unit (807th Pioneer).⁴⁴ And there were African American gravediggers, to which I'll return in Chapter 4.

Students

> Let us remember that our country has a future as well as a present, and that the colleges and universities, in a very real sense, hold that future. The great process of teaching and learning, which are as necessary as preparation for war, must go on.
> —Edwin A. Alderman, president, University of Virginia, ca. 1920⁴⁵

Eight months after America entered the war, the *Richmond Times-Dispatch* proudly announced, "Schools and Colleges are doing their part." The editors pointed to the million dollars that Virginia students raised in cooperation with the YMCA and YWCA. Although obviously biased, the paper concluded, "No other colleges in the country have given so liberally." As with most cultural trends in Virginia during this period, the article outlined the gift giving by gender and race: reporting that the men raised the highest amount, followed by the women, and then a mixed-gender group of "colored students." These students saved their money by "trimming down" social affairs (in the case of the women), giving up "party frocks" (again, the women's contribution), curtailing fraternity banquets (the men), and demonstrating an unsurpassed "spirit and sacrifice" (the African American students). The highest contribution from a woman's college was made by Sweet Briar College.⁴⁶

Unlike in subsequent 20th-century wars in which exemptions to the draft were allowed, students were expected to serve in World War I. The only student exception was someone who, before May 18, 1917, had been preparing for the ministry. Accordingly, the day that America officially entered the war, the Virginia Military Institute (VMI) announced that it was going to graduate its senior class one month early. This would give the army additional officers, who were in short supply. That year, VMI expected to graduate 59 student soldiers who would have had no difficulty in obtaining commissions after their newly set May 15 graduation date.⁴⁷

In addition to providing student soldiers, four hundred institutions of higher education across the country acceded control of their curriculum to the U.S. government for the duration of the war. They were converted into military schools because there wasn't sufficient time or space to enroll American men into the handful of specialized military academies. The transition of authority on college campuses resulted in radical alterations to the administration and curriculum of several Virginia colleges, including the University of Virginia. As a "war college," it began offering limited classes designed for their "practical value to the men when they go into service."[48] All students who qualified for military service as of October 1, 1918, were inducted into the Student Army Training Corps (SATC). These students attended college tuition-free, received free room and board, and were paid $30 a month based on their rank of private in the U.S. Army.

At the University of Virginia (UVA), one observer described the change after the imposition of military training exercises as follows: "All of the talk of aristocratic ease of the student life at the University, the midday rising, and early morning going-to-bed are institutions of the past." Instead, the students began classes at a previously unheard of 8:30 a.m. so that they could spend their afternoons at military training, intramural athletics, and physical training.[49] A series of black-and-white photographs

Students' Army Training Corps at the University of Virginia, March 9, 1918. Note the Thomas Jefferson statue in the background (Holsinger Studio X06068B3, Special Collections, University of Virginia Library, Charlottesville).

taken on the UVA grounds in the summer and fall of 1918 reveal the training regime. Row after row of students in uniforms march in strict formation, some even equipped with rifles, accompanied by their superior officers every ten or so rows. The presence of real rifles was significant because there was a severe shortage of weaponry, and many of the soldiers in training at Virginia's camps used wooden substitutes. The UVA students marched through and around "Thomas Jefferson's University" and occasionally stopped to line up in front of patriotic spots, such as a bronze statue of Jefferson or his famous rotunda. In some of the photos the shadow of the photographer standing on a ladder is visible, alerting the viewer to the posed nature of these propaganda shoots.

Depending on their physical fitness and academic performance, students were sent to one of three military "finishing schools": officers' training camps, noncommissioned officers' training camps, or regular camps for privates. Virginia was home to dozens of military academies to train all abilities and ages, from young boys (e.g., Woodberry Forest Academy) to college students (e.g., Virginia Polytechnic Institute and State University, better known as Virginia Tech). The oldest state-supported military college in the country is Virginia Military Institute (VMI), located in Lexington. In 1917, the superintendent of the school, General Edward M. Nichols, was appointed as the first chair of the Virginia Council of Defense. In the fall of 1918, a Student Army Training Corps was established. VMI was the only college in the entire country that did not have to hire outside instructors to assume command of this new unit; its own faculty was sufficient.[50] It did supplement regular instructors with occasional special guests, such as when a Canadian officer who had served with distinction at the Battle of Vimy Ridge in France visited in the fall of 1917.[51] By the end of the war, VMI had trained about 1800 cadets for service; more than 82 percent of VMI students and graduates between the ages of 18 and 40 served in the military during World War I.[52]

VMI sent 40 corps members to the nearby campus of Washington and Lee University (W&L) four afternoons a week in the spring of 1917 to drill the W&L student body.[53] On May 12, when the War Department asked the president of W&L to furnish 36 volunteers, 75 newly trained students stepped forward. They reported for duty and were sent to train at Camp Crane in Allentown, Pennsylvania. The site was designed to train ambulance drivers, mechanics, orderlies, and, later, gas mask instructors; many of the volunteers at this camp were conscientious objectors. The W&L students were eventually shipped out to Liverpool, England, for duty, enduring a brutal Atlantic crossing on which the temperature dipped to 24 degrees below zero.[54] And while these students rarely raised a weapon during the war, their service was invaluable.

Other schools were converted to facilitate military operations. The University of Richmond agreed to transfer its 291-acre campus to the federal government between May 1918 and June 1919 for use as General Hospital No. 22. After November 11, 1917, the name of the hospital was changed to Debarkation Hospital No. 55, as it provided care for wounded soldiers returning from abroad.[55]

Although they could not serve as soldiers, women enrolled in Virginia colleges contributed labor and money. At Virginia College in Roanoke, students supported three French orphans for five years, and faculty members "adopted" at least one Belgian soldier, meaning that they wrote to him regularly and sent him knitted goods and a box of items at Christmas.[56] In a more lighthearted vein, the vice president of the college allowed her students to dance with soldiers during their brief sojourn in town while waiting between trains.[57] It isn't possible to precisely quantify the impact of these gestures on morale, but it was not insignificant. Moreover, the small break with established social mores such as not dancing with strange men was a harbinger of more dramatic changes to come after the war, such as female suffrage and increased employment options for women.

Faculty and students at the State Normal School for Women at Harrisonburg (today's James Madison University) focused their efforts on raising money to give to other organizations, such as the Red Cross and the Salvation Army. Each student gave the relatively large sum of ten dollars toward the fund, and faculty agreed to contribute a percentage of their salary. In addition, the college reported that 100 percent of their student body formed and joined a Junior Red Cross chapter. These women knitted socks, sweaters, and rag rugs and put together scrapbooks for patients and collections of clothing, or layettes, for refugees, such as Belgians and Serbians, who were fleeing their war-torn countries. The home economics department made a silk flag for the local Red Cross chapter.[58]

The Red Cross's efforts extended well beyond that of college volunteers. This large charitable organization was founded in 1881 by Clara Barton and on the eve of the war was the nation's official disaster relief agency. Its work ranged from establishing emergency hospitals to driving ambulances (at home and abroad), from delivering troop meals to nursing sick citizens, and from promoting public health campaigns to providing food provisions to the sick and dying.[59] The organization also raised large sums of money to fund its "net of mercy." As one propaganda poster put it, "Join [the Red Cross] Yesterday Today Always *The* Greatest Mother."[60]

In 1918, SATC was established across the country. The goal was to establish a military unit at every college in order to train at least one hundred men at each for the service.[61] Several years earlier, the Reserve Officers' Training Corps (ROTC) had been created; it was reestablished after a brief hiatus in 1919, whereas the SATC was not continued after the war. Designation as an SATC school meant that eligible high school graduates could enter these institutions of higher education and receive instruction in military drills and tactics alongside their academic study. Their academic studies were to include "theoretical military instruction," mapmaking, international law, and a mandatory one-hour-a-week course on the "underlying issues of the war."[62]

Dozens of Virginia colleges, universities, junior colleges, and "normal" schools (teaching colleges) hosted SATC units. These included the all-black Virginia Union University and Hampton Institute.[63] Virginia Union encouraged "every colored man prepared to enter college" in 1918 to enroll in SATC. The campus boasted an "unusually thorough and well balanced study in college, theological, and academy departments."[64] Virginia Union even advertised in a Nashville, Tennessee, paper that it had been authorized as an SATC site and encouraged more southern black men to take advantage of the "Board, Clothing, Free Tuition and One Dollar per Day [salary]."[65]

African American teachers in Virginia's industrial schools (or "training schools") were also enlisted in the state's preparedness plans. Two days after the United States entered the war, a headline in a Richmond paper read, "Colored People Join Preparedness Campaign." The state school inspector, Arthur D. Wright, planned to mobilize the "Home Makers Clubs," run by African American women, to cultivate home gardens and preserve the bounties from them by canning.[66]

When it came to training black men, American military leaders were hesitant. The racist and restrictive attitudes of many whites during that period made integrated training rare. The U.S. Army was not integrated until 1948, so African Americans who served during World War I did so in separate units, sometimes commanded by white officers (e.g., the 371st Infantry), a mixture of white and black leaders (e.g., the 369th Infantry, and the 365th through 368th Infantry), and only occasionally by all black officers (e.g., the 370th Infantry). In January of 1917, a Richmond politician, Giles B. Jackson, presented a petition to the chair of the Senate Committee on Military Affairs to urge Congress to establish a school to train black soldiers.⁶⁷ Jackson had been born enslaved 64 years earlier but went on to become an attorney, entrepreneur, land developer, newspaper publisher, and a "civil rights activist in the conservative mold of his mentor, Booker T. Washington."⁶⁸ He was serving as the head of the Negro Division of the U.S. Employment Service in Washington, D.C., when he suggested a separate training facility in Fort Des Moines, Iowa. For the time, this "Negro West Point" was a radical first step toward ensuring that African American men would receive the military training that they needed to serve with distinction, as they had previously in every major American war.⁶⁹

Since the fighting units were segregated, the military decided to begin the racial separation during training. In Newport News they constructed Camp Alexander, named after Lieutenant John Hanks Alexander, who fought in the Ninth U.S. Cavalry, to house African American labor battalions and shipyard stevedores. As during previous American wars, black soldiers were often given the most undesirable assignments, including sanitation duties and the responsibility of burying the dead. More than 57,000 black soldiers embarked from this camp for France. Of that number several thousand were from Virginia, and almost six hundred black Virginians died during the war (mostly from disease and training accidents).⁷⁰

Many southern whites were frightened that training and arming blacks would lead to violence within American communities. An isolated incident in Texas, on August 23, 1917, heightened these fears. Black soldiers in the 24th Infantry training at Camp Logan shot and killed 17 white civilians after 80 to 150 African Americans marched toward downtown Houston to protest racist treatment. The white paper expressed ignorance as to why a black crowd would react negatively when a "negress was arrested," the alleged catalyst for the violent riot.⁷¹ Putting this incident in context, that year, 1917, 36 African Americans were officially lynched in the United States. Many of these victims were murdered by local citizens who took the law into their own hands after an arrest. Texas had one of the highest lynching rates in the country. While this incident seemed to confirm the fears of many whites who thought that arming black soldiers would lead to uprisings, the majority of black soldiers served their country honorably and with distinction. This service came despite the constant racism and harassment that they suffered at the hands of white soldiers and many American communities. In sharp contrast, French soldiers welcomed these troops and praised them for their bravery. After the war, France erected several memorials to all-black units, something the United States has yet to do.

In the end, only 20 percent of African American trainees saw combat in France, compared to 66 percent of AEF soldiers as a whole.[72] In other words, black soldiers served at a third the rate of whites. However, some of these black troops were among the first to see actual combat because their units served under French command, such as the 369th Division, which conducted raids with the French 16th Division in the Argonne Forest in the spring of 1918. Although the French forces mistreated their own African colonial troops, they claimed to be "colorblind" when fighting alongside AEF troops and embraced black American troops.[73] In contrast, African Americans fighting in U.S. units under white commanders often experienced racial injustices. Sergeant Major Charles Holston Williams, with the 811th Pioneer Infantry, explained the reception he found as "an intense race feeling among our own Americans, supposed to be our comrades in arms."[74] After the war, Williams founded the Hampton Institute Creative Dance Group at the historically black college of the same name in Hampton, Virginia.

Because of the racist fears of many white commanding officers in the AEF, most African American soldiers served in noncombat positions, such as laborers, drivers, or stevedores. The last category included longshoremen, who loaded and unloaded ship cargo in Norfolk and Newport News. Other black Virginians, such as Sandy Thurston from Louisa County, served as cooks. Thurston was just 22 when he was drafted and sent to train at Camp Dix in New Jersey. In 2014, when I was giving a public talk about World War I in Virginia, two of his children came up to talk with me. After I recovered from my surprise that the children of a man born in 1896 were still alive, I asked them about his service. Like many veterans, he didn't like to talk about it much, but he had mentioned to them that he cooked meals for the troops. Later I found Thurston's 1919 answers to the war questionnaire handed out to returning veterans on the Library of Virginia's database. He answered the standard questions, where he trained, what ship he traveled on to and from Europe, what his "attitude toward military service" was ("trying hard to defend my country"). He briefly answered a question about how his camp experience affected him: "I was call up to do my bit." When asked about his "impressions" from taking part in the fighting he replied, "It made me a stronger and a better man in life than I was before in sival [civil] life." This optimistic answer is admirable, if not sycophantic, given the abominable treatment of African American veterans abroad (they were not permitted to march in an Allied victory parade in Paris) and upon their return home (when some black soldiers who wished to retain their commissions were labeled "deficient in moral fiber").[75]

Medical Personnel

> Realizing that patriotism and loyalty should be paramount in the breast of all American citizens at this time and feeling ... that loyalty for my country and the desire to serve here in this critical period, I am herewith offering my service for the Army Medical Corps should there be a need for a Negro physician for that branch of the service.
> —Dr. Urbane Bass, 1917[76]

In addition to segregating soldiers, African American doctors and nurses were forced to work in separate wards to care for the wounded and dying black servicemen. One of the first black doctors who reported for duty at Fort Des Moines was Dr. Dana Olden Baldwin from Martinsville. He served in France with the 92nd Division, 317th Sanitary Train, and with an ambulance corps. Upon his return to Virginia after the war he opened "St. Mary's, a 27-bed, private hospital for African Americans."[77] He continued to see patients until 1971, when he died from a stroke. Perhaps the most famous black doctor from Virginia was Dr. Urbane Francis Bass. Dr. Bass was born in Richmond in 1880 and earned his medical degree from the Leonard Medical School at the Raleigh Institute in North Carolina (today Shaw University). He moved to Fredericksburg a few years later, in 1909, determined to open up a medical practice in his home state. In 1916, despite being two years too old for the draft, he proactively contacted the U.S. secretary of war to offer his services "should there be a need for Negro Physician [in the Army Medical Corps]." His offer was accepted and he received a commission as a first lieutenant in the Medical Reserve Corps, reporting for duty at Fort Des Moines in the fall of 1918. He left for France with the all-black 372nd Regiment of the 93rd Division on March 30, 1918. Six months later, on October 6, 1918, his legs were severed by the shrapnel from an exploding artillery shell. After saving many lives he was unable to save his own; he died from blood loss the next day, before he could reach a hospital.[78] Two striking memorials were erected in his honor. The first is in a military cemetery: he is the only African American officer buried in the Fredericksburg National Cemetery, alongside white officers in "Officers Row."[79] The second is a beautiful stained-glass window at the Shiloh Baptist Church in Fredericksburg, where he had attended services. A year after his death he was posthumously awarded the Distinguished Service Cross for administering "first aid in the open under prolonged and intense shell fire until he was severely wounded and carried from the field."[80]

Another category of medical specialists who were treated as social

Stained-glass window designed in honor of Dr. Urbane Bass placed in the Shiloh Baptist Church, Fredericksbug (photograph by Stephen Miller, 2016).

inferiors was women. Although women had founded medical colleges in America as early as 1848, the combination of wartime conditions and the all-male composition of fighting units relegated women to secondary roles as nurses, not surgeons or physicians. Despite efforts to limit their exposure to direct warfare, these women were often on the front lines, alongside the troops and doctors, risking their lives to rescue and heal American troops. Hundreds if not thousands of Virginia women worked as nurses at home or abroad. Several of the base hospitals located in France originated in Virginia. For example, Base Hospital 45's staff was drawn primarily from Richmond and headed by a local doctor, Stuart McGuire. The staff included 24 physicians and surgeons, 153 enlisted men who worked as orderlies and clerks, 6 female stenographers, bookkeepers, dietitians, technicians, and artists, and 65 registered nurses from Virginia.[81] The last group was headed by Ruth Robertson, a Canadian nurse who was appointed the chief nurse for the base hospital in November 1917. In announcing her appointment to this challenging post, the position was described as requiring a "combination of qualifications never before so precisely outlined and consequently never before so difficult to secure." Fortunately, she exhibited the necessary skills, including "familiarity with battleground emergencies," "ward work on an immense scale," and firsthand field experience. Her foreign citizenship was at first a barrier, but Dr. McGuire argued that she had experience unmatched by "anybody in Virginia."[82] During the war a relationship blossomed and they were married in August, after the war ended. Another Virginia woman, Anna Elizabeth McFadden, left her job at Garfield Memorial Hospital in Winchester to travel to France in 1917 to provide assistance. She served at Base Hospital 1, a navy medical outpost with over five hundred beds.[83] After the war, the Medical College of Virginia recognized the contribution of female nurses and agreed to admit women into training programs as physicians and dentists.[84] And today the McGuire Veterans Administration Hospital in Richmond is the second-largest building in Virginia, dwarfed only by the 3.7 million-square-foot Pentagon. The hospital was named after Stuart McGuire's father, Hunter Holmes McGuire, a well-known Confederate Civil War surgeon.

In accordance with the times, the medical hierarchy in Virginia was organized around white doctors. Throughout the state, medical societies, academies of medicine, and hospitals recruited doctors to serve abroad and, just as importantly, hired men to remain in Virginia to care for returning casualties and domestic health incidents. The military doctors treated a wide range of corporeal maladies resulting from exposure to poison gas, shrapnel, bullets, and malnutrition. They also would have been well aware that troops often suffered from infestations of lice, venereal disease, and psychological trauma.

What no one expected in 1918 was the devastating health consequences of a worldwide influenza outbreak. Over half a million civilians died in America from a disease that was given the incorrect geographical moniker "the Spanish Flu"; another 30 million died worldwide, and half a billion people, a third of the planet's population, were infected. One of the most surprising aspects of the outbreak was that the fatality rate was highest in young adults, most of whom died after the influenza virus invaded their lungs and caused pneumonia. This virus was highly contagious, spread by coughing, sneezing, touching, and even talking (if spittle flew). The vectors of transmission were poorly understood. In Alexandria, for example, someone started a rumor that the flu had originated in the soil that the Virginia Shipbuilding Corporation stirred up as it commenced construction.[85]

Public health officials tried to control the transmission of the virus by limiting large public gatherings and encouraging people to wear masks and to stop shaking hands. This slowed but did not stop the return of the disease in fall 1918 (there had been a mild outbreak that spring). Worldwide populations, including Virginia's, were severely impacted well into the summer of 1919. During these critical months the war ended, troops returned home in tightly packed ships, thousands of injured soldiers convalesced in overcrowded hospitals, and Americans hosted parades and other celebrations to welcome back their soldiers. Throughout these celebratory moments, the flu continued to claim victims.

In fact, many Virginia communities lost more citizens to the flu than to any war-related cause. In Loudoun County a plaque memorializes the 30 "glorious dead" from the community who died in the war. A third of these men died from influenza or its related fatal accompaniment, pneumonia. Of these ten soldiers, five died in France or while in transit back home, while the others died during training at Camp Lee or at other installations in the United States. The local paper reported on dozens of other influenza deaths that occurred among civilians, despite the decision to close the schools, suspend church services, and advise people to avoid public gatherings.[86]

One soldier who worked at the Virginia Shipbuilding Corporation in Alexandria that deadly fall remembered the shocking speed at which the virus could kill. Robert L. Lake (1886–1971) was at breakfast one morning with four men; at noon one of them was missing and Lake was told that he had fallen ill earlier that morning; by 4:00 p.m. the same day, the patient was dead. That death was one of the harbingers of an outbreak that killed 74 men and two women in its first two days. Lake reported avoiding the same fate by drinking an "old Indian remedy" that included doses of rye whiskey, Bermuda onions, and quinine pills that left him and two of his friends "stinking like polecats."[87] While Lake fortunately survived, many of his colleagues did not.

Lake and other survivors in Alexandria had to dispose of dozens of dead bodies. They wrapped each corpse in gray blankets and laid them side by side on the floor of an old brick church with a tag attached to each with next-of-kin information. Lake estimated that there were 345 bodies and as director of purchasing at the Virginia Shipbuilding Corporation it was his responsibility to find coffins. He quickly bought every available one in Alexandria and had to search in larger cities for the rest.[88]

Women's Land Army

> Last year people had to be educated up to the need for gardening: This year they realize not only the need for gardening, but that they must be their own gardeners. And, as man labor on the farms is becoming less and less obtainable, the farmers are realizing that the crops must be harvested by women, and they are evincing great interest in the Woman's Land Army of America.
> —Juanita Massie Patterson, April 12, 1918[89]

The Women's Land Army originated in Britain, where the government recruited women to help bring in the fall harvests of 1915 due to a shortage of male farmers. One editorial, which was reprinted in Virginia papers, opined that women in Britain who did not help till the fields were comparable to traitorous men who were derelict in their duty or deserted.[90] In Virginia, female students at dozens of colleges initiated this domestic "army" during their 1917 summer vacation. The students and faculty at Randolph-Macon Woman's College in Lynchburg contributed large sums of money and countless hours of service to the war effort. The sophomores organized themselves into a civilian "militia" that subjected themselves to "rigid discipline," "endured privation" in everyday needs to redirect money and supplies to the war, and sewed a nine-by-15-foot flag to fly over a campus building. They also made sateen dresses from a cotton fabric woven like satin with a glossy surface for French orphans, pillows and curtains for the YWCA hostess house at Camp Lee, and one hundred blue denim comfort kits for the troops at the camp for Christmas.[91]

Randolph-Macon Woman's College raised two units of "farmerettes," with six girls in each ready to work during the summer months. A farmer nearby in Pittsylvania County welcomed the young women to his farm, where they "lived independently, did their own cooking, made their home in two small frame houses on the farm," and then planted and raised half an acre of beans and peas, later drying and canning these items and threshing an additional 70 acres of wheat.[92]

By the spring of 1918, military leaders and politicians realized that they needed to systematize this work beyond American colleges. Accordingly,

Promotional poster for a summer school at the University of Virginia to train "The Women's Land Army of America," 1918. The two-week course was designed to teach women how to farm (Special Collections, University of Virginia Library, Charlottesville. Broadside 1918.W66).

the Council of National Defense met in Washington, D.C., with the Women's Land Army of America, the National League for Woman's Service, and the National Woman's Trade League to outline a plan for a national army of female workers.[93] Mrs. Malvern C. Patterson (nee Juanita "Neta" Massie), a wealthy woman living in Tuckahoe with her husband and several servants, was appointed the head of the Woman's Land Army of Virginia. She oversaw a network of county-based "Land Armies." These female workers planted crops and worked directly with local farm bureau agents.[94] The University of Virginia offered a two-week training course for "farmerettes" in the summer of 1918. In Loudoun County, Charlotte Haxall Noland, the founder of the Foxcroft School in Middleburg, recruited girls and women to the Loudoun Land Army of farm workers. She hoped to fill 590 positions vacated by male farmers who had been drafted into the military. As the winter crop ripened in 1918 the *Hamilton Enterprise* "reported a county wide shortage of 73 year-round farm hands."[95] More women were needed. During the summer of 1918, Noland and her sister, Rosalie Noland, successfully recruited more than one hundred women to do farm work.[96]

Famous women were recruited to promote these efforts. A Richmond paper's society page reported that "The Governor's Lady" (Marguerite Inman Davis, wife of Governor Westmoreland Davis) was assisting with the peach crop in Northern Virginia. She was part of the Land Army of Loudoun County, where she and her husband had lived before they moved to Richmond. While peaches served an obvious function as food, more importantly the nonedible pits were used in gas masks. Some communities placed red, white, and blue barrels on street corners to encourage residents to donate fruit pits and nuts; the pits were burned to produce charcoal and carbon, which neutralized poison gas. It took at least two hundred pits to produce enough carbon for one gas respirator.[97]

The sisters were soon given "military" ranks in the Land Army. In their rank as Colonel Charlotte Noland and Major Rosalie Noland, they organized five weeks of fruit picking, potato digging, stone hauling, road mending, barn whitewashing, and other agricultural tasks during the fall harvest, supervising women from multiple states. Although these young women began as "unskilled laborers," Colonel Noland reported that by the end they proved "their industry and enthusiasm" could match that of "the most earnest workers of today," by which I take it they meant male laborers.[98]

Military leaders and the media spared no effort in trying to entice women to volunteer. One newspaper column praised the "delicately nurtured women [who] have gone forth from their homes to work to release

The Women's Land Army packing peaches in Northern Virginia, August 1917. One of the crates reads "Blue Mountain Peaches" (photograph from the Department of Agriculture. National Archives Identifier 512802).

their husbands for the colors." Furthermore, the male reporter admonished that "we must have no [female] idlers, no drones, in this great time of action, and right bravely will the women and girls answer the summons."[99]

Men who claimed conscientious objector status—a category not available in the first draft, but later introduced as an option—were put to work in the Virginia fields, but not without a disapproving notice in the paper. The county agents at the State Agricultural College in Blacksburg (today known as Virginia Tech) worked to place 112 such claimants, who were described as men "who cannot see their way clear to fight even for freedom and democracy."[100]

Red Cross

> If possible, the women were more complexly organized than the men. Here again the [Virginia War History Commission] volume gives the

facts of the manifold processes of the increasing war works of the Virginia women. If the names of men predominate in this [1924] volume, this fault may be set down to a habit common to wars and common to newspapers. This volume gives first-hand evidence that a preponderance of men's names does not mean a preponderance of men's work in war time.

—A. K. Davis[101]

When I first started researching the role of the Red Cross in Virginia during the war, I was amazed by the amount of knitting that its members did. The Red Cross chapter of Brunswick, Virginia, reported modestly that "the knitting habit became popular among the women and girls, and many serviceable sweaters, scarfs, and socks were made."[102] But if they were anything like their sisters in the Appomattox chapter, this brief summary was the tip of the iceberg. In that county, where General Robert E. Lee had surrendered to General Ulysses S. Grant half a century earlier, the members knitted 505 sweaters, 322 pairs of socks, 60 petticoats, 75 bed shirts, and over a hundred sheets and pillowcases.[103] The Fauquier County chapter estimated that it made 208,388 "knitted articles" between April 1917 and April 1919.[104] I wasn't even sure what half of these items were or how you went about making them, like knitted spiral puttees, waterproof money belts (was this really possible using yarn?), and gun cases (apparently sheep's wool is very versatile).[105] Knitting was just the beginning of these women's war contributions.

Red Cross chapters throughout the state made hundreds of thousands surgical dressings (the women in Accomack County alone made 82,406 gauze wipes), bandages in every shape and size (triangular, tailed, abdominal, etc.), hospital garments (pajamas, bed socks, and "helpless case" shirts for amputees), and large quantities of "miscellaneous" items (picture puzzles, storybooks, gun wipes, comfort kits, and property bags).[106] After a while I began to question how millions of unstandardized pieces of equipment were successfully organized and delivered to the intended recipients. As a case in point, the products produced by home-front knitters fell under the direction of the CPI rather than the Quartermaster Corps, which was the official source of troop equipment.[107] Later I learned that many of these items never made it abroad but rather rotted in domestic warehouses or were fodder for mice.[108]

Some Red Cross chapters in Virginia mention shipping boxes of home-made supplies to soldiers at Camp Lee. Sometimes these offerings ended up in surprising places. The Chesterfield Red Cross chapter shelled and canned three acres' worth of navy beans and boiled down blackberries into jam and shipped them to the Red Cross hospital in St. Die, Vosges, France. There the food offerings were sent into Germany to help feed French prisoners of war.[109] On holidays, women in Virginia chapters sent Christmas cards to American troops at home and abroad. Some chapters made sure to supply their own drafted sons and husbands with a handmade wool sweater and two pairs of socks before they left home.[110]

The supplies required for this domestic production required funding. The Red Cross women answered that call as well. Fund-raisers included dances, bake sales, and sales of cut flowers and canned vegetables.[111] The headlights of cars were sometimes used to light up evening events to maximize the hours available for fund-raising.[112] Virginia Red Cross chapters also raised funds to support children abroad (notably in Belgium, France, and Serbia), to provide traveling soldiers with food and refreshments at canteens, and to provide injured soldiers with Christmas gifts.[113]

The Red Cross was one of the largest women's organizations in Virginia, but there were countless other female-led groups. Khaki Clubs organized rooms in churches where soldiers could find "a reading, writing and smoking room, a piano, current magazines, newspapers, and tobacco." Female members acted as chaperones and entertainers.[114] Groups like the United Daughters of the Confederacy (UDC) organized during or after the Civil War came to support the Great War cause. In Franklin County, the Jubal Early Chapter of the UDC united with the Red Cross to do charitable work for the domestic war effort. But one does have to wonder if the Godmothers League or the Women's Auxiliary to the Howitzers' Association were necessary subentities, given the plethora of other civic clubs.[115]

Women Workers

> Late hours, idle mornings, dainty clothes, bonbons, and gossip are just a few of the peace-time luxuries which American womanhood is asked to put away without moth balls, not that the call has come for the full utilization of her services in the wining of the war.
> —*Richmond Times-Dispatch*, November 11, 1918[116]

If you read through the questionnaires and papers collected in the 1920s by Virginia's War Commission, you would think that women's work during the war was restricted to socially expected tasks like knitting for the Red Cross or gardening (versus the more masculine "farming"). This false impression was created from a standard set of questions posed to community authors, which segregated the efforts of women into "War Work and Relief Organizations" (to include the Red Cross, Salvation Army, and a handful of other groups populated predominantly by women) and occasionally a subquestion about the contributions of "The Colored People" (to include similar but segregated women's organizations).

To the contrary, women served multiple roles during the war, highlighted by a December 1, 1918, newspaper headline in the *Richmond Times-Dispatch*: "Women at Man's Work: Fair Ones Brought to Industrial Fronts."[117] In the decades after the introduction of the social construct the "Cult of Domesticity," which encouraged middle- and upper-class women to stay at home, away from the filth of industry, many Virginians considered sending women into the workplace a radical notion. But as "man-power" dried up after the summer of 1917, women started doing more and more jobs that were once considered the sole province of men. A Lynchburg paper revealed some of the social tensions behind this change: "Lynchburg banks have been forced to employ women to take the place of men who have gone to war." Twenty local women volunteered to work in a Lynchburg overall pants factory to cover the labor shortage.[118]

The truth was that women were filling in for absent men in a multitude of ways in Virginia factories and businesses. At Penniman, a factory town in York County near Williamsburg, women worked long hours to pack artillery shells. This was tedious and dangerous work, and not just because of the explosive nature of the material. Unfortunately, these women were soon afflicted with TNT poisoning, which turned their skin yellow, resulting in the moniker "canary girls." This coloration reflected a more serious sickness: bad coughs, sore throats, nausea, and vomiting. Many women fell ill, others died, and some became sterile.[119] Women who served in the Women's Munition Reserve at Seven Pines in Henrico County also faced grave risks as they worked at the bag-loading plant packing smokeless powder for the ordnance department.[120] Community historians glossed over these hardships and simply reported, "The wheels of business were kept running [by women] when man power was reduced to the minimum."[121]

The wartime employment equation should have been simple: replace the absent male workers who were serving abroad or training in domestic camps with females who remained at home in their communities. But restrictive educational opportunities and social expectations left many Virginia women without postsecondary degrees and lacking the relevant skill sets to step in to the vacated positions. So the first order of business had been to train women for these jobs. In Richmond, the Woman's Working

Reserve was organized in the summer of 1917. More than 170 women who had never worked outside of the home enrolled in a two-month class in typewriting, "office methods," and other business topics. They met at John Marshall High School, and 140 successfully completed the courses and proceeded to fill positions vacated by men.[122] In Charlottesville, the University of Virginia offered a two-week training school, tuition-free, to train women for the Women's Land Army of America. A publicity poster illustrated two women carrying a basket overflowing with vegetables, water, and a hoe, wearing blue outfits that were vaguely naval in design (with a white folded collar). Behind them a woman rides on a horse, carrying a large American flag, invoking an image of Joan d'Arc.

There are numerous untold stories about the role of women during the war. Some are just now seeing the light of day, a century later. For example, Blanche Stansbury Caton (1888–1968) of Alexandria worked as a "fingerprint girl" for the U.S. Navy. She and her colleagues used fingerprint records to identify sailors who had committed a crime or deserted. Despite her own military career, her Arlington Cemetery gravestone still simply lists her as the "wife of" a major.[123]

Among the states, Virginia had the fourth highest number of women who worked for the Navy, with a total of 1,067 (the highest was New York with 2,329).[124] The first Virginia woman to enlist in the Navy was Kathleen Virginia Venable Michaux of Richmond. She died from the flu one month before the signing of the Armistice. Another Navy woman was Lula May McDonough Thrift (1892–1918) of Leesburg, a "yeomanette," though the military preferred the designation "yeoman (F)."[125]

Women also worked for the Navy as camouflage designers. By the summer of 1918, naval officers had come to the realization that "complete invisibility" for their ships was impossible, given the efficacy of the German submarines. But a lieutenant commander in the British fleet developed a technique called "a baffle scheme" (or "dazzle camouflage") which used strongly contrasting colors to distort the ship's number, direction, speed, and overall mass.[126] Since American shipyards were producing a large number of vessels, the U.S. Shipping Board and U.S. Navy took charge of implementing this new painting system. They established over one hundred "district camoufleurs," who were personally appointed and trained other artists in a school dedicated to this craft.[127] One branch of this instruction was the four dozen female cadets in the Women's Camouflage Corps.[128]

Unlike their male counterparts, Virginia women had to demonstrate suitable appearance and character for their positions. And while the military insisted on gender-specific titles, like "Lady Marines," the public, surprised by the addition of women to these roles, came up with their own nicknames, like "marinettes." Unfortunately, these female recruits, like Fanny E. Laycock of Leesburg in the Paymaster's Department, were discharged after 1919.[129] The navy (and the army) returned to being single-sex institutions until the advent of World War II.

By substituting women in clerical positions at domestic military headquarters, their male counterparts were freed up to go over to France or, as Bessie Hays explained about her service, "release[d] ... to do the things that [women] could not do."[130] Conversely, Sarah Ethel Hunter, from Richmond, signed up as a stenographer because her family had no man to send, thereby representing her family with her own service.[131] Anna Lewis Jones of Alexandria worked as a stenographer for the American Expeditionary Forces. And still other women went to the front, where they treated patients, "took dictation, fried doughnuts, drove ambulances, and operated switchboards."[132] Several of these women were first-generation immigrants, such as Katie Mercedes Hoban, a daughter of Irish immigrants living in Portsmouth.[133]

Immigrants

> We here in America believe our participation in this present war to be only the fruitage of what [Washington and his associates] planted. Our case differs from theirs only in this, that it is our inestimable privilege to concert with men out of every nation what shall make not only the liberties of America secure but the liberties of every other people as well.
> —President Wilson, July 4, 1918[134]

Virginia immigrants are often superficially envisioned as British expats searching for new lands for younger sons or escaping religious or political persecution. In truth, the flow of nonnative peoples to the land mass later referred to as "America" on a 16th-century world map began long before John Smith's 1607 landing and continues today. In the 2010 Federal Census, the largest ethnic population in Virginia, based on shared ancestry, is English (representing around 25 percent of the state's population), followed by African (about 20 percent), German (about 10 percent), and Irish (10 percent).[135] The early 20th-century commonwealth contained a similarly diverse group of citizens. To use just one demographic measure, within dozens of individual variables counted by the

1910 census (like "native white persons w/both parents born in Holland" or "naturalized foreign-born white males of voting age") the number of "white males of voting age of foreign parentage" in Virginia increased from 6,290 in 1910 to 15,362 in 1920.[136] This increased ethnic diversity changed the face of the soldiers drafted into the AEF. Ironically, the descendants of the continent's first inhabitants were not eligible for the draft because they did not become citizens of the United States until the "Indian Citizenship Act" of 1924.[137] While Native Americans were not required to sign up with the Selective Service, they did serve in the armed forces and, in other cases, volunteered for duty at home and abroad.

Sometimes we assume that only American cities are sites of large immigrant communities, places like New York City or other large New England cities. Virginia's urban sites, like Lynchburg, with 30,000 residents, are much smaller but still diverse.[138] In that moderately sized city, a third of the population was African American in 1910.[139] Foreign-born residents totaled less than one percent of the city's population but included a diverse set of nationalities, such as the 138 Russians, 26 Canadians, ten Turks, 46 Germans, and seven Austrians. In all, hundreds of men and women living in Lynchburg in the 1910s were foreign born or first-generation Americans. Moreover, "white native residents with both parents born in another country" included 75 additional first-generation Germans, 135 Russians, 134 Irish, an Austrian, and several dozen other nationalities. All of the males in these families between the ages of 18 and 25 were eligible for the first draft in the summer of 1917. Fortunately, in that first round of draft picks, Lynchburg filled its quota of 311 soldiers by counting its 337 servicemen who were already serving in the National Guard or the army.[140] But some of these men served after the second draft on March 30, 1918.

A large number of immigrants living in the state capital of Richmond were drafted into the AEF. That one Virginia city registered 71 men from Italy, 94 from Russia, 17 from Greece, 24 from England, and a number of men from Poland, Ireland, Canada, Brazil, Denmark, Holland, Lebanon, Sweden, the West Indies, and China. Despite the suspicions of some, 21 men from Germany and Austria, considered by the Selective Service Act to be "enemy" aliens were nevertheless registered to fight against the Central Powers. This blend of "old immigrants" who arrived in the middle of the 19th century from northern and western Europe and "new immigrants" from eastern Europe and non–European countries, resulted in a multi-ethnic fighting force. Some of these men, such as Ramchandra Shelka from India, who served in the Thirtieth Infantry Regiment after his machine gun training at Camp Lee, fought in frontline units, while others like Bombay-born Mohammed Jaffe worked at Camp Stuart and remained in Virginia for their wartime service.[141]

A powerful symbol of America's reliance on foreign-born civilians and military personnel occurred during a ceremony held in Virginia, at George Washington's home. On July 4, 1918, Woodrow Wilson made a pilgrimage to the home and tomb of America's first president to discuss the status of the war efforts and his hopes for a peaceful future. Notably, he invited 27 foreign-born citizens, each one from a different nation, to join him at Mount Vernon for an event that was billed as "the greatest of Independence Days." Wilson deliberately selected the powerful association of Washington's home and the Fourth of July to welcome these immigrants "not only as citizens in the eyes of the law, but as Americans, in name, in principle, and in belief—one people and one country."[142] The surnames of the draftees from nearby Alexandria reported in the newspaper just days before President Wilson's arrival hinted at the ethnic backgrounds of the Virginia forces: Vermillion, Jaeger, Shreve, Guiseppe, Henkel, Thomasson, Niswander, Mingin, Grillbortzer, and Saffelle.[143]

Children

> Twenty Million Children in [the] United States Who May Share in Patriotic Task of Gardening and Helping the Nation to Win War
> —*Richmond Times-Dispatch*, April 12, 1917[144]

The Victorian cultural milieu, which viewed elite women as delicate souls who should remain unsullied by industrial forces by remaining in the home, maintained that children were similarly pure and innocent. Oxymoronically, during this same era some authors and politicians believed that children were savage and immoral and supported child labor without adequate safety provisions. Despite the contradictions, the American government wholeheartedly endorsed the use of children to convince adults to support the war.

Children were the ultimate "advertisement" for engendering patriotism and an alignment with broader political goals. In Virginia, a wide range of social organizations recruited children to spread a message of patriotism and support for the war. The obvious recruits were the children in the Boy Scouts and Girl Scouts. In 1917, both organizations were relatively new, having been founded in 1910 and 1912, respectively. The Boy Scouts were founded by Robert Baden-Powell in Britain. While serving as an army officer, Baden-Powell realized that his men lacked leadership skills and resourcefulness. In his effort to teach his men these techniques, he was surprised to find that military readiness skills caught the attention of young boys. Soon thereafter he published *Scouting for Boys*, and within two years membership in the newly formed Boy Scouts reached into the tens of thousands. Chicagoan William Boyce introduced the group to America after a London Boy Scout came to his aid while he was traveling.

While the mission statement of the Boy Scouts does not talk explicitly about military training, one rural Virginia scout leader made the connection clear in an editorial in his local newspaper. He mentioned that members of his community had been asking whether scouting principles were adaptable to war conditions. Quoting the constitution of the Boy Scouts of America he replied, "Technical military training and drill shall not be included for the reason that they are not equal in value or as suitable for boys of scout age as in training for good citizenship."[145] This disclaimer did not stop the author from concluding, in the same article, that the 324,489 boys currently enrolled in the scouts were a "large army." Indeed, they were encouraged to

Two unidentified boys, possibly Mrs. Mamie Hill's sons, from Charlottesville, dressed as soldiers, October 7, 1918 (Holsinger Studio Collection, X06826A2, Special Collections, University of Virginia Library, Charlottesville).

"train," just like their older, army counterparts. In the summer of 1917, several hundred acres of land in Washington, D.C., was provided to a troop of boys to march and train with shovels, rakes, and hoes (in lieu of rifles).[146] Men who were unable to serve in the military because of their age or a physical disability were encouraged to become troop leaders.[147]

But how do you convey such a devastating and complicated conflagration as war to a child? First, Virginia schools held war assemblies where children were taught about the causes and advancements in the conflict. Patriotic songs were sung during these events and often supplemented by "Sunday Sings" in the community.[148] Next, the children read the speeches given by President Wilson and other leaders. Younger children were asked to make patriotic drawings and "booklets," while older children were instructed on how to promote the sale of war bonds and how to garden and conserve food. Finally, the children were given recipes based on meat and wheat substitutes to bring to their mothers. These booklets contained questionable instructions on how to make gingerbread cake without sugar and recommended eating prunes instead of candy.[149]

The motto of both the Boy Scouts and the Girl Scouts was "Be prepared." Accordingly, scouts of both genders were encouraged to create "garden armies" and hold parades. On Virginia's Eastern Shore, a Boy Scout troop was awarded a medal for the potatoes that they dug.[150] Like members of adult charitable groups, the children were encouraged to make items to give to the troops and, on occasion, European refugees, such as Serbian youths. Here, the shared scouting mission was divided along gender lines. Girl Scouts were encouraged to knit garments, make scrapbooks for ailing troops in hospitals, and sew Christmas stockings for the patients in the naval hospital. Boy Scouts made checkerboards, built bedside and drawing tables, and constructed wooden splints for setting injured limbs.[151] On one occasion Boy Scouts carried more than 750 patients to an emergency hospital in Richmond erected to handle flu cases.[152]

These busy children also sold Liberty bonds, war savings stamps, and thrift stamps. Over the course of two years, four loans were taken in the form of bonds (in the amount of billions of dollars each) with interest ranging from 3 to 4.5 percent.[153] After the war ended there was one last "Victory Liberty Loan" released on April 21, 1919. Members of the public were encouraged to buy these bonds to support the Allied cause. The publicity posters for these financial stimuli did not mince words, stating, "That Liberty shall not perish from the earth: buy liberty bonds" (with an illustration of the Statue of Liberty engulfed in flames and menacing biplanes flying overhead).[154]

Despite this admonition, the bonds sales for the First Liberty Loan were not strong. So the government planned a sophisticated marketing barrage, hiring movie stars, famous artists, and even pilots to perform acrobatic stunts over small towns. The Boy Scouts and Girl Scouts joined in enthusiastically, rallying around the slogan "Every Scout to Save a Soldier." In the fall of 1917, about 270,000 Boy Scouts and their leaders across the country announced a goal of raising $50 million worth of bonds within four days for the Second Liberty Bond. These efforts included a house-to-house canvas, bond posters in store windows, parades, and even the construction of camps in public parks and squares where buglers would play to call attention to their efforts.[155] Sometimes, children would erect a faux camp alongside a parade route or on the grounds of a training exercise. They displayed posters in these temporary camps, urging the public to buy war bonds or stamps. By the end of October 1917, the combined efforts of scouts, local banks, and citizen volunteers had raised over $45 million in Virginia subscriptions to the Second Liberty Bond. This amount was double that of Virginia's neighbors: North Carolina raised about $21 million, while West Virginia subscribed about $22.5 million.[156]

When a third bond effort was required, one aspiring political cartoonist, 12-year-old Desmond Wray of Richmond,[157] submitted a sketch to his local newspaper. Realizing that some Virginians might be wondering why the first and second bond efforts were not sufficient, he drew a stout Uncle Sam in a rowboat, holding an ax over a monstrous face labeled "Kaiser" in one of three life preservers floating next to the boat. The caption reads, "The third time they never come up," as a smiling sun looks on approvingly from the horizon.[158]

Across the country and in local communities throughout Virginia, "four-minute men" rose to the occasion to speak to church congregations, theater audiences, and other public gatherings about the importance of buying bonds. They received the nickname because they were encouraged to keep their patriotic comments short and to the point. In Richmond alone, 59 men volunteered for this effort.[159]

Some of the fund-raising efforts were downright bizarre. One such idiosyncratic effort was devised by the national fuel director and asked school children to "Tag Your Shovel" on January 30, 1918. A school board report raised more questions than answers: "A delegation of school pupils tagged the shovels of Governor H. C. Stuart and Mayor George Ainslie; each child tagged the family coal shovel; fuel conservation jingles were composed by the pupils and published in the daily newspapers."[160] To interpret this strange ritual it helps to remember that in the 1910s many

Virginia homes were heated by coal, stored in metal buckets with small tin shovels to dig out the pieces. Clearly this advice was aimed at conserving that precious resource. But "tagging" a shovel? Sure enough, after a little bit of searching, I found the headline "Who Will Tag Mayor Ainslie's Shovel?" The subtitle was more informative: "School children want honor of decorating coal scoop at Executive Mansion."[161] A follow-up article clarified that the tags read "save a shovel full of coal" and teachers across the country, not just in Virginia, received bundles of these slogans to distribute to students.[162]

Even if you didn't sign up for a scouting group or tag a shovel, Virginia children were expected to assist in a multitude of ways. In Newport News, the Jewish Girls' Service Club furnished refreshments[163]; in Petersburg, the Girls' Protective Association was founded to care for "delinquents" found throughout the city. This state of affairs was blamed on the "wartime instability" and "immortality" of this Virginia city, located adjacent to the fast-growing and large-scale training site at Camp Lee.[164] Other children visited troops in the hospital.[165] One of the grandest gestures was the Thrift Day Parade, held on March 23, 1918, in Richmond. This large event included army and navy units from Camp Lee and most of the local civic organizations. Children marched alongside these citizens and afterwards followed up with pleas to local businesses and households to buy War Savings Stamps.[166]

World War I posters filled with children were clearly an important element in the national and local war council's playbook. These richly illustrated missives targeted both young and old audiences. The work of preparing for and supporting the troops was clearly a statewide effort. But who was behind these pieces of propaganda in Virginia, and what strategies did they employ?

Defense Council

> Council of Defense has fine War Record—Activities Assume Wide Scope—Numerous Undertakings Are Carried Out—Virginia's Participation in World Struggle Now Object of Attention—Some Accomplishments.
> —*Richmond Times-Dispatch*, January 19, 1919

Sometimes the breadth and depth of civilian efforts during the Great War is underappreciated. Poring through local newspaper articles, letters, diaries, and the less common photographs of Virginians working in their homes during the war reveals the unending tasks on the domestic front that kept industries functioning efficiently. These home-front efforts were coordinated by the Virginia Council on Defense, of which there were two iterations.

The first Virginia Council of Defense was established on April 26, 1917. This followed a year after the creation of the Council of National Defense, an august organization that included the secretaries of war, the navy, the interior, agriculture, commerce, and Labor. Their task was to organize the country in the eventuality that America went to war.

Every state in the union had these councils. In Virginia, the first Council of Defense combined the Agricultural Council on Safety and the Industrial Council of Safety. The second was organized in February 1918 (under the leadership of a new governor) with a new array of subcommittees and modifications to the distribution of power and authority within the group. Virginia's council focused on the stimulation of agricultural pursuits, the conservation of the resultant crops, the adequate distribution of labor, and the production of more wartime materials, such as steel. It made no secret of its goal to "arouse the patriotic spirit in the State."[167]

It would be impossible to detail every aspect of this council's work between 1917 and 1919. One committee after another passed hundreds of resolutions, held thousands of meetings, and spawned a surprising number of supplementary groups. In the end, it's hard to imagine any Virginian, regardless of their age, sex, or race, who didn't belong to several groups.

For example, the council created subcommittees to organize female volunteers. In Virginia, Mary Cooke Branch Munford of Richmond was appointed the state chairman of the women's committee. The heads of 64 separate female organizations were invited to join her; they in turn created new subcommittees within the Virginia Division of the Woman's Committee of the Council of National Defense.[168] A "Working Force of Negro Women" was also created, but mentioned in the council's papers only as an afterthought.

The women's first task was to encourage Virginia women to sign a Food Pledge card created by Herbert Hoover to encourage food conservation. The "Negro Woman's" committee promptly sent in 38,000 signed cards as part of their pledge to cooperate with the Food Administration. Women from both segregated committees quickly proceeded with other goals: establishing an employment service bureau for girls and women, teaching women to can their food surplus, organizing "milk stations" to improve child welfare, and a multitude of other household-related tasks.[169] General William Tecumseh Sherman was not targeting civilian efforts like vegetable canning or knitting when he suggested waging a "hard war" against the South (in 20th-century terminology, a "total war" that targeted combatants and noncombatants).[170] But by the fall of 1917 the French prime minister Georges Clemenceau understood that his military strategy equated foreign policy with his home policy: "At home I wage war Abroad I wage war.... I shall go on waging war."[171] For other scholars, "total war" implies the struggles on the battlefield as well as the cultural traditions, economic policies, and legal judgments that support war.[172]

State Guard

> [The State Guard] are as a rule men of large affairs and of the highest standing in their communities; they have rendered the State a signal service in affording to our people at home protection at great personal sacrifice to themselves when our National Guard, forming part of the army of the United States, was at war.
> —Governor Westmoreland Davis, January 14, 1920[173]

The Virginia Council of Defense had another important mission: to create a State Guard to replace Virginia's National Guard units after they were deployed to France. During the summer of 1917, the Council of Defense helped to organized more than 30 Home Guards (defined as units that would only serve within the city or county where they formed) and 31 units of Virginia Volunteers (units that could serve anywhere within the state). With the National Guard under federal military control for the duration of the war, the Home Guards took up their duties under local police control. Both groups of domestically serving soldiers were primarily staffed by teenagers, older men, and men who were exempted from the draft. This last category included men whose crucial civilian occupations, such as industrial plant employees or postal workers, disqualified them from being drafted. The Lynchburg State Guard included 68 enlisted men and three officers in the winter of 1918; each of the officers along with 19 enlisted men were eligible for the draft; the remaining 49 had been exempted for one of the reasons mentioned above.[174] In some cases, foreign-born men served in these units, such as Isadore Passamaneck, a Russian tailor who served in the Second Company, Richmond Grays.[175]

While most of these men were as ardent as their military counterparts, they were last in line to receive supplies. Thus, many of these units were equipped with antiquated firearms, some from the Spanish-American War, and whatever uniforms could be spared. The First Company, Richmond

Grays, included 64 enlisted men, a surgeon, and three officers. But they only had 63 "olive drab coats and trousers" and 61 hats.[176] And the Winchester State Guards had 84 officers and enlisted men but the officers had "no belts or side arms, stating they were unable to purchase revolvers, notwithstanding several efforts to make such purchase."[177] And yet these units performed vital functions within Virginia: providing security for prisoner transport (e.g., Company D of the Richmond Light Infantry Blues escorted a bootlegger to jail), raising money for Liberty Bond and War Saving Stamp drives (e.g., the Brambleton Guard of Norfolk), aiding civil authorities during emergencies (e.g., the Hopewell Rifles assisting the police in controlling a riot in Hopewell on October 4, 1918), and many other crucial protective services.[178]

The Home Guard units were deactivated six months after the declaration of peace, but requests for funding and supplies continued through the spring of 1919. In Lynchburg, the captain of the State Guard wrote to "our contributing members and friends" to plead for "summer weight breeches" to replace their wool uniforms and for "two indoor target rifles" so that they could continue to train.[179] These units were reinstated in World War II to perform similar services. The legacy of the Great War State Guards continues today in the Virginia Defense Force, a 1200-person volunteer force that assists the National Guard and Virginia civil authorities during natural disasters and emergencies.[180]

Military Chaplains

> In retrospect, the speaker imagined King David walking as did the chaplain that first evening [at Fort Myer] down the long line of barracks crowded with men at supper ... three-quarters of a mile long ... and the streets afterwards alive with men during the few minutes before the bugle sounded.
> —Unnamed Virginia chaplain, July 30, 1917[181]

Both the Virginia Defense Force today, and the Virginia Council of Defense in the past recruited men to serve as military chaplains. During the Great War the council hoped to provide a chaplain for each Virginia regiment. To qualify, the religious officiant must be under 40 years old, be a regularly ordained minister of some religious denomination, in good standing with his church, and obtain recommendations from at least five other accredited ministers from the same denomination. Chaplains received $2,000 a year for their service, the rank of a first lieutenant, and an additional $150 for the maintenance of a horse (the officer was responsible for buying the horse). Perhaps in recognition of the importance of veteran chaplains who had already seen and mentally survived the horrors of war, the recruitment effort gave preference to those who had served in the Spanish American War "if not now too old."[182]

By mid–May 1917, the U.S. Army was desperately recruiting chaplains. To increase interest in the open positions, it defined the role broadly, beyond simply "preaching terrible sleep-producing sermons to tired soldiers." Instead, they wanted "good mixers" who could keep the men "amused and interested" while monitoring their moral discipline. As if that wasn't a difficult enough task, the army hoped that chaplains would steer soldiers away from "rum shops and dives" and prevent suicides.[183] All the while the applicant should not take his position of moral authority too seriously. He had to be "one of the boys," not aloof with "ponderous dignity." One minister displayed these undesirable traits and, as the story goes, during his Sunday service in a Virginia training camp, the soldiers began a poker game behind some bushes not more than 30 feet from the chaplain.[184]

Dozens and possibly hundreds of Virginia men of the cloth answered the call in both the State Guard and the regular army. For example, Walter Russell Bowie, rector of St. Paul's Episcopal Church in Richmond, traveled to France to serve as an army chaplain at Base Hospital No. 45. There the Reverend Bowie visited, aided, and tried to comfort patients, although he sent a series of sermons back home to Richmond, where he described the wards as "places of pain" and "a little lurid glimpse into hell."[185] The Union Theological Seminary, also in Richmond, furnished a number of chaplains as well as camp pastors for soldiers in the training camps. Another Richmond clergyman, the Rev. L. Valentine Lee, returned to the city after spending a month at Fort Myer and gave a speech about the "clean living of the men" he worshipped alongside. This public lecture was held at St. Paul's Episcopal Church where the Reverend Lee expounded on the "high moral tone of the camp, the absence of profanity, the clean living of the men."[186] One hates to question the word of a clergyman, but newspaper headlines revealed obvious divergences from this ideal, including outbreaks of sexually transmitted diseases, violent encounters among soldiers (often involving racial prejudice as a catalyst), and rising rates of prostitution in towns located adjacent to these camps.[187]

Perhaps as a result of these social trends, the U.S. Army decided that chaplains needed additional, nontheological training. It established Camp Taylor as a "chaplains' school" in Louisville, Kentucky, with the express purpose of teaching clergymen how to "give intelligent advice to soldiers" on military matters.[188] This was the one of first integrated schools in the army. A Winchester pastor, from the Methodist Episcopal Church, was a student there. He was sent to serve as the chaplain at Camp Devens, Massachusetts, with the 151st Depot Brigade.[189]

To assist with religious matters on the home front, chaplain aid societies were founded. Portsmouth organized a branch in August 1918, co-chaired by two women. As part of their duties they distributed rosaries, medals, scapulars (sacramental objects made from two panels of wool that hangs from one's neck), prayer books, and New Testaments at various military installations (such as the nearby naval hospital and marine barracks). They also furnished newly established missions at these sites with altars, flowers, candles, and other religious paraphernalia.[190]

Even though they rarely raised a rifle, chaplains served on the battlefields of Europe and occasionally lost their lives there. For example, the Rev. James Cannon, III, of Blackstone was assigned to the Tenth Engineers, First Division. He regularly risked his life to search for and carry back the wounded while under heavy artillery fire. During the Meuse Argonne campaign he joined a battalion and fought alongside the troops. He was awarded the French Croix de Guerre and a Bronze Star for his bravery.[191] And the minister at the Methodist Church in Clifton Forge served in the Battle of Saint-Mihiel. The Rev. Andrew Davidson Brown, a white chaplain, served in the predominantly African American 92nd Division, a practice reminiscent of a century earlier when antebellum plantation owners passed laws to require enslaved communities to have a white minister present, alongside the enslaved one, to prevent potential revolts. In another instance, a Virginia National Guard lieutenant, Thomas McNeill Bulla, a chaplain of the 116th Infantry Regiment, died at age 37 from wounds he sustained in the Meuse Argonne offensive on October 17, 1918, after he "exposed himself to enemy fire by moving across no man's land" to help wounded soldiers. In the early 21st century the on-post chapel at the World War II–era Fort Pickett (Blackstone, Virginia) was rededicated in Chaplain Bulla's honor and his descendants attended the ceremony.[192]

There were many religious associations conducting theological work during the war. One, the American Bible Society, was determined to place a Bible in the hands of every soldier. As one propaganda poster put it, "To Win this War the Boys at the Front need Strength of Spirit." The poster described the "Khaki Testament" that they wanted to place in every soldier's kit. A Richmond paper announced a visit from a chaplain at St.

Thomas's Episcopal Church who was bringing "army and navy edition[s] of New Testaments, bound in olive drab linen." Sure enough, they were camouflaged Bibles.[193]

Chaplain Thomas McNeill Bulla. In April 1917 he became the chaplain of the Third Battalion, 116th Infantry Regiment, 29th Infantry Division. After many acts of bravery to rescue wounded soldiers, he was the only chaplain of a Virginia regiment to lose his life in the war on October 15, 1918 (courtesy Virginia National Guard).

3

Vestiges

> The volume will take its place as the chief authority on the subject, and will be essential to every student of the period. No other survey of the State's activity in the war has appeared heretofore.... The War History Commission is fortunate in having as its editor Mr. Davis, who has given himself to the task with whole-hearted devotion; his enthusiasm has arisen from a sincere conviction of the justice of the war, and of the duty of the State to perpetuate the memory of the sacrifices attending it.
> —Anonymous book review of "Publications of the Virginia War History Commission," by A. K. Davis, 1926[1]

When Arthur Kyle Davis and his colleagues sat down in the 1920s to compile information about Virginia's role in the war, they imagined a multivolume series that would include firsthand accounts of community involvement from hundreds if not thousands of Virginians. Davis was born in Petersburg, the son of a professor who founded Southern Female College of Petersburg in 1863. After his father died, Arthur Kyle, or A.K. as he was known, took over the presidency of the small college, where he remained for more than half a century. On January 7, 1919, Governor Westmoreland Davis (no relation) appointed A.K. as chair of the Virginia War History Commission. The commission established city- and county-level committees to distribute and administer surveys to veterans and to collect additional records of civilian activities within each of 121 regions. These early ethnographers hoped to compile these responses into a comprehensive set of books. In the end, only seven were published, between 1923 and 1927, before the funding and support for the project petered out. Many additional, unpublished documents are stored in the Library of Virginia's archival collections.[2] The last two volumes in the series, titled *Virginian Communities in War Time,* document wartime activities on the home front, ranging from the expected, like Red Cross supply drives, to the unusual, like Virginia colleges sponsoring Serbian orphans.

As I searched to discover what remained of these people and their charitable groups today, I wondered, is there anything left to visit? Or Virginians who have yet to be recognized for their efforts during the war? Are there already World War I memorials in plain sight that are overlooked today? The answer is yes to all three questions.

In this chapter I use the two primary travel routes within wartime Virginia—railroads and rivers—to explore the extant vestiges of the conflict. In the following pages I take a trip along an old railroad line, search the capital city for traces of the war, seek out Germans and German Americans in the mountainous communities, trace the connection between the Great Dismal Swamp and the Great War, and see if I can interest my five-year-old twins in any of this legacy on a road trip to a rural community.

Charlottesville

> Down the enemy or he'll down you.
> In this, the World's Greatest War.
> Victory depends on your deeds.
> In your victories Democracy is guaranteed
> Strict discipline is essential.
> In discipline lies the key to success.
> Over there are soldiers of the highest discipline.
> Now let's go.
> —Wartime holiday card[3]

Even with the advent of GPS and constant geographical monitoring apps, I find it helpful to begin geographical explorations with something that you know, or think you know. So I began my quest for World War I remnants with my current home in Charlottesville and the surrounding county of Albemarle. Located in central Virginia, an hour west of Richmond, the county was known in the 1910s for its farmlands, apple orchards, rock quarries, and factories, like the Woolen Mills located along the Rivanna River.

Early on in my research I located the county's official World War I memorial. Most county and municipal governments in Virginia have one: a commemorative statue erected to honor those who served. In Charlottesville, on the lawn of the former whites-only high school (today a county office building), a chunky boulder is carved to resemble its thinner, marble counterpart, which is commonly erected at the graves of military veterans. Two bronze plaques explain that it honors the men and women from the city and county who served in the armed forces. The use of the complete term "World War I" and the inclusion of women was my clue that this memorial wasn't erected until after World War II and was inscribed at a time when local communities were trying to, belatedly, recognize the work of women during the first war.

I found other local memorials in churches and cemeteries and even as entire buildings, such as "Memorial Gymnasium" at the University of Virginia. Today, few people recognize the connection between the honorific term "memorial" on buildings, bridges, and roads from this era and the Great War.

I almost missed the most dramatic World War I memorial in Charlottesville, "The Aviator," because I thought it was simply a representation of Icarus, from the Greek myth. In 1918, the president of University of Virginia hired a nationally known sculptor, Gutzon Borglum, to craft his interpretation of a fallen alumnus pilot, James Rogers McConnell. McConnell, "Mac," as he was known to his friends, attended the University of Virginia between 1908 and 1910. He met his death in the air during an aerial dogfight, which inspired Borglum to draw his inspiration for the statue's design from the myth of Icarus, who flew too close to the sun on wings made of wax. The end result was a rather shocking male figure, poised on a globe, about to leap into the air with spread wings. Flying nude, his only accoutrements are his fighter pilot's helmet, a knife on his waistband, and lace-up boots. I am not alone in walking by this memorial without initially realizing that it honored a World War I pilot.

I realized there must be more memorials or physical evidence of World War I from a county that sent hundreds of men to train for the war, several dozen of whom never returned. So I hit the road, deliberately selecting an older highway that ran parallel to the railroad tracks. Known colloquially as Route 29, one of its other names is "Seminole Trail," a nod to the pathways of earlier inhabitants of the region. Its formal name is "29th Infantry Division Memorial Highway." While this designation was appended to a long stretch of road in 1993 to honor the unit that landed on Omaha Beach during World War II, the 29th dates back to World War I. As previously noted, this division was known as the "Blue and Gray" because of its makeup of National Guardsmen from both the North and the South; it served with distinction during the war.

I didn't see much century-old physical evidence from the World War I era on my drive, unless you count the occasional historic farmhouse, some of the older pine and oak trees, or the coal buckets on sale at the

"The Aviator" erected in honor of James Rogers McConnell (1887–1917). Designed by Gutzon Borglum, 1919. Part of the inscription around the base reads, "Soaring like an eagle into new heavens of valor and devotion" (photograph by Lynn Rainville, 2015).

Covesville Antique Store. An architectural historian once taught me that old stores in rural communities often have a distinctive façade, not fancy but like the roof of a saloon in an old western ghost town: rectangular blocks of wood, stacked like blocks, with a half circle resting across the top to provide space for printing the shop's name. This architectural technique usually dates to the late 19th or early 20th century, so I kept an eye out for those features.

In North Garden, situated near Albemarle County's center, one veteran, Hobart Clements, erected a personal memorial to his fellow soldiers: a flagpole accompanied by a large boulder that stood in the front yard of his home. A plaque on the stone contained a short eulogy: "Dedicated to those who fought in any war and to the thousands of broken-hearted mothers all over the world."[4] Mr. Clements was drafted when he was 22 years old. After his return from the war he returned to his profession as a lumber man and wood worker, specializing in repairing antique chairs until his death in 1994. Surprisingly, his gravestone does not include any reference to his wartime service; this appears to reflect the irrelevance of the war to his surviving children rather than his own longtime interest in commemorating the war on his property.[5]

I headed further south through the winding back roads of the county and soon reached the town of Alberene. The name combines "Albemarle" with the surname of James H. Serene, who cofounded the Albemarle Soapstone Company in 1883. While most of the residents of Alberene were farmers, access to the railroad brought various industries. Thus the male residents here in 1917 were millworkers at the local soapstone quarry (e.g., Ernest Allen, age 30 in 1917), lumber workers (e.g., Joseph Preston, age 36), railroad engineers (e.g., Robert Lee, age 28), and electricians (e.g., Urbane Jean Brochu, age 18). Each of these men registered for the draft.[6]

Alberene is one of multiple spots in Virginia, including the town of Schuyler and a quarry in Orange County, that are home to industrially mined soapstone and talc deposits. These crude materials were transported via the railroad for use by the navy and army.[7] By early 1917, Virginia was the worldwide leader in soapstone production. The product was used in laundry tubs or sinks and in the manufacture of talcum powder, soap, and lubricants.[8] Soapstone and talc were also placed on the inside of tires, prior to installing the inner tube, to decrease the impact of heat on the tire rubber.[9] Demand for this material increased as trucks became a more common vehicle for transporting wartime supplies within the commonwealth.

On my way back home, I drove through the historic communities of Browntown and Irish Road to an old African American cemetery named after the nearby church, New Hope. Here I found two World War I veterans who served in segregated units. James Lewis Woodson was in his thirties when he was drafted. His headstone lists his death date as October 19, 1918, with no additional information. That month, numerous American regiments and hundreds of Virginians participated in the largest and deadliest operation of the American Expeditionary Forces in the war: the

Meuse Argonne offensive. I have not been able to find any additional information about his service, a common difficulty since a 1973 fire burned most of the service records for World War I veterans at the National Personnel Records Center in St. Louis. I couldn't help but wonder whether he lost his life serving his country during that deadly fall battle.

Hunter Hilton Tapscott survived the war, but it left him emotionally scarred. He was only 21 when he registered on June 12, 1918. Several months later, in September, he was drafted and served in the Twelfth Field Battalion at Camp Lee, serving in the 112th Provisional Replacement Company. He lived to age 50, which at first I interpreted as a positive: he had survived the war. But then I looked up his death certificate and learned that he died of "chronic alcoholism," possibly stemming from the emotional trauma Tapscott experienced in France.[10]

Richmond

> Patriotic Richmond women at 100 or more stations scattered over the city will offer for sale to-day small American flags, the proceeds from the sale to be devoted to a home war-relief fund, to be used for hospital purposes in such emergencies as may arise.
> —*Richmond Times-Dispatch*, April 4, 1917

In contrast to the back roads of Alberene, I thought that it would be easy to locate remnants from the war in the state capital. But I soon found that even the "obvious" examples of World War I–era material culture were often ignored or misunderstood by the general public, myself included before I started this research. A couple of Christmases ago, I was visiting a Richmond botanical garden, famous for its seasonal lights and decorations. That year the theme was reproductions of famous architectural landmarks, using only plants. I saw a tall bell tower made out of some type of seed, a straw-like substance, and miniature pinecones and thought nothing of it. Only later did I realize that it was a floral replica of the official Virginia memorial to the Great War.

The brick and mortar version, the Carillon Tower, stands in Byrd Park, about a dozen miles away, near the James River. Better known today for an annual Nativity Play that has been celebrated at the site since 1946, the red-brick tower originally contained a World War I museum in its lower stories. The collections on display included troop memorabilia (uniforms, weapons, and medals) as well as posters and other wartime artifacts. Due to a leaky ceiling, in 1964 this collection was transferred to the Virginia

War Museum in Newport News. At the top of the tall tower 66 bells were hung at a cost of $75,000, about a million in today's dollars. Richmond citizens selected the melodic feature so they could imagine their lost loved ones were "still speaking ... waiting on heaven's bright shore for reunion at the last."[11]

I was off to a strong start in my hunt: here was the symbolic heart of Virginia's efforts to commemorate the war. Moreover, Richmond teemed with war memorials. At the southern end of the city, I found the ruins of a bridge from the Civil War; to the east, also located along the river, is Tredegar Iron Works (known by most people for its use as a gun foundry in the 1860s); just west of that site is Hollywood Cemetery (with its famous 90-foot pyramid to honor the Confederate dead); and three miles to the east are the steps of the "White House of the Confederacy" (home of Confederate president Jefferson Davis during the conflict). The perception that Virginia's military history was, or should be, focused on the Civil War had dogged me throughout my research. But as an anthropologist, I was certain that the war—in which 93,000 Virginians had served, tens of thousands of civilians had worked on or at in-state training camps, and hundreds of thousands of Virginians had aided the war effort through manufacturing or modified domestic production—would be commemorated through physical evidence in more ways than just a bell tower.

I decided to start with an easy task: find World War I veterans in nearby cemeteries. I already knew from my search of rural Albemarle that while the gravestone didn't always list an individual's wartime service, very often the family requested the freely available and distinctive military gravestones. These markers often feature distinctive symbols or inscriptions about military units and were easy to locate among the civilian motifs like urns and willows or roses. I started with one of Richmond's most august and largest cemeteries: Hollywood. While it contained thousands of Confederate dead, surely there would be important personages from the Great War buried there as well. I cheated. I Googled it, and quickly found the cemetery's own "Notables" page designed to "honor and commemorate the lives and contributions" of historically important burials. Three American presidents (technically correct, counting Jefferson Davis the chief executive of the transitory and doomed Confederate States of America in this group of "American" presidents), six Virginia governors, and dozens of "other notables" were listed alphabetically. The list contained Civil War soldiers, politicians, Supreme Court justices, merchants, engineers, and professors—but not one World War I veteran.[12]

However, more in-depth research turned up dozens of World War I–

era heroes and contributors buried in the graveyard, of whom several went on to notable public careers. For example, John Fulmer Bright (1877–1953), a politician and physician, served as a colonel in the National Guard and 16 years as mayor of Richmond. During World War I he was stationed in Alabama.[13] Similarly, Julian Vaughan Gary (1892–1973) served in the U.S. Army and later in the Virginia House of Delegates and the U.S. House of Representatives. And finally, John Abram Cutchins (1881–1976) was a lawyer who joined the Richmond Light Infantry Blues and earned the rank of captain in 1916 during the Mexican border expedition. During World War I he rose through the ranks to lieutenant colonel and won the army Distinguished Service Medal for his "duty of great responsibility" as assistant chief of staff in the AEF.[14] In addition to gravestones for individuals who served during the war, the cemetery played an important role in the annual reunions of one specific group of veterans: physicians and nurses. Base Hospital 45 was organized in Richmond, and then shipped out to Toul, France. For more than 50 years, its alumni memorialized deceased comrades from the unit at graveside ceremonies here.[15]

And now I had another lead: Base Hospital 45. Surely there would be something left from a large field hospital that was organized in Richmond and at nearby Camp Lee before the surgeons and nurses shipped out to France. I didn't realize the sheer number of "base hospitals" that the United States ran during the war, 238, nor did I realize the immense organization that went into training the staff, assembling the supplies, and finding a suitable location along the front for opening a field hospital.[16] Base Hospital 45 was founded by Stuart McGuire, a renowned surgeon and former president of the University College of Medicine (1905–1913) and president of the Medical College of Virginia (1914–1923). Dr. McGuire came from a family with a predilection for aiding soldiers. His father, Hunter McGuire, was the physician who successfully amputated Stonewall Jackson's arm after he was hit by friendly fire (the famous Civil War general died from pneumonia a week later). The younger McGuire followed in his father's occupational footsteps and opened a private sanatorium, a precursor to Richmond's Medical College of Virginia, at St. Luke's in Richmond. He was already 50 years old when the United States declared war, but still he accepted the responsibility of leading Base Hospital 45. Soon thereafter he appointed Ruth Robertson as the chief nurse. As mentioned earlier, they were married the summer after the war ended, he age 52, she age 40.

The hospital team spent four months mobilizing and training before embarking from Camp Lee for France on July 10, 1918. The Base Hospital that they ran in Toul was lauded by French officials as "the best organized and equipped institution in France."[17] Dr. McGuire and his colleagues treated 17,438 casualties, but only 350 died, a remarkably low 2 percent wartime death rate. The original plan had been to erect the hospital far behind the front lines, where it would be safe from artillery shells and the slow but occasional moving of the front line. Instead, it opened just a few miles west of the front lines and ended up serving as both a base hospital and a triage and evacuation facility. It operated out of a repurposed French building in Toul; nothing remains of it there today, and the ambulances, stretchers, and furniture are long gone, but what about back in Richmond?

I had a lead: the Medical College of Virginia (MCV) is today a modern-day conglomerate originally founded by Virginia doctors from Hampden-Sydney College in 1838. In 1917 the growing hospital merged with the University College of Medicine (then headed by Dr. McGuire) to form MCV. Today the MCV campus and the associated Virginia Commonwealth University School of Medicine sprawl over many city blocks. The historic center is easy to find, since it takes the form of an Egyptian temple. The "Egyptian Building" was built in 1846 and served as the first permanent home to MCV (at that time a division of the Hampden-Sydney College medical department).

Surely this architectural oddity, one of the first Egyptian revival–styled buildings in America, with its reed-bundle columns and winged falcon god hovering protectively over the entrance, would contain something that related to the war? Disappointingly, no. In the end, the remnants of medical service during the war boiled down to more plaques and memorial windows. The first is a bronze memorial tablet in a stairway of an old medical building, honoring the doctors and nurses of Base Hospital 45.

When this tablet was unveiled at a banquet in 1941, the speaker's talk focused not on the hospital veterans but on "Behind the Scenes in the Second World War." Commemorated in conjunction with the 21st annual reunion of these medical veterans, the two-and-a-half-foot-wide, one-foot-tall bronze plaque includes a bas-relief image of the hospital at Toul and the names and ranks of 347 individuals who served with the unit in France. Dr. McGuire, then 74 years old, was ill and did not attend the dedication.[18]

In a commemorative act that tied together the decades of McGuire family medical service, this World War I plaque was placed on a wall in the Hunter McGuire Memorial Annex, dedicated to Stuart's father. The senior McGuire, who died 14 years before the war's outbreak, is memorialized just below the plaque with a bust.

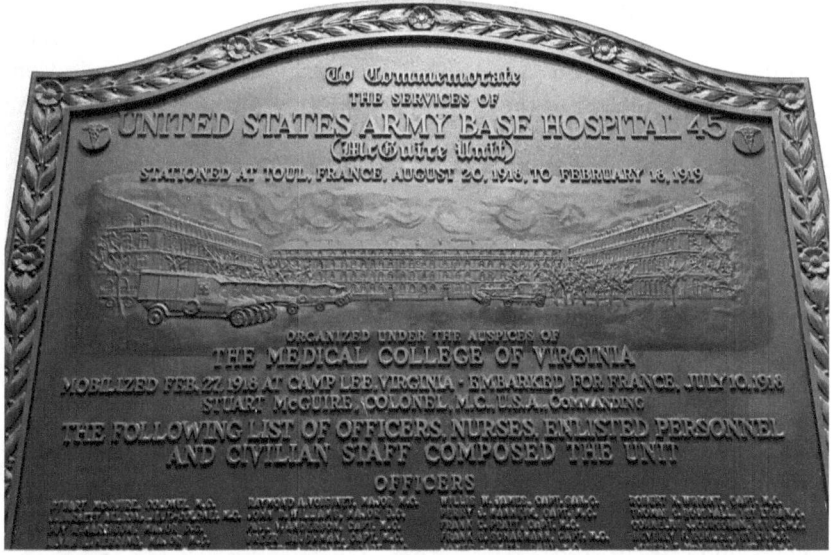

Tablet honoring Base Hospital No. 45, run by Richmond doctors and nurses. The plaque includes an engraving from a photograph of the hospital along with the names of the officers, enlisted personnel, nurses, and civilian staff. The memorial hangs in McGuire Hall on the campus of the Medical College of Virginia in Richmond (photograph by Matt Digan, 2016).

Remarkably, one of the current MCV partners, Virginia Commonwealth University, has saved some of the medical equipment that McGuire and his colleagues used a century ago.[19] These artifacts include dental equipment, a chamber pot and water flask used during the influenza outbreak, and even German medical tools.[20] These items were on display in 2014 in a temporary exhibition mounted for the centennial of the start of the war.[21]

Were there other buildings from or memorials to World War I preserved in Richmond? I was a bit stumped. Tourism materials for Richmond focus largely on the Civil War period, its top-notch museums are better known for ancient artifacts and contemporary art, and the various historic homes tend to focus on pre–20th-century lifestyle. So I crowd-sourced the problem online, turning to a website that I created back in 2014 to collect information about World War I memorials in Virginia. I added a post asking local residents to contact me if they knew of any Great War memorials in their communities. I put an all-points bulletin out through social media and used old-fashioned phone conversations to spread the word further.

The first response came when a colleague sent me a photograph of a large picturesque window in his synagogue, Beth Ahabah, the largest and oldest in Richmond. As one might expect in a religious institution, this window emphasized the peaceful resolution of the conflict, not the horror of combat. The colorful stained glass was donated in 1921 by H. S. Binswanger and was consecrated as an act of thanksgiving for peace following World War I.[22] The base of the window contains an optimistic wish which was not to be: "Commemorative of peace resulting from the World War." The individual panes represent patriotic elements such as red, white, and blue shields and crisscrossed American flags, alongside the Star of David and a reproduction of the Ten Commandment.

Next a friend sent me a photograph of a memorial at St. Paul's Episcopal Church, also in Richmond, where none other than Robert E. Lee and Jefferson Davis had worshipped. Its bronze plaque is elegantly trimmed with carved roses, and an eagle perches at the top, holding the requisite olive branches. Three stars lie below the eagle, and the inscription is split into two parts by a pair of heraldic shields with crosses and rows of

Memorial Window at the Beth Ahabah Synagogue (photograph by Brian Groban, 2017).

rosettes. The first half of the text reads, "In grateful and loving memory of those from the fellowship of this congregation who made the supreme sacrifice during the world war," while the second lists the names of three men who died in the war (an additional 83 members served in the war).[23] The last two sections thank the "noble" civilian congregants for their patriotic service and concludes with a quote from the Bible (John 15:13): "Greater love hath no man than this, that a man lay down his life for his friends." There were 137 other churches in Richmond in April 1917; many of those extant have similar plaques.[24]

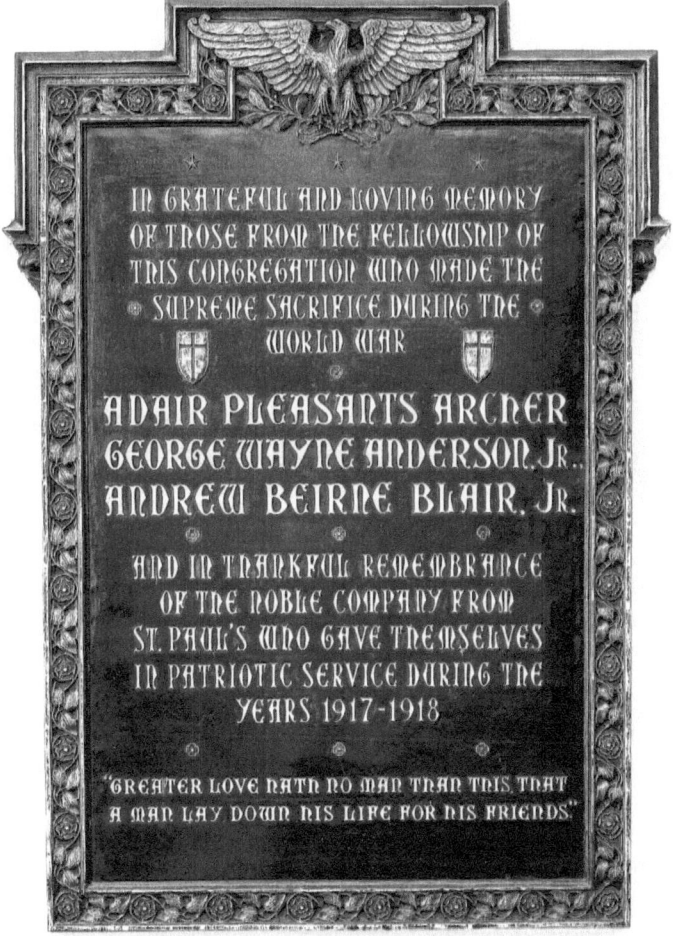

Plaque to honor the Richmond soldiers who died in the Great War at St. Pauls's Church (photograph by Brian Groban, 2017).

The largest remnant of World War I activities within the city of Richmond is, of course, the railroad itself. In the 1910s, Richmond was one of the largest railway hubs in Virginia. A 1910 railroad map reveals the stops that led from the capital south to the crucially important wartime city of Petersburg.

Camp Lee

> Three months ago the site on which now stands Camp Lee consisted of fields of rowing crops and acres of wooded lands.... To-day the same fields and woods have been converted into a city for the accommodation of about 50,000 people.
> —*Richmond Times-Dispatch*, September 20, 1917[25]

Petersburg and eastern France share several features: wheat fields, stretches of woods, and man-made craters. The craters along the Western Front are well known. Some measure hundreds of feet in diameter; they were created by huge charges of ammonal, which threw bits of soil, rock, and men up to four thousand feet in the air.[26] It is sobering seeing the extent of the damage along the infamous western front, a stark reminder of a war in which one participant alone, the United States, produced and exported 222 million pounds of ammunition.[27] To this day there are large stretches of countryside in eastern France that are forbidden zones, where uncalculated tons of unexploded ordinance, consisting of dud high explosive and gas shells, grenades, cartridges, and other types of munitions, still make them precarious to tread.

Petersburg's landscape also contains a scar from a massive explosion. The Battle of the Crater was fought on July 30, 1864, during the Civil War siege of Petersburg. In an effort to end the stalemate before Petersburg, soldiers from Pennsylvania who had been coal miners before the war dug long mine shafts under the enemy's lines and set explosives there. Although the resulting explosion blew a huge gap in the Confederate defenses, the Union Army was unable to capitalize on the southerners' initial shock and was bloodily repulsed. The 170-foot-long, 120-foot-wide, 30-foot-deep scar on the landscape is still visible today.

There are other striking parallels between the siege of Petersburg and warfare on the western front. Both conflicts featured stalemate and trench warfare. The mine under the Confederate lines, much like those placed under the German lines by the British at the Somme in 1916, was a failed but spectacular attempt to break the stalemate.

Just over half a century later, World War I battles were being fought using tactics similar to those of the American Civil War. Thus, the Petersburg battlefield was selected as the location of Virginia's first Great War training camp. Named in honor of the Virginia general, Camp Lee was built in the summer of 1917, just months after the United States initiated the first Selective Service Act. Over the next two years, 60,000 troops passed through the camp. The first batch included troops from Virginia, West Virginia, and Pennsylvania; together they served as the 80th Division and left for France in May 1918. A second batch arrived later and served with the 37th Division. The 1918 population of the camp, at about 40,000, qualified it as the third largest "city" in Virginia, behind Richmond and Norfolk. The number of soldiers far outnumbered the available supplies, so many trained with wooden sticks instead of rifles.[28]

Before the troops arrived, 13,000 workers labored over a few short months to erect the hundreds of buildings and roads necessary for the army's needs. To accommodate the large population, the military selected an empty spot with sandy soil that had been used for growing peanuts. Following the same basic design used in the 32 other training camps across the country, the Camp Lee planning team decided on a horseshoe-shaped center, with row after row of barracks filling in the "blocks" radiating from the center. While this horseshoe pattern was unique to Camp Lee, dozens of other training camps in America were designed along the same basic lines: two miles by one mile in size, with about 1600 buildings and requiring hundreds of miles of electrical wiring, heating pipes, and millions of square feet of lumber to accommodate tens of thousands of men.

The camp architects and builders put lots of time into planning every detail. One minor element of the overall design hints at this complexity: ten thousand signs to orient the inhabitants, from named barracks (how else would you keep track of your bunk?) to street signs (most unimaginatively labeled with numbers). One reporter estimated that the wood for the signs required several hundred thousand feet of lumber. The labor, transport (Camp Lee is not near the wooded forests of the Virginia Piedmont), and carpentry for the signs alone presented a huge logistical challenge.[29] Other tasks included the construction of more than 1,500 structures (including a police barracks, hospitals, and stables), one of the largest water tanks in the country, and 15 miles of roadways. This construction effort required 40 million feet of lumber, 20 railroad cars of nails, and a 14,000-person construction crew.[30] And after everything was up and running there were about 20,000 light bulbs that needed changing!

The daily life of a soldier at Camp Lee was not as exciting as one might think. A historian of the 313th Field Artillery Regiment, stationed at Camp Lee in the fall of 1917, described his average day: "Work settled down to the routine of carefully planned schedules of intensive training, interrupted by innumerable and apparently unavoidable details, such as psychiatric examinations ... campaigns for the sale of Liberty Loans bonds and endless paper work in connection with War Risk Insurance and allotments of pay."[31] In an effort to alleviate the drudgery of garrison life, the camp planners included recreational options in their design, including a library, theater, and hostess house.

Even though almost a century had passed, I thought that it would be easy to find the material residue of World War I at Camp Lee. So I arranged a visit to the site, today called Fort Lee and home to the U.S. Army Combined Arms Support Command/Sustainment Center of Excellence, a bureaucratic way of saying that they keep track of things, from people to supplies. The current post population is only 3,393 people,[32] just a fraction of the 57,000 who lived there at the height of mobilization in 1918.

I hoped to find plaques, statues, barracks, and maybe a mess hall or the "Hostess House" from World War I. But I hadn't looked closely enough at the historic photographs of the site: the buildings were all wood. In the end, only one survived: the Davis House. This nondescript 19th-century square farmhouse was requisitioned as the headquarters for the 80th Division at the start of the war. Later, Major General Adelbert Cronkhite, the division commander, moved into it and Petersburg residents nicknamed it "the White House" (both for its color and for the status of its resident). After the war ended, it was purchased by Gordan R. Davis—hence its current name—and remains in use at the military installation.[33]

One of the other physical remainders from World War I is actually a Civil War–era feature: miles of practice trenches. While it is a popular misconception that trench warfare was invented by World War I generals, this military phenomenon predates the western front and the First World War. In 2016, a retired National Guardsman helped me get access to the nonpublic areas of Fort Lee in order to see what was left of these open-air tunnels. They were a bit of a letdown, an unremarkable series of serpentine ditches that cut through the woods. It was hard to imagine the blood-curdling screams, the deafening explosions, and the stench of real-life battle while standing in a newly wooded expanse of riverine land, which today provides beautiful scenery for a spring hike.

Before I returned home, I stopped in Petersburg, the nearby city. Its major products in the 1910s were tobacco, peanuts, trunks and traveling bags, and lumber and timber products.³⁴ During the war, this city hosted military parades, complete with recreational activities, as a show of appreciation for the troops' service and to raise money. For example, on May 20, 1918, the Red Cross and the Women's Patriotic League hosted a visiting French battalion; local Greek Americans gave $510, with "every Greek in the city, so far as known, giving something."³⁵ When the war broke out this central Virginia city had a population of about 35,000, a substantial increase from its prewar population of 25,000. Like many Virginia communities during the war, the population increased dramatically as labor needs increased.

In addition to supporting the efforts of Camp Lee, one of the Petersburg high schools was converted into an emergency hospital, the site of the Petersburg Red Cross chapter headquarters.³⁶ Another school, Southern College, a junior college for women, was led by President A. K. Davis, who later served as the head of the Virginia War Commission. But none of these schools have commemorated their wartime uses through plaques or statues.

Petersburg is, however, home to one of the most iconic types of World War I statues in the country: "The Spirit of the American Doughboy." Originally designed by Ernest Moore Viquesney (1876–1946), the son of French immigrant sculptors, the mold was used to create over 140 such statues out of various materials including stone, zinc, and pressed copper. Each features an American soldier wearing an era-appropriate uniform, helmet, boots, and ammunition pouch. The man also carries a bayonet mounted on a rifle and is often depicted in the act of throwing a grenade as he strides through a "no man's land" of barbed wire. The statue is most often mounted upon a plinth that contains plaques identifying the local World War I dead. The iconic design was even used to create miniature doughboys to serve as lamp bases or door prizes at fund-raisers.³⁷ The only official Viquesney statue in Virginia is in Petersburg and was erected on Armistice Day 1928. The inscription implores "Lest We Forget" and attributes the gift to Petersburg Post No. 2 of the American Legion, which "affectionately dedicated" it to "our comrades who marched out with us during the World War and did not come back."

Hampton Roads

> The war activities of the government are greater and more important in the Hampton Roads district than in any other district along the coast. On the Norfolk side are the navy-yard at Portsmouth, the

Spirit of the American Doughboy statue in Petersburg. Designed by E. M. Viquesney in 1920. Dedicated by Petersburg American Legion Post No. 2 on Armistice Day, 1928 (photograph by Stephen Miller, 2016).

extensive terminals at Pig Point, the great Naval base at Pine Beach and other works of importance.
—*Richmond Times-Dispatch,* June 30, 1918[38]

The Virginia veterinarians who bred and raised the war horses at the Front Royal depot used railroad cars to ship their much-needed front line resource 40 miles east to Manassas. There the cars headed either north to Alexandria to catch the Richmond, Fredericksburg, & Potomac (RF&P)

Railroad south to Richmond or they headed due south to Orange or Gordonsville, where they caught a spur that took them east to the main North–South RF&P line. Eventually they ended up in Newport News, alongside tens of thousands of other equids and thousands of men who were waiting to ship out. Here ships made hundreds of trips to and from Britain and France, bringing supplies and, later, troops to aid in the fight.

Navigation has always been key in this region of Virginia. Home to one of the world's largest natural harbors, it is the spot where several rivers end their run from the mountain runoffs to the west and empty into the Chesapeake Bay and, from there, into the Atlantic Ocean. Collectively, this large body of water is known as Hampton Roads; "roads" is short for a "roadstead," a body of water sheltered from rip currents or tides. This region has contained a dense concentration of military installations, ships, and personnel since the 17th century when European Americans settled its shores. The roadstead enabled ships of all sizes to anchor safely while they waited their turn to enter one of the 12 piers at Newport News or one of the five piers at Norfolk.[39] As the ships unloaded their supplies and passengers they would have required the services of citizens in the nearby coastal cities of Hampton, Norfolk, and Portsmouth.

During the Great War, military planners worked to secure river access to these communities. One of the solutions was to hang several steel nets across strategically important bays along the eastern seaboard. In Hampton Roads, one was located between Fort Monroe (located adjacent to Old Point Comfort) and Fort Wool (located to the south). Authorities were concerned that enemy submarines would set mines to blow up passing vessels, so mine sweepers dragged large metal objects to preemptively detonate them.[40] These efforts are part of an often forgotten naval war fought on the American side of the Atlantic.[41]

Months after the November 11, 1918, Armistice, the January 22, 1919, issue of the *Alexandria Gazette*, following an article about the "largest hog on record" (with its blood and offal alone weighing 150 pounds), was a story about a "discarded submarine net." The news bite explained that the British warship *Warrior* had become entangled in the defensive feature leftover from the war. These wartime nets had become an inconvenience for Virginia fishermen. A month after the Armistice, the Bay Fisherman's Association in Heathsville pleaded with naval authorities to remove the net from across the mouth of the bay, which was preventing edible fish from entering.[42] The steel net that guarded New York harbor had been removed. By December 9, 1918, but for some reason the Virginia nets stayed in place for several weeks longer.[43] The one guarding the entrance to Hampton Roads was not removed until January 11, 1919, two months after the western front fell silent.[44]

Today this region is the heart of a multibillion-dollar shipping industry, centered around Huntington Ingalls Industries, the owners of the old Newport News Shipbuilding company. Huntington Ingalls is the largest employer in Virginia, and many of its 20,000 workers are third- and fourth-generation shipbuilders.[45] The explosive growth in the local economy and attendant increase in population began in 1915 when America began shipping large quantities of supplies to the Allies. And then, between September 1917 to April 1919, 677,435 tons of supplies were shipped overseas from Newport News, with an additional 805,654 tons from Norfolk. Even something mundane, like storage space, was built on a massive scale in this vicinity: Norfolk alone provided over four million square feet of storage space for military equipment, food supplies, and equids.[46] Not surprisingly, military planners decided to build four training camps nearby, just south of Newport News, in order to take advantage of this critical land/sea crossroads.

These camps—Camp Stuart, Camp Hill, Camp Alexander, and Camp Morrison—served a variety of purposes, as embarkation and debarkation hospitals, storage depots, magazines and hay sheds, stevedore training facilities, and animal stables. As might be expected in the Jim Crow era, Camp Alexander was segregated for "the organization and training of colored engineer troops."[47] In addition to the camps, there were animal embarkation depots, quartermaster general supply depots, ordnance depots, supply bases, and engineering depots. Almost a hundred thousand men passed through these camps on their way overseas, creating a lot of pressure on the residential and business infrastructure in the region. Accordingly, Hampton Roads residents played an important role in managing relationships between civilians and soldiers.

While some soldiers stayed only briefly, arriving from training camps across the eastern seaboard and soon thereafter embarking at Newport News for their transatlantic voyage, others trained in nearby camps for weeks or months before their departure. Social tensions frequently arose from the pressure on food resources, the rise and fall of labor demands and resulting employment opportunities, as well as overcrowding in several of the local communities. To alleviate these tense interactions, many locals opened up their homes and businesses to welcome soldiers and sailors. On the other end of the hospitality spectrum, the U.S. Army commandeered the rooms of the elegant Hotel Chamberlin during the war for its officers.

Norfolk, located just south of Newport News, devised a "Take a Soldier Home" program, which aimed to feed soldiers in local homes on Sunday evenings. The charitable outreach was so successful that one soldier recalled, "I never saw such a town and such people ... that's the fifth invitation today and I can't hold another bite."[48] Many of these same households opened their doors and rented rooms to laborers who required lodging above and beyond the local commercial capacity. Cars were still a novelty mode of transportation in the 1910s, and drivers in Norfolk placed signs in their windshields advertising transportation for soldiers and laborers. The inexpensive fare, five cents, or a "jitney," resulted in the nickname jitney buses.[49] Local citizens were on hand both for emotional ship sendoffs and the more routine marches to and from transports. For example, the North End Girls' Water Brigade handed out food and drink to the soldiers as they marched past.[50] Even more remarkable, given the humid Virginia summers, local donors purchased 6100 gallons of ice cream and fed 83,000 men after one soldier expressed a heartfelt desire for "honest-to-God ice cream."[51] Hampton Roads residents contributed large sums of money to the Victory Loan campaign, to the six major bond drives, and to creating a fund to assist Armenians.

Wartime ship building resulted in an almost 80 percent increase in shipyard employees, from 7,000 in 1917 to 12,500 by 1919.[52] These workers and their dependents needed housing, groceries, schools, businesses, and places to worship. The U.S. census indicates that the population of Newport News almost doubled between 1910 and 1920.[53] Some entrepreneurial residents started renting out rooms which led to "every little shanty [becoming] a habitable home and a veritable gold mine for its owner."[54] Boarding houses resorted to a technique popularized during the California Gold Rush referred to as "hot-bedding," whereby renters took turns sleeping in the same bed by managing their work schedules. After the United States entered the war, the difficulty in housing laborers was seen as a security risk. In 1918, the president of the Newport News Shipyard, Homer L. Ferguson, testified before the U.S. Senate that the housing shortage left him unable to fulfill government contracts for new ships.[55] A solution had to be found.

Ferguson made a deal with the government: if the Emergency Fleet Corporation of the U.S. Shipping Board would finance new homes, his company would buy land, supervise construction, and manage the financial arrangements of either renting or selling the houses. The initial $1.2 million appropriation was approved on January 11, 1918, and prominent architects and a sanitation engineer began designing "Hilton Village."[56]

Construction of Hilton Village, Newport News (photograph by Griffith, August 1, 1918. Newport News Public Library).

The community planners took a new approach to a federally subsidized housing project: planning every detail from the style of the houses to the distribution of commercial buildings within the community. Two of the architects, Francis Y. Joannes and landscape architect Henry V. Hubbard, applied innovations in fire safety, lighting, ventilation, and convenience to their planned village.[57] Hubbard stated explicitly that he was trying to avoid the typical wartime housing, which he viewed as "little better than scrap" and a "reproach upon the country." Instead he argued that "the married man with a family" needed a "proper house, rightly situated and arranged."[58] A broadside from the Old Dominion Land Company picked up on this theme when it advertised its "acre home sites" and argued, "An owned home ... [a]wakens the best impulses in every member of the family," "[d]evelops the family's will power and builds character," and "creates morals." The company advertisement concluded enthusiastically that home ownership "makes for good citizenship."

Curiously, in the midst of this American patriotic fervor, the architects used styles from the early 20th-century English garden cities movement, resulting in blocks of row houses with steeply pitched roofs (unnecessary in the mild Tidewater climate) that looked like a scene out of a Elizabethan village. Inside, these Tudor revival homes featured modern conveniences: hardwood floors, "Murphy beds" (hinged boards that fold out from a wall), dining-room cabinets, bedroom wardrobes, floor heaters, and a coal range for cooking and heating.[59] Similar to George Pullman's efforts decades earlier in his planned Chicago community, the architects included a commercial district, which originally contained stores, a bowling alley, a state-of-the-art movie house, a lodge hall, a billiard parlor, and a hotel for visiting guests. Land was set aside for churches, a school, and a park; other planned features were not initially completed: a community garage, a railroad station, and an apartment complex.[60]

Land clearing and construction began in April 1918 on a forested patch of 65 level acres conveniently located two miles north of the shipyard. Without any preexisting roadways or buildings, the team could plan every element of the design, from gridiron street plans to uniform, narrow building lots (ranging in width from 25 to 40 feet). To counteract the narrowness, the lots were deep (up to 130 feet) so that the tenants could have gardens, an important feature given wartime food rationing. By the end of 1919, over three hundred buildings had been built, but they were only available to white home buyers and their racially homogeneous families. Jim Crow policies were still firmly in place, despite the thousands of African American Virginians who were serving their country during the war. Ironically, three decades earlier, when Huntington purchased the land for his Old Dominion Land Company, he selected a neighborhood that was predominantly African American, believing that men of any race could be taught the necessary skills to build ships. Decades later, African Americans were heavily engaged in the shipyard but restrictive, Jim Crow–era, ordinances prohibited these skilled laborers from obtaining specialized jobs and supervisory positions, and severely restricted where they could live.

Suffolk and the Dismal Swamp

> The heart of the great Dismal Swamp of Virginia is not more than twenty miles from Norfolk and the grounds of the Jamestown Exposition. The region is virtually unknown even to those residing on its borders, and nine-tenths of the people of Tidewater Virginia are more familiar with the subject of Alaska or Borneo than they are with that of the Dismal Swamp.
>
> —*Times Dispatch*, November 4, 1906[61]

Suffolk has a long history of European-American settlement: mapped by Captain John Smith in 1608, settled in 1620, the county seat since 1755. Centuries earlier, Native Americans lived here and it was their forced food contribution that fed Captain Smith and led to tensions between the two groups. It lies just to the west of Hampton Roads and, like many of the communities in that Tidewater region, it is fed by a tributary river, the Nansemond, named after the original native residents.

In the 1910s, Suffolk was a gateway to Norfolk and Portsmouth and a major railway exchange point, a key strategic position during World War I. A 1918 topographic map shows a grid-like collection of railway lines, leading into and out of Suffolk in all directions. The muted browns and greens of the fields and soils on the old map change to blue, weed-like clumps in the east. This natural feature, the Great Dismal Swamp, has one of the most storied histories of any Virginia waterway. None other than George Washington surveyed the marshy lake and suggested draining the feature to create a north–south canal connecting the Chesapeake Bay with the Albemarle Sound (just to the south, in North Carolina). Multiple groups have used this bayou to disappear, most notably as part of the Underground Railroad and as a community for escaped slaves. For one World War I veteran, it was a place of refuge and income. Captain Bill Crockett, originally from the Eastern Shore, served in the Coast Guard and as a merchant marine. Like many returning veterans, he had trouble finding secure, full-time work. Instead, he lived in the swamp, working occasionally as a lumberman.[62]

Suffolk has a second claim to fame: it is the self-proclaimed peanut capital of the world. Its sandy soils were not suitable for other crops.[63] Today, the city has what it believes is the "first peanut museum in the world." A few years before the Great War began, an Italian immigrant named Amedeo Obici opened the Planters Nut and Chocolate Company in Suffolk. He, like his American-born male counterparts, was required to register for the draft. Obici filled out his draft registration card on September 12, 1918, at his Suffolk residence. Just two months before the Armistice, it is unlikely that he was ever called up to train or serve in the U.S. Army. But his card demonstrates that the draft was far-reaching and included foreign-born men. When he died in 1947, Obici was buried in the town's historic cemetery, Cedar Hill. His body, and that of his wife, Louise, were later exhumed and moved to a hospital that he founded in her honor.[64]

Another Cedar Hill "resident," a World War I soldier cast in bronze, was moved more than once before arriving at a final resting place. This metal sentinel was originally located at the intersection of North Main Street and Milner Street in Suffolk. The large number of visitors to this urban intersection necessitated the move of the life-sized doughboy to the median at the entrance of the Cedar Hill Cemetery. The statue was commissioned by the local American Legion and crafted by New York sculptor Joseph P. Pollia (1894–1954). Like Obici, Pollia was born in Italy and immigrated to America as a child. He is better known for his Civil War statue *Equestrian Statue of General Thomas 'Stonewall' Jackson*, which stands at the Manassas National Battlefield Park in Northern Virginia. He specialized in statues of soldiers, most of whom clutch their weapon in one hand. The Suffolk soldier has his weapon at his side while he pensively stares into the distance. While he is in uniform, he isn't wearing his helmet (that too is held at his side) or his jacket (held in his other hand). Unlike the spirited militarism of many other Virginia memorials to the war (like the Petersburg example), the title of this one conveys its more sober reflection on the conflict: "Doughboy at Rest."

Bronze plaques adorn two of the statue's four sides. One contains the names of men from Suffolk and Nansemond County who "died in the service of their country in the Great War." As with most of the Virginia military memorials, the names are segregated by race, with the "colored" section as usual at the end. The other shows an eagle standing on top of a stars-and stripes-emblazoned shield and clutching two American flags in its talons. The bird hovers above a poetic inscription that reads, "Those who died for love of country sleep peacefully—those who live to carry on hold high the torch that lights the flame of patriotism in the hearts of our children." This plaque is dated 1931; Pollia finished the statue two years earlier, and it was dedicated two weeks before Memorial Day 1931.

After the war ended, Suffolk welcomed home its soldiers, living and dead. First came the survivors. On the Fourth of July 1919, the town hosted a Welcome Home Day for the returning white veterans. A town historian unabashedly reported that the "white soldiers, sailors and marines" were welcomed to a "sumptuous repast" and a "street dance" on Washington Square. They estimated that the crowd that day was the largest the city had ever seen.[65]

Two months later, on September 1, all of the "colored" veterans were welcomed "by the people of the community." At first I misread that statement and assumed that the "community" included both black and white citizens. But the next sentence made it clear that the parade was a segregated one hosted for and by African Americans.[66] Black troops who were willing to sacrifice their lives for their country were welcomed home adhering to contemporary segregated social expectations. Decades later, African American officers during World War I used the skills that they developed as military leaders within this segregated fighting force to advocate for social change during the civil rights movement.

Suffolk men who fell in battle did not come home until the autumn of 1920. As with most of the dead from the Great War, there was no time to transport bodies amidst the fighting. Instead, the American dead were buried in mass graves at or near the battlefields and exhumed after the war once permanent cemeteries were selected in France, Belgium, and Great Britain. Bodies were identified by deciphering rudimentary dog tags or by collating data from uniform insignia and personal effects. The U.S. government eventually decided to offer grieving parents and spouses three options: burial abroad (near where their loved one fell), internment in Arlington National Cemetery (for individuals who served in military units), or a hometown burial in a local cemetery.

In Suffolk, the first body to be returned home for burial was the white soldier Edward B. Walters (November 7, 1920), shortly followed by an African American soldier, Ben Freeman (November 14). In a sobering testament to the sacrifice of this small Virginia community, "for some time after this nearly every week bodies of ex-service men arrived."[67] Several families decided to bury their sons at home rather than in European cemeteries, such as W. E. Baker, who was buried in Arlington National Cemetery and Herbert R. Holloman, who was buried in Richmond. Thus, Virginians took full advantage of the U.S. government's offer to bring the bodies of their relatives back home for burial.

Shenandoah Valley

> The Shenandoah: "Daughter of the Stars"
> Thrifty intelligent people have made the county and entire section one of national fame.
> —A. K. Davis, 1927[68]

All of the Virginia estuaries that lead to the Atlantic begin further west in the Blue Ridge Mountains. The western quarter of the state contains Mennonite and Quaker communities, Scotch-Irish and German settlements, and the sons of British settlers who headed west in the 18th century to obtain land grants. The region was originally settled thousands of years earlier by Iroquois-speaking tribes. In the early 20th century, a new wave of German immigrants was arriving to join second- and third-generation German American families. In fact, Loudoun County's German residents first arrived during the Revolutionary War, when they served in Armand's Legion, recruited by authority of Congress during the summer of 1777 and composed of men who could not speak English. Their descendants still live in Lovettsville, where the community first settled. Dozens of these men served in the American army during World War I.[69] But in other communities, newly arrived Germans and multigeneration German Americans were watched carefully by the authorities.

In fact, accurately assessing the wartime opinions of Virginians of Germans ancestry is difficult. In the decade after the end of the Great War, very few Virginia counties admitted to charitable opinions of Germans.[70] But before America entered the war, public opinion in Virginia was mixed. While many communities supported the Allied cause from the beginning of the war in 1914, other citizens' loyalties lay elsewhere. A resident of Hopewell explained, "The sympathies of our people were with the Allies, yet one often heard Germany defended in the early days of the war. When the powder plant at Hopewell was opened, many of our young men went to work there, and a godly minister rebuked them, saying: 'You have gone to make powder to kill Germans.'"[71]

When the German blockade-running submarine *Deutschland* narrowly evaded capture to make a transatlantic voyage to the then neutral United States, some of the residents of Nottoway County recalled, "The crew of the German submarine that slipped into the United States harbor was rather applauded over its escape. But alas! the time soon came when our people could not believe that they had held such sentiments."[72]

These anti–Teutonic sentiments eventually developed into full-blown hysteria and, in some communities, hatred for German residents. Many Virginians were on high alert to catch "traitors." In an unusual example, neighbors of German American George Vogt, in Luray, felt compelled to post a circular "to whom it may concern" that referenced "slanderous reports" of his antipatriotic actions. The typed letter assured the community that "Mr. Vogt and family have lived among us for years and we have always found them good, lovable, law-abiding citizens, and they have now willingly, at the call of their adopted country, given their first-born, Geo. Vogt, Jr., to fight to uphold the dignity of our own beloved U.S."[73] The letter was "signed" with the printed names of 78 of the Vogts' neighbors. Even when immigrants sent their sons to fight on behalf of America, there was still suspicion. The citizens of Giles County summarized their reaction to the actions of the "imperial German government" in 1916 and 1917: "[We] became indignant. As news of sinking ships became more and more frequent the feeling against Germany grew more bitter, and when the Lusitania was sunk the spark was fanned to a blaze, and it needed but the word of our great war President, Woodrow Wilson, to fire the nation. That word was given on April 6, 1917."[74]

Some anti–German sentiment made its way into the Virginia school curriculum. In Clifton Forge, the school curriculum paralleled local ambivalence about the participants in the world war: "The schools played no little part in the city's wartime activities. While there was some feeling manifested towards the opposing nations in war, yet it did not develop into exceeding hatred." But local language teachers did cease offering German, and history instructors focused on Germany's "past greatness" rather than her present condition.[75] And in Lynchburg, school administrators banned the study of German culture all together.[76]

In the Piedmont county of Albemarle "the Mayor and other city officials at once took action to arouse public sentiment and outlined plans for keeping watch against possible damage by the German element in our midst." Anti-German citizens spread rumors that German American residents were going to poison the city reservoir or burn railroad bridges. Local authorities posted soldiers at the bridges and asked volunteers to guard the reservoir; in the end, the fearmongers reluctantly concluded, "Our citizens of German descent behaved with perfect propriety," with only a brief mention of "one or two" who were "interned for a short while."[77] The location of their confinement is lost to modern memory.

Abingdon

> To the men and women of Washington County who answered the call of duty in the way of right and liberty.
> —Inscription on stained-glass window,
> Washington County Courthouse, 1919

As this chapter illustrates, there are hundreds of memorials to the Great War in the Old Dominion. But what use are stone remnants if they are hidden in plain sight and ignored or misunderstood by passersby and residents. Or worse yet, visitors notice them and remain unconvinced that the war deserves any further study or appreciation. So I decided to conduct the ultimate test: bring along my five-year-old twins on a research trip to see if I could interest them in my hunt for vestiges of World War I heritage and tales of Virginia's military and civilian achievements from that era. In this book I have tried to discuss the actions of Virginians throughout the

3. Vestiges

state's diverse geographical and cultural regions. But I was missing stories and contributions from a remote region, Southwest Virginia. So I planned a trip to rural Washington County, three hundred miles from the state capitol.

As every tourism director knows, one strategy to attract visitors is to mention a connection to a famous person. And while George Washington didn't sleep here, apparently Martha did; witness the Martha Washington Inn and Spa in Abingdon. Tourism trick number two: add something haunted. A quick Internet search revealed that the Martha Washington Inn is considered, by some, to be one of the most haunted places in Virginia. The inn was built originally as a home for General Francis Preston (a hero in the War of 1812) and his large family; two decades later new owners purchased the home with the intention of turning it into a women's college; three decades later the nation was embroiled in a civil war and the building was used as a hospital. Martha Washington College was eventually able to reclaim the use of its buildings and grounds after World War I and continued to function as a school until its closure in 1932. Three years later, the Martha Washington Inn opened for business, with some extra features. These spectral add-ons include a phantom horse (that

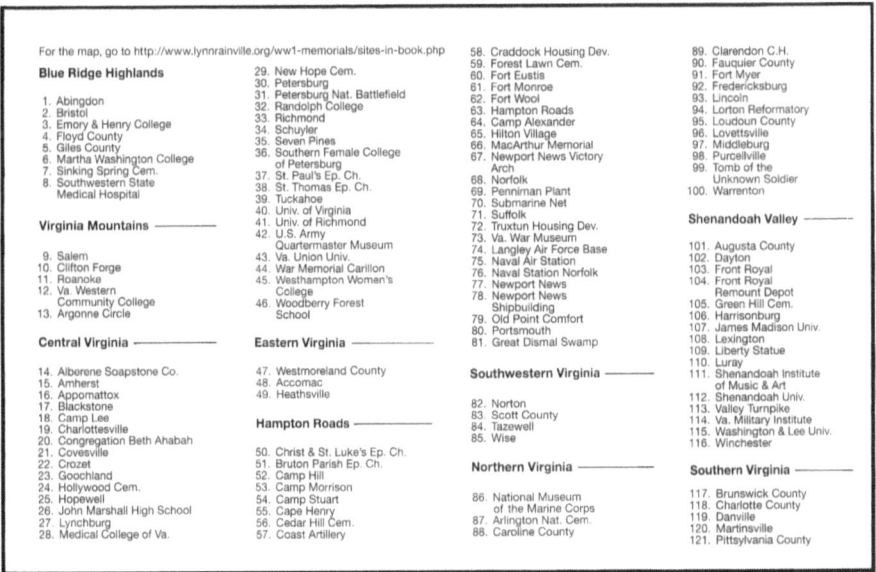

Regional distribution of the sites and communities mentioned in this book. An online map accompanies this list and provides the locations of each place (layout by Rick Britton).

belonged to a mortally wounded Union soldier), a Confederate soldier (shot dead in front of his girlfriend in her college dorm room), a violin-playing girl who mourns the death of a beloved solider, and a haunted tunnel that connects the inn to the nearby Barter Theater.[78]

Alas, my historic sleuthing debunked most of the details in the sightings mentioned above. And, sure enough, the only "sightings" related to historic eras that were popular with modern audiences, so no World War I ghosts. To get historically accurate details I was going to have to visit some local experts. First stop: the Historical Society of Washington County. Added bonus: it was across the street from a cupcake bakery. Maybe it wasn't going to be that difficult to interest my twin daughters after all.

At the historical society I learned a plethora of interesting and unusual details about this small town that appeared, at first glance, to be off the beaten path. I quickly learned that I wasn't thinking about the right "path." For over two centuries, Abingdon had been hosting travelers as they headed west on the Great Wilderness Road. One of these travelers, the famous pioneer Daniel Boone, called the spot "Wolf Hills" after his dogs were attacked by feral canines. And during the summer of 1780, a local militia, known as the Overmountain Men, formed nearby and set off across rural routes from the Abingdon Muster Grounds to chase and capture British forces in the area. Local accounts credit the battle in which they participated on Kings Mountain in South Carolina as the beginning of the end of the American Revolution. By the mid–19th century, railroad tracks reached the town, delivering passengers and freight and loading salt, lumber, and other southwestern Virginia products. Today the main line, named the Virginia Creeper after a native plant and the speed of the railway on the steep tracks, has been converted to a popular bicycling and walking trail. The Abingdon seal sums up these local assets: agriculture (symbolized by the head of a cow and a leaflike object that I assume is tobacco); education (symbolized by theater masks and a candle illuminating a book); lumber (symbolized by a wagon wheel and an axe); and icons relating to the town's origin (symbolized by a wolf, a mountain pass, and a fort).[79] Strolling down the historic lanes in person, I found history on every block: old churches, federal-style domestic architecture, handmade red bricks, and graveyards. But I needed a clue to find its World War I–era history.

I turned to one of my stand-bys, A. K. Davis's seven published volumes about Virginia during the Great War. Elizabeth Litchfield Stuart submitted 16 pages about this area to the chronicling effort and concluded,

"The population of Washington County was practically united in patriotism."[80] Every time I read a boast like that I wonder about the definition of "practically." Did the small African American population support a war that required them to serve in segregated units without access to most combat positions? Were there really no German Americans living in the community with conflicted loyalties?

Mrs. Stuart's summary of local wartime contributions reminded me that a hundred years ago there were three colleges in Washington County: two for women and one for men. The students at the two female colleges, Martha Washington College and Stonewall Jackson College, joined the Red Cross, raised money to support European children in war-torn countries, and donated funds to the YWCA war fund. Emory and Henry was the only men's college in the area during the 1910s. During the war, the majority of its 183 students served in the Student Army Training Corps and 104 of these recruits remained in the ROTC after the war ended. Six students lost their lives during the war (three were killed in action, three died while in other service). From the War Commission reports I learned that on April 22, 1918, Count Charles de Chambrun, the great-great-grandson of the legendary French military officer who fought in the American Revolution, the Marquis de Lafayette, planted a tree on the college grounds.[81] Trying to locate a nondescript century-old tree occupied my daughters for quite some time. Not only did we fail to locate the arboreal memorial; we also did not succeed at finding an on-campus gateway erected in honor of Second Lieutenant Harry Clay Williams (Emory and Henry class of 1910; Columbia Law School class of 1918), who died on November 6, 1918, in Base Hospital No. 8 of septicemia from an infected wound.[82] Later, when I placed a call to the college archivist I learned that the beautiful archway erected by his classmates and built from Tennessee marble had been taken down decades earlier.

I was striking out on the campus of Emory and Henry so I drove a dozen miles back to the Historical Society of Washington County. Its collections included a wide array of memorabilia from the war, which provided a small window into Abingdon's contributions. One of the carefully preserved artifacts was a bronze medal awarded to John Jesse Henderson.[83] Above the spread wings of an eagle was the inscription "United States Forces" and a rainbow-hued ribbon that connected the lapel pin at the top (with a shield, stars, and a bundle of 13 arrows) to the cross-shaped bottom piece of metal (decorated with an eagle, a heart-shaped shield, and the inscription). It took a little bit of research to figure out why Henderson was awarded a medal. He was one of two thousand men drafted from Washington County. A photograph taken in October 1917 showed dozens of these men enjoying a meal at John P. Wilson's farm, just before they boarded trains for Camp Lee. Henderson was 21 years old, living in Saltville, and working in a paper mill when his number was called and he too ended up in the Petersburg training camp. While at Camp Lee he wrote to his parents, complaining about the quotidian nature of chores and bureaucracy. Unfortunately, Private Henderson died on March 12, 1918, before he left the training camp, raising more questions about how his actions resulted in a medal.[84] The artifact itself does not contain any additional clues, but a short announcement in a Richmond newspaper after the war might shed some light. As of July 1919, the State of Virginia had not taken any steps to issue medals to service members, so local groups, such as the Howitzers' Association, was distributing its own medals to members of its battalion.[85] At least 40 African Americans from Washington County went to Camp Lee to train. One of these men, nicknamed "Black Jack" Hall, was the first man in the community who refused to claim any exemptions from serving. Having passed his physical exam and being questioned whether he wanted to claim any exemptions, he replied, "No, I want to go!"[86] Many of the men from this community were given a "comfort bag" (with some handmade supplies) from a local church and a box lunch from their Red Cross chapter before they left on the train for Camp Lee. Seven of these recruits lost their lives abroad.[87]

While in Abingdon I visited a large historic cemetery to see if I could find any of the names of the World War I dead. The official Virginia tourism page summed up the Sinking Spring Cemetery history in a paragraph that began, "[This] Cemetery is the final resting place for Brig. Gen. John B. Floyd, Lt. Col. W.W. Blackford, Civil War era Richmond newspaper editor Robert Hughes, and over 30 Confederate soldiers are interred in the 'Unknown Confederate Dead' section of the cemetery."[88] By now I was well used to the Civil War homage so despite the absence of any World War I mention, I went to review its tombstones in person. Although it took over an hour of running up and down row upon row of headstones, I succeeded in finding the final resting places of several World War I veterans. At the very edge of the cemetery there was Hubert Ray Hagy, one of six children and the only son in his immediate family to reach adulthood. Unfortunately, he died in 1918 from wounds received during a battle in France. Several rows away was the grave of Frank Robinson, who died around the same time. His stone, like his memory, was fading away. I could barely decipher the crossed rifles at the top of his stone, and the eroded inscription could be understood only after much effort: "Died ... From

Wounds Received in the Battle of Argonne Forest France ... Machine Gunner."

I was able to locate three other World War I veterans and a handful of ex-servicemen from other 20th-century wars. And then I noticed that there was another cemetery across the road. It was a black cemetery, originally used to bury enslaved laborers on a nearby plantation. There I located John Cooke, a private in the 155th Depot Brigade who lived until 1942. That unit was stationed at Camp Lee for the duration of the war and helped process new recruits, providing uniforms and equipment, and processing discharges at the end of the war.

At the end of the day I was happy with my World War I discoveries: almost a dozen gravestones (most with some new details about the men's service during the war), photographs, a medal of honor, and some newspaper clippings. But there were more fortuitous connections ahead. First, there was an informal memorial in the restaurant where we ate dinner. Near the restrooms at the back was a black-and-white photograph of a man in uniform. The only identification on the photograph was the name, "Arthur Speece Withers." By now I could easily recognize an American uniform from World War I. I looked him up in a handful of online databases and learned that he was born in Abingdon, drafted at age 23 (and again in his 50s during World War II), and enlisted on February 13, 1918. He left the service almost a year later, on February 3, 1919, and soon thereafter was hired by Emory and Henry College as a teacher. Later he married Bernice Ruth West, moved to North Carolina, where he taught at High Point Technical College, and died in 1985 at age 90. I only realized later, when I was sorting through my photographs, that the outside of the restaurant where we ate retained its 19th-century bas-relief name high above on the third floor: "Withers." Arthur's father, Salmon "Sam" Withers, operated a hardware store in this building from 1890 to the 1950s. Now I knew why they had hung up a portrait of Arthur. I just wished that the portrait's caption had explicitly referenced his World War I service.

Later, while checking out, I realized an historic connection to World War I at our hotel. After I rang the bell for service, my eyes roamed over the lobby. I saw a fragment of a letter written by Woodrow Wilson. As he was the U.S. president who declared war on Germany, this was an unexpected and direct connection to World War I. But unless the Martha Washington Inn shared my obsession with the war, why was it featured prominently in the lobby? Reading further I found a photograph of a slender woman dressed in a long white dress, Edith Bolling Galt, better known as Edith Wilson, Woodrow's second wife. They were married just months before the United States entered the war. Edith was born in Wytheville, Virginia, 50 miles northeast of Abingdon, and, in 1887, she briefly attended Martha Washington College to study music. During the war, she promoted gasless Sundays, meatless Mondays, and wheatless Wednesdays as part of the wartime rationing efforts. She even hosted a herd of sheep on the White House lawn, thereby saving manpower to mow it and, later, auctioning the wool for the benefit of the Red Cross.[89]

Perhaps the most remarkable World War I connection in this rural Virginia town was a fluke encounter. As I was driving out of town along Abingdon's brick-lined Main Street, I noticed a large recreational vehicle with a political slogan soliciting votes for a lieutenant governor candidate in the November 2018 election. Two men exited the vehicle and proceeded with a photo shoot, the younger man posing in front of the courthouse. I was curious: why were they using the Abingdon courthouse as a backdrop? Was he from there? I stopped to ask and learned that he was from Virginia Beach, hundreds of miles to the east along the coast. He picked Abingdon for the publicity shots because he wanted to promote jobs in small towns, which seemed ironic to me, knowing that in Abingdon's prime a century ago Washington County was one of the ten most populous counties in Virginia. It was too much to hope that they had come for the World War I–era Tiffany window of which they were unaware until I pointed it out to them. Just as I was giving up on any World War I connection, the candidate's campaign manager recalled an earlier occupational experience, decades ago, when he was called out on an ambulance run to pick up one of the last surviving African American veterans of the war at his Norfolk home after he had a stroke. Although he could not remember the name of the patient or the exact date, he hazarded a guess that this incident took place in the 1990s. Since the last American veteran died in 2011 at the remarkably old age of 110, it's possible that the patient in the 1990s was one of the last living Virginia veterans.

In my research I had a spotty track record of finding actual burials from World War I, but after having spoken with hundreds of Virginians over the course of two years, it was clear that the memory of those soldiers and civilians had not yet faded.

4

Remains

> Because you died, I shall not rest again,
> But wander ever through the lone world wide,
> Seeking the shadow of a dream grown vain
> Because you died.
> —Vera Brittain, 1918[1]

There is no easy way to comprehend the number and impact of World War I dead. On a global scale, over 11 million men lost their lives; this does not count the civilian casualties, which might be as high as 7 million. Of France's total population, one in 20 was killed; in British villages some parents lost multiple sons. Because it entered the war later, the United States' troops and families did not suffer as horribly as their European counterparts, but the daily fear of losing loved ones was as high as any other country between 1917 and 1919. I use the year 1919, months after the signing of the Armistice on November 11, 1918, because American deaths continued after peace was declared. These additional deaths came from wounds sustained during the war, wartime illnesses (especially from the influenza epidemic), and the always unexpected and tragic accidental deaths while soldiers were still in uniform.

There is no master list of Virginia deaths during or as a direct result of World War I. One effort to tally these lost lives was conducted in the 1920s as part of A. K. Davis's War Commission work. When Davis and his colleagues reached out to Virginia's counties and cities, one of their goals was to document a complete "list of the dead." But the task turned out to be difficult. One contemporary account, a 1920 newspaper article, summarized their understanding of the number of Virginia casualties from the war: 1,635 deaths and an additional 4,452 seriously wounded men. The report differentiated between officers and enlisted men, with casualties among the enlisted men much higher: 1,564 enlisted men dead and 4,255 wounded versus 71 officers dead and 196 wounded.[2]

Using more recent technology, this list and other sources were used to create an online database titled "Virginia's Military Dead." It provides basic information for each wartime death: name, rank, cause of death, location, and date deceased (when known), residence, gender, race, service unit, and occasionally additional notes. Curated by the Library of Virginia, this list contains 3,706 records for deceased service members, five of whom were female nurses. The discrepancy—the database list of dead is more than double the length of list from the 1920s—is largely due to differing definitions of a "Virginian." Is that someone who was born in the state? Enlisted from Virginia? Died in the state? In the library dataset, the criteria for a "Virginian" appears to be the soldiers' hometowns or the residence of their surviving kin at the time of the veteran's death.

To put the Virginia deaths in context, about 116,000 Americans died from combat, wounds, or illness while training for or fighting the war.[3] In the 1920 Federal Census, about 2.3 million people lived in Virginia; the population size of her southwestern neighbor, Tennessee, was almost identical. These two southern states sent similar numbers of soldiers to the war (Tennessee sent 91,836, while Virginia sent 93,499). They both suffered the same number of fatalities, each state losing about 3,800 men and women. While each of these estimates relies on multiple assumptions about one's definitions (e.g., whether or not it includes mortalities in 1919 from wounds suffered during the war), it appears that Virginia's troop contributions were in line with her similar-sized southern neighbors. In the end, Virginia troops were credited with providing 2 percent of the United States military force during World War I.[4]

Virginia is divided into 95 counties and 39 independent cities. Dividing the number of political entities by the estimate of 3600 deaths, it appears that each community lost, on average, 28 citizens due to wartime service. An informal check of the average number of deaths listed on the World War I memorials that I located throughout the state confirms this estimate: most Virginia counties or independent cities lost between one and two dozen soldiers. This estimate does not include the large number of civilian deaths from the influenza outbreak. Although it is hard to obtain precise numbers (pneumonia and other diseases were often conflated or co-occurred with the flu), several hundred thousand Virginians contracted the flu and about 15,000 died from it between 1918 and 1919.[5]

To visualize the Virginians who died during the war, I took a representative sample of one hundred war dead. Within this group, 49 soldiers died from disease, not the fighting. Another 29 were killed in action and 13 died from wounds sustained during a battle. Somewhat unexpectedly, ten drowned; most likely these casualties were sailors on ships or died due to accidents in port. Fewer than five soldiers died in accidents either at training camps, at the front, or in transit to and from France. A few in my sample of one hundred died at the hands of others. Murder, it seems, did not take a vacation even during wartime. And while the number of people within my survey is statistically insignificant, a small percentage committed suicide or were executed for crimes.[6]

While the dead went to their final rest, tens of thousands of injured and ill Virginians returned home. One newspaper reporter estimated that 32,202 sick and wounded men arrived in Newport News between February and August 1919 alone. In a strikingly honest description, the reporter wrote that these men were "gassed, armless, legless, many of them wrecks for life."[7] Others, "in pitifully large numbers," were transported back home in steel cages due to their "mental derangement." Initially, these tragic cases were cared for in the Newport News National Soldiers' Home or nearby General Hospital 43, but unfortunately few were destined to recover fully because their malady, "shell shock," was not yet fully understood.[8]

A health warning to protect oneself against the "Spanish Flu," more accurately "influenza" (*Richmond Times-Dispatch*, October 15, 1918).

Battling the Influenza Epidemic

> Dear Jessie.... I am well hope you all the same ... will tell you that miss Leaner hariet was bearied last sunday at sterling it was ofel sad

> she was only sick a few days ... be share and let me no if any of you all get sick.
> —Margaret Thornton writing to her daughter about the influenza epidemic in Loudoun County, 1918[9]

Many of the noncombat deaths were due to influenza, a disease often given the geographically incorrect moniker the "Spanish Flu." The name was applied during the spring of 1918 as the disease spread throughout Europe. Unlike other countries on the continent, Spain lacked a media blackout on reporting the subsequent deaths caused by the epidemic and, as a result, it became closely associated in the public's consciousness with the quickly spreading sickness.[10] As with today's flu cases, the virus was always present in some form or another, but when people congregated in large numbers or spent more time indoors with closer contact and less air circulation, it spread more easily. Each year the virus mutated, resulting in different strains. In 1918, the strain was more deadly for young and otherwise healthy individuals who lacked some of the resistance that older people had from surviving earlier outbreaks.[11] The deadly 1918 strain initially reached American soil among a handful of sailors who returned home to Boston. Within two weeks, it had spread to the civilian population with thousands being stricken.[12] Within a week the virus reached the commonwealth. By the time it ended, in the spring of 1919, state officials classified the epidemic as "the worst disaster that ever befell the State of Virginia."[13]

In Virginia, the flu season in the spring of 1918 appeared to be normal. People of all ages fell ill, but deaths were most common among infants and the elderly. The summer passed uneventfully, with more scattered flu deaths but no public health emergency. Then on September 13, as the scorching hot summer came to an end, a new inductee at Camp Lee came down with symptoms of a severe respiratory disease. Because of the large number of men at the camp—almost 48,000 soldiers in residence—a single case would not have initially raised alarms. But before doctors could accurately diagnosis the illness, ten more cases were reported at the camp. Within just four days, the number grew to five hundred and then doubled within the next 48 hours. To handle the growing number of cases, squad rooms within each barracks were turned into infirmaries. Sheets were ripped in half and hung around cots to try to provide makeshift quarantine conditions.

With available treatments officials could do little to stop this raging epidemic except try to limit large gatherings. Accordingly, the commanding officer at Camp Lee, Brigadier General Charles A. Hedskin, closed down the post's social halls (the YMCA, the Knights of Columbus hall, theaters), forbade public gatherings and visitors, and forced the sick to wear masks. But he decided against a general quarantine at the camp; some of the most important battles of the European war were being fought in September and October of 1918, and with the high casualty rate among American troops at battles such as the Meuse Argonne offensive, the general was under a lot of pressure to keep the troop supply line moving. Only the officers' training school at Camp Lee was quarantined.

Medical reports compiled by the U.S. surgeon general indicate that the worst of the Virginia influenza outbreak began around September 26 and ended around October 20, 1918. During that time, there were 5,370 documented cases in the Virginia training camps, of which 719 turned into pneumonia. Among the pneumonia cases, 201, or 27.5 percent, died. Without the complication of pneumonia, the death rate for all of the entire 5,370 flu cases was only 3.74 percent.[14]

The 48,000 men at Camp Lee were not training in a vacuum. They regularly visited nearby Richmond and Petersburg for food and entertainment. Public health officials were very concerned about this situation. But, again, a public quarantine or restriction of troop access was not adopted. Instead, city health officers waged a public education campaign. They produced posters and pamphlets for distribution in schools, businesses, and public places. These posters encouraged standard hygiene practices: wash hands, cover mouths when coughing or sneezing, don't spit, and use a handkerchief. And like other maladies from this era, the posters equated civilian weaknesses with military failures. One poster admonished, "Coughs and Sneezes Spread Diseases; As Dangerous as Poison Gas; Spread of Spanish Influenza Menaces Our War Production." When entering public theaters, Americans were warned by Commissioner of Public Health John Dill Robertson that "influenza frequently complicated with pneumonia is prevalent at this time throughout America," and he advised individuals suffering from colds to "go home and go to bed until you are well."[15]

These actions were not enough to prevent the spread of the disease from Virginia training camps into nearby cities. By the end of September, local officials had connected the rise in flu cases with the crowded conditions found in army barracks. Accordingly, the new recruits of the Students Army Training Corps in Richmond were housed in outdoor tents instead of indoor quarters. Military officials pledged to promptly care for any trainees who fell ill.[16] Despite these prophylactic measures, the

Richmond Health Department reported 85 cases of the flu in just one day, October 1, between the hours of noon and five o'clock.[17] The progression of the disease in Richmond followed a now familiar pattern: within days, hundreds of people had fallen ill and local nurses were overwhelmed. Public health officials turned to the Red Cross to recruit more nurses. They also lectured schoolchildren on how to prevent the disease. Despite these admonitions, by October 5 more than two thousand cases of influenza were reported in Richmond.[18]

To combat this astronomical increase, Richmond instituted a series of bans on public gatherings, closing churches, schools, and soda shops. But public officials could not agree whether proper ventilation in public spaces was sufficient to halt the disease's spread. So instead of banning public gatherings, some Virginia communities banned common drinking cups or communal communion cups.[19] These measures failed to halt the rapid rise in new cases, so public officials began canceling events, such as a conference of four-minute men and a YWCA conference.[20] They even cancelled the Virginia State Fair, originally scheduled to open on October 7. And then, ironically, both Dr. T. L. Driscoll, a clinician in the U.S. Public Health Service, and Dr. Lawrence T. Price, the director of an emergency hospital, fell ill.[21]

In central Virginia, the epidemic did not level off until the third week in October; a milestone measured by the still grim tally of 13 deaths on October 22, which was the first decline in casualties since the outbreak.[22] Finally, by the end of October, new cases were decreasing across the state and the epidemic seemed to have run its course. After a couple weeks of debate, on November 5, Richmond lifted the closure order on many public places and the next day school children returned to their classrooms, movie theaters reopened, and soda fountains could serve from their taps again (as opposed to the bottles that they had been forced to substitute).[23]

While the worst of the epidemic was over, the virus returned for another bout of cases in early December. As the flu does each year, it petered out by the end of winter. But the final statistics were sobering: during the fall of 1918, 20,841 patients were diagnosed with influenza in Richmond; 946 died. In the spring of 1919, an additional 132 people died from the flu in the city.[24]

Although the influenza crisis captured the attention of most politicians, Virginians were dying of other diseases in 1918 and 1919, including the mumps, measles, tuberculosis, diphtheria, scarlet fever, and cerebrospinal meningitis.[25] One army report estimated that 4 percent of Virginia draftees were rejected because of thyroid disease.[26] An even larger concern was venereal disease. As early as 1914, the American Social Hygiene Association started warning the public about venereal diseases. After the United States entered the war, an anti-VD campaign ramped up, equaling other propaganda efforts like the selling of war bonds. One wartime pamphlet asked, "How could you look the flag in the face if you were dirty with gonorrhea?"[27] Some safety campaigns even encouraged masturbation ("you won't go crazy") in lieu of sexual interactions. VD was of particular concern in the training camps; each month the camp surgeon submitted a monthly report on any outbreaks. This report was based on the results of the semimonthly physical examinations and contained data on prophylaxis, neglect of duty, etc.[28] Before the men were allowed to risk their lives, they were given complete physicals to ensure that they were healthy.

Waiting for News

> Mr. and Mrs. Charles Dawson ... received official notice that their son, Private Franklin L. Dawson had died from wounds received in battle. Further particulars are expected to follow in letter from his two brothers, who are yet overseas.
> —Virginia newspaper, ca. 1918[29]

Throughout my research I have tried to imagine what it was like on the home front during the war. How did families like the Dawsons, mentioned above, handle the daily worry that their three sons might not return from the war? Over the course of the 20th century, the efficiency of daily news notifications has increased so rapidly that it took some research to figure out just how Virginia families learned about distant events during World War I. This research changed my perspective on the Virginia fatalities. It's one thing to look up the names of the dead a hundred years later and see the final tallies of who lived and who died. But Charles and Henrietta Dawson would have paid close attention to every newspaper and feared receiving a telegram each of the 486 days between the time when Franklin was drafted and his death overseas. And after they received that notification they would, of course, have worried about their other two sons, Charles Carline and Sewell Randolph, until they returned home safely in 1919.

To better understand what relatives went through as they waited for their sons and daughters to return, I read through the letters between Aphelia "Affie" Yerby Holladay, a 57-year-old Richmond woman, and her two enlisted sons, Percy and Phillip. Where did she go each day to catch up on local news and check on the latest casualties? How did she keep abreast of the military happenings that meant life or death for her sons? In between the letters that she received, Affie spent dozens of days not knowing if her sons were alive or dead. Her younger son was drafted in the first round, on June 5, 1917. Her older son didn't wait for his number to be called; he enlisted on March 29, 1918, and joined his brother at Camp Lee. Affie's nephew, Clayton Yerby, wrote a letter to his aunt after he heard that Percy was leaving for training soon. "I hear you are about to make the supreme sacrifice for which mothers are made," he wrote. "It is hard,— oh so hard to give your boy up, and words are non-comforting things, but you raised him to give honor and nobility to the world and to uplift mankind."[30] It was a heavy duty for a 25-year-old and a daily worry for his mother. Clayton assured Affie that there was a "splendid chance of his returning unscathed—a hero of mercy," but Affie confessed to her son in a later letter that his departure was "the hardest day of my whole life."[31] And keep in mind this initial departure was simply a 25-mile trip to Camp Lee for training; initially Percy was able to return home to Richmond on weekends for the first few months of his service.

While waiting at home, Affie hung two blue stars in her window. This tradition originated in 1917 when U.S. Army Captain Robert L. Queisser designed a service flag in honor of his two sons who were serving in the war. The original design was a rectangular banner with thick red border and a white backdrop for a five-sided star. During World War I, a blue star signified military service, while a gold one indicated the death of a serviceman. Later, in 1928, mothers who lost a son in the war organized into a national group called the "Gold Star Mothers" that fought for the right to reclaim their children's bodies and bury them back home on American soil.[32]

After training at Camp Lee, both of Affie's sons were shipped to Europe. These three family members made an effort to stay in touch via regular letters and the occasional telegram. Most of Mrs. Holladay's correspondence with her sons is on small pieces of notepaper, much of it marked with the logos of the YMCA or the Knights of Columbus. Like the distribution of Bibles (by the American Bible Society) and books (by the American Library Association), these organizations gave out free stationery in an effort to boost morale, encouraging and enabling soldiers to write home more often.

Troop mail was censored, but it was still an important way for families to stay in touch over the long months apart. Affie's sons, Percy and Philip,

Percy Holladay and his fiancée, Mary Caroline Holladay, April 28, 1918 (Virginia Historical Society, "Memories Book," Mss1.H7185 h377).

complained that sometimes their mail wasn't being received, perhaps due to overzealous censors or an overwhelmed censorship office, which didn't have time to read through all of the letters.[33] The letters that did get through came addressed to "Mrs. W. H. Holladay" with a postmark that read, "AEF Passed As Censored," indicating that there may have been blacked-out sections (or even sections cut out). Despite the army censors, the Holladay sons were able to impart many of their personal thoughts about their experiences in the war to their family. After serving abroad for just a few months, Percy wrote to his parents, confessing that he "was more homesick than ever before." His brother, Philip, concluded that war was "the most horrible and unsatisfactory way of settling international or internal questions." It was through these letters that Affie learned, long after the fact, that her sons had fought in the deadliest American battle of the war, the Meuse Argonne offensive; spent time in a French hospital for severe diarrhea; and narrowly avoided the fatal-complications of pneumonia.[34]

The worst news, of course—the news a mother like Affie would have dreaded each day of her sons' deployment—could not come in a soldier's own hand. Neighbors and community members probably first learned of a local death through the newspaper. Most Virginia newspapers had daily columns dedicated to announcing the wartime deaths of local as well as famous citizens. For example, the June 22, 1918, issue of the *Richmond Times-Dispatch* carried a "Roll of Honor." The subtitle explained that it was a "list showing men who were killed or injured on French soil." That day, 38 individuals were listed, with deaths from action, wounds, diseases, severe wounds, or wounds of an undetermined magnitude. Dead marines were listed separately; 127 names were recorded on that day. These casualty numbers spanned the entire AEF, and then the paper specified individual deaths by name and residence. On that day four of the dead were from communities in each corner of the state: three privates—Floyd H. Whitmore (Milton), Harris Clarke (Glenmour), Charles H. Woodbury (Norfolk)—and one sergeant, Harvey C. Graves (Blacksburg).[35]

Families were notified of nonlethal injuries via letters. When the news was more urgent, a serious wound or a death, a telegram was sent. Domestically, the Red Cross and various women's groups helped finance and assist soldiers who wanted to send a message home. This most often occurred when a solider fell ill during his training or in transit to and from the camps. For example, in Danville, the Red Cross maintained a canteen that met all regular passenger and troop trains. They estimated that over 375,000 passengers passed through the city over the course of two years. Among this number about six thousand were sick or wounded. Many of these men asked to send telegraphs, and the Red Cross funded these requests to the total of $4,801.[36]

As the war wound down, telegrams were also used to notify families about their sons' return schedule. Seven months after the war ended, the Salvation Army sent Mrs. Holladay a "Night Telegram" on behalf of her son Percy: he had arrived safely in Philadelphia, and was en route to Camp Dix in New Jersey. Eight days later, on June 9, 1919, her other son Philip sent a Western Union telegram informing her that he would be "home last of week. Maybe. Sent to another camp writing."[37]

The Dawson Family was not as fortunate. The War Department announced 4400 recent casualties in the *Washington Times* on Friday, December 13, 1918. This large number was a result of a major push that fall to win the war, which included some of the deadliest battles for American troops.[38] Franklin L. Dawson died from wounds that he suffered while fighting with the 80th Division, 318th Infantry in Souilly, France. No records survive from his brothers, who may have heard firsthand how Franklin died. If we are to judge from the movements of his unit that fall, he would have been part of a massive movement of troops that participated in the Meuse Argonne offensive. Between September 15 and 25, the 80th Division traveled north 32 miles, from Ligny-en-Barrois to a position along the front just north and west of the infamous battle site of Verdun.[39] On the day Franklin died, October 11, the First Army Field Order at Souilly called for the troops to hold their ground and prepare for further attacks.[40] Colonel Robert P. McCleave, chief of staff in the Third Division, described the enemy's resistance that day as "very obstinate."[41] More than two months after he was killed in battle, Franklin Dawson's parents learned of his fate on that day of heavy fighting.

Burying the Dead

> In Flanders fields the poppies blow
> Between the crosses, row on row,
> That mark our place: and in the sky
> The larks still bravely singing fly
> Scarce heard amid the guns below.
> —John McCrae, "In Flanders Field," 1915

Families like the Dawsons had a difficult decision to make as they slowly came to terms with the loss of their loved ones: where would they bury the body? In past wars, most corpses were buried in mass graves at or near the site of battle. Sometimes an effort was made to retrieve the bodies of high-ranking officers or other symbolically important corpses, but it was extremely rare for a body to be retrieved from a distant battlefield and returned to the deceased's place of origin.

Obviously, disposing of wartime corpses was not a new challenge. Even when battles were fought on just one nation's soil, debates emerged over when, where, and how to bury the dead. This occurred 50 years earlier in America, at the close of the bloody Civil War. In 1865, the railroad lines did not reach every battlefield nor did they have refrigerated cars (to better transport bodies during the summer heat). Instead, most enlisted men were buried in mass graves near where they fell. Gradually, mothers and wives banded together to demand the return of their loved ones.⁴²

In World War I, the grim task of burying the millions of dead continued for many years after the end of hostilities. Most of the Allied forces decided not to repatriate their dead, instead burying them in battlefield cemeteries, usually segregated by nationality. The Americans had to decide whether their dead should be buried alongside other nationalities, in separate American cemeteries abroad, or, in a never-tried-before strategy, shipped home en masse on ships for burial on domestic soil in the States.

When the United States entered the Great War, the government promised enlisted men and their families that it would repatriate the bodies of dead soldiers. In anticipation of the large number of fatalities, the American Graves Registration Service was created within the military and tasked with the retrieval, identification, transportation, and burial of deceased Americans.

Exhuming American bodies from a French battlefield for shipment back to the United States. The soldiers are cleaning off the coffin with a brush to try to decipher any identifying marks (*Graves Registration Service*, 3: v3p114, Library of Congress).

From the military's standpoint immediate identification and burial were matters of accounting and morale. Nothing was more depressing to the front line soldiers than to see unburied dead around them. The men, and a handful of women, who died during combat posed a logistical and ethical dilemma for their surviving comrades: how to safely and properly care for their corporeal remains while still fighting for one's life. There are countless examples of soldiers risking and in some cases losing their lives to pull a comrade's body back to the relative safety of a trench or defensive position. Even if a soldier died after being evacuated to a field hospital, his colleagues must still decide how to dispose of the body in a safe manner for the living and in a respectful way for the dead.[43]

Temporary burial sites were created that ranged from hastily dug, individual internments to mass graves that served as short-term solutions until war's end. Various military units were responsible for managing these interim resting places, including sanitary squads and pioneer infantry regiments. There were 37 pioneer infantry regiments during the Great War, 16 made up of African American troops and 21 that included white troops. These "workhorse" regiments were given more advanced technical training than other labor battalions and often included specialists such as mechanics, farriers, grooms, and carpenters.[44] Eugene Ragland, an Albemarle County resident mentioned in Chapter 2, served in the 807th Regiment of the pioneer infantry.[45] This unit was praised for its "cheerfulness" while "suffering much" from sleeping in the rain and mud and being short on rations.[46] These skilled African American laborers were deployed abroad to assist the Graves Registration Service. This assignment was considered by soldiers to be one of the worst details due to its grisly task.[47] After the war ended, more than six thousand black pioneer infantrymen (in the 813th, 815th, and 816th Regiments) were sent to Romagne-sous-Montfaucon to collect and bury the bodies of the fallen from the Meuse Argonne offensive. The work of retrieving decomposing bodies was difficult enough, but the pioneer infantry regiments were also forced to live in primitive conditions, which put them at risk of illness and death. Despite the hardships, African American troops buried over 23,000 bodies on foreign soil.[48]

Military chaplains also played an important role: administering last rites, saying prayers over the hastily dug graves and, in some cases, helping to dig them. At the Meuse Argonne battlefield, the Episcopal Rev. Hal Kearns took charge of one burial detail, writing, "Our men were falling in such numbers that it was no longer possible to send those who had made the great sacrifice back to burial grounds in the rear; they must be buried on the battlefield."⁴⁹ These mass graves were marked carefully on field maps so they could be located after the war. When possible, prayers or services were conducted at the site, but one chaplain recalled, "Often we worked under such heavy shell fire that there was opportunity to utter only a word of prayer as we lowered the bodies into their temporary resting places."⁵⁰

After the war ended, burial details were sent back into the field to exhume these bodies for proper burial in a more permanent location. Often, African American units were asked to do this unpleasant and unpopular task. Burial groups were supplied with rubber gloves, shovels, stakes to mark the location of graves, canvas, and ropes to tie up remains, among other tools and materials. Men remarked that it was "the most dreadful experience I've ever had." One chaplain assigned to this detail described the post-traumatic effects of such work as causing "a trying of the nerves ... and a curious kind of irritability that was quite infectious."⁵¹

In the American Civil War, soldiers sometimes pinned notes to their clothing or scratched personal information onto their belt buckles so their bodies could be more readily identified in the event of their deaths on the battlefield. Half a century later, the U.S. Army passed a regulation that assigned each soldier an aluminum identification tag.⁵² A decade later, in 1916, the regulation was modified to require two circular tags, one to remain with the body and the other to file as part of the burial record. These "dog tags" helped the military gravediggers identify the bodies so that the gravestones could be accurately inscribed.

By the end of the war, approximately 70,000 of the 116,000 dead American troops were buried in over 2,300 cemeteries located in or near dozens of European battlefields. This included 15,000 men who were buried in individual graves.⁵³ Despite the distribution of graves over such a large area, Secretary of War Newton D. Baker promised the nation that the dead would eventually be returned home for reburial. Matters were complicated, however, by the politics of varying U.S. groups and Allied nations about whether to repatriate the dead to individual family graves or rebury the dead in large national cemeteries. After a public backlash against leaving American bodies abroad, in October 1919, the War Department announced that it would give parents the choice to return the bodies of their sons or have them reinterred in the nearest American cemetery in Europe.

In the end, this promise of domestic burial cost the federal government over $30 million, a figure that would have been much higher had not many families agreed to let their children rest abroad in newly built

American cemeteries.[54] In France, Britain, Belgium and Italy, the United States negotiated the long-term lease of hundreds of acres of land in order to bury its dead in "American cemeteries." To manage this monumental mortuary task, Congress founded the American Battle Monuments Commission (ABMC) in 1923. President Harding appointed a seven-member committee to honor the American armed forces through monuments and memorials abroad, chaired by the former head of the American Expeditionary Force, General John J. Pershing. During his three decades as head of the ABMC, Pershing presided over the design and construction of eight American cemeteries in Europe and managed the complicated logistics surrounding the reburial of tens of thousands of Americans.[55]

In order to serve the needs of the mourners and adequately remember the fallen men and women, each ABMC cemetery included a chapel, ornamental landscaping, a battlefield map, and some form of a memorial statue. All retrieved bodies were buried under military-issued marble gravestones, while the names of the missing and presumed dead were inscribed on the walls of the chapels. Although the United States gave mourning kin the option to bring their child or spouse's body home, they hoped to make the foreign cemeteries attractive enough that Americans would pick the less expensive option of burying their fallen abroad.

The chair of the Commission of Fine Arts, Charles Moore, was the catalyst behind the designs of the American cemeteries in Europe. In designing these sites he was clearly influenced by Arlington National Cemetery, as he suggested that uniform white marble headstones situated within "gentle wooded slopes" would produce "the desired effect of a vast army in its last resting place."[56] The democratic nature of these identical gravestones emphasized the egalitarian ideal of American society, while the symmetrical blocks and paths within Moore's planned landscape suggested a predictable and thereby soothing route through the cemetery. Moreover, the orderly rows of headstones at these foreign cemeteries created a parklike atmosphere that arose out of the 19th-century rural cemetery movement and dovetailed with the founding of "memorial parks" in the United States.

Over the course of the 1920s, the ABMC hired well-known architects to communicate its aspirations in stone: "to perpetuate the deeds of its sons ... and help to preserve the glorious record of America's achievement in the World War."[57] This grandiose goal required skilled craftsmen like French architect Paul Cret, who had emigrated to the United States in 1903 to apply his beaux-arts method to design neoclassical buildings and sculpture. This style, common in museums and federal buildings of

Washington, D.C., would have been very familiar to its post–World War I American audience.

One the most impressive of the eight American burial sites in Europe is the Meuse Argonne American Cemetery, located at Romagne-sous-Montfaucon in the Argonne forest of northwestern France. The Meuse Argonne Cemetery was formally unveiled 20 years after the United States entered the war, on Memorial Day 1937. More than 14,000 marble gravestones lie in orderly rows, a sharp contrast to the chaos and corporeal devastation that covered the fields during the infamous Meuse Argonne offensive in the fall of 1918. On a visit in 2015, sponsored by the ABMC, I was walking up and down rows of gravestones and I noticed the dead of a familiar division, the 29th. Captain Robert Y. Conrad was identified as an officer from Virginia who served in the 116th Infantry Regiment, 29th Division.[58] Months later, at the Library of Virginia, while reading through scrapbooks containing newspaper clippings and obituaries, I came across the headline "Capt. Conrad Killed." I learned that he was from Winchester, served in the National Guard, and died on October 8, 1918, during the 47-day battle. The newspaper highlighted Captain Conrad's Confederate heritage; his father, Major Holmes Conrad, "served with distinction" in the southern army.[59] One of Conrad's war buddies sent a message to his wife, informing her that he had seen the captain fall in battle at Malbrouck Hill. Later, the War Department sent a formal notification, and he was awarded a posthumous Distinguished Service Cross for leading his company while under assault, "capturing many prisoners and machine guns," and suffering a mortal wound "while leading a charge on a machine-gun nest."[60]

Captain Conrad's gravestone contains a military inscription standardized after the Civil War: the name of the deceased, his rank, his birth and death date (if known), his military unit, and any commendations (such as a medal of honor). In the ABMC cemeteries gravestones are of two types: a three-dimensional cross or a rectangular post with a Star of David at the top.[61] In domestic cemeteries, these two symbols, Christian crosses and Jewish stars, are inscribed within a small circle at the top center of the stone. As with his compatriots, there is no personalized epitaph for Captain Conrad. The American military decided to prohibit additional language, such as a biographical inscription, in order to encourage an egalitarian ethos in which the stones of generals are the same as those of foot soldiers.

Another Virginian buried abroad is wagoner Joseph Stump from Copper Hill in Floyd County. Stump served in Company B, Seventh Machine Gun Battalion, Third Infantry Division, and received the French Croix de

The Meuse-Argonne American Cemetery in France. The marble headstones mark the graves of 14,246 Americans who died in the Great War, most of whom lost their lives during the Meuse-Argonne offensive in the fall of 1918. Every Memorial Day French and American flags are placed at each gravestone (photograph by Lynn Rainville, 2014).

Guerre with a Silver Star for his actions at the Battle of Chateau-Thierry. In June 1918 he was "conspicuous by his great bravery in the defense of Chateau-Thierry and was gloriously wounded at his post of combat."[62] He was buried near where he died at the Aisne-Marne American Cemetery, another ABMC burial ground.

Canadian Lieutenant Colonel John McCrae's (1872–1918) famous poem "In Flanders Field" honors a battlefield where his close friend and former student had died. Years later, land near this site was given by Belgium to the United States to create the Flanders Field American Cemetery; it was officially dedicated on August 8, 1937.[63] Entering past thick, squat columns adorned with eagles and ornamental globes, walking down the tree-lined gravel paths, and standing in a perfectly manicured grass lawn, the observant visitor will notice the grave of a Virginian: Lynchburg resident First Lieutenant George Preston Glenn (1894–1918). Like that of many aviators, his war was brief, lasting only 28 days. He trained in three countries (America, Canada, and England) before reporting to the Petite Synthe Aerodrome in France. He was assigned to the 17th Aero Squadron, in which he flew a Sopwith Camel biplane, and his colleagues described him as "a son of Virginia" and "a charming fellow." On July 20, 1918, Glenn was escorting a Royal Air Force squadron to Brussels when he and his squadron were attacked by five Fokker D.VIIs. Glenn was "last seen [at 20,000 feet] diving." Glenn was shot down one day before his 24th birthday and died shortly thereafter in a German prisoner of war camp.[64]

Many families of other Virginians who died abroad requested that the remains of their loved ones be repatriated for internment at home. Franklin Dawson, mentioned earlier, was buried in the Sharon Cemetery in his hometown of Middleburg, Virginia. The short marble obelisk at his grave mentions that he died from "wounds received while in action."[65] Similarly, Second Lieutenant Wilson Brown Dodson's gravestone in the Forest Lawn Cemetery reads, "Killed in action in France." Dodson, who attended the University of Virginia, later served in Company A, 16th Infantry, First Division, and lost his life on October 8, 1918, during the Meuse Argonne offensive while leading his platoon in an attack on Hill 272. He received the Silver Star for his bravery and is honored on a memorial plaque erected in his hometown of Norfolk City. Captain Conrad's domestic commemoration is a little more complicated. Although his family agreed to leave his remains in France, two years after his death officers and members of Company I, First Virginia regiment, held a memorial service for the Winchester officer. On October 10, 1920, the veterans, known locally as "Capt. Bob's" company, gathered at the Mount Hebron Cemetery. The company bugler played "Taps" "at the foundation of a monument to be erected in the cemetery in memory of Capt. Conrad."[66] Despite their intentions, there is no evidence today of a memorial in the Mount Hebron Cemetery.

Other Virginia families decided to bring back the bodies of their dead loved ones for burial in America's official national military graveyard, Arlington National Cemetery, located in Northern Virginia. One of the most famous gravestones at this site, the Tomb of the Unknown Soldier, dates to World War I. On Memorial Day 1921, unidentified remains of four bodies were exhumed from American military cemeteries abroad. During a somber ceremony held in Chalons-sur-Marne, France, on October 14, a highly decorated World War I veteran, Sergeant Edward F. Younger, selected one of the caskets containing an unidentified serviceman by placing a spray of white roses on it. These remains were shipped to Washington, D.C., where they lay in state in the U.S. Capitol for three days until November 11, when President Harding presided over their reburial. Unidentified remains were selected to emphasize that "a plain soldier" could "typify the greatest among the nation's heroes."[67] Located in the newly created Memorial Amphitheater, the memorial was a simple block of masonry, unlike the carved tomb of today. The 50-ton marble neoclassical sarcophagus was unveiled in 1932.[68]

During several of the subsequent 20th-century American wars (World War II, Korea, and Vietnam), an unidentified service member killed in action was selected for reburial at this gravesite to represent all of the fallen from the conflict. With advances in genetic identifications from DNA samples, the crypt was re-dedicated in 1999 to honor America's missing personnel instead of unidentified remains.[69] To this day, an honor guard formed in 1926 watches over the tomb 24 hours a day, 365 days a year. They train for up to a year, taking rigorous tests before qualifying to serve as tomb guards. The first female guard was appointed in 1997.

Sergeant Witchie of Fort Myer, Virginia. He is blowing "Taps" at the Tomb of the Unknown Soldier, Arlington National Cemetery. The wreath was presented by the Gold Star Mothers of Missouri on September 21, 1930 (National Archives, form V-5, file no. 95398).

Dozens of Virginia families decided to bury their World War I veterans at Arlington. One of these burials is Cismont native Frank Nelson Lewis, who served as a captain in the Fourth Infantry, Third Division. He received the Distinguished Service Cross for gallantry during a battle at Cunel on October 5 and 6, 1918. Captain Lewis was severely wounded in both arms and legs and yet continued his command, leading his company in a successful attack. He succumbed to his wounds months later in a French hospital on January 6, 1919. His body was shipped back to Virginia and he was interred at Arlington on March 3, 1921.[70] Another Virginia widow, Mary Peck, the wife of Captain Myron Hall Peck, erected a marble cross at Arlington in honor of her husband. The inscription begins, "In loving memory of my dear husband" and outlines his service in France, including the posthumous honor of receiving the "French Croix de Guerre with Palm and the Distinguished Service Cross."[71] Captain Peck was commanding the Second Engineers in the fall of 1918 in Saint-Étienne-à-Arnes when one of his reconnaissance parties failed at a mission. When Captain Peck went to complete the search, he was struck by a shell fragment and died within minutes. He was temporarily buried in a nearby cemetery where he fell before being exhumed and reinterred at Arlington.[72]

Erecting Gravestones

> They Live, the beautiful, the dead,
> Like stars above our head.
> —Gravestone inscription for
> Russell Snyder (1892–1918)

Each American family that lost a relative in World War I had the option of requesting, free of charge, a headstone from the U.S. government—a tradition that began with the Civil War.[73] While the style has changed slightly over the generations, from outlines of shields (for Civil War Union soldiers and veterans of the Spanish-American War) to pointed stones with the Southern Cross (for Confederate veterans), the headstones remain easily identifiable by their bright white marble and simple construction. In a country that usually reserves white for weddings, this stone choice stands out among more common dark gray granite monuments of the 20th century. The morphology of the stone reveals the war. In the case of World War I veterans, curved white stones were the most common.

Families were not required to select these governmental-sanctioned stones. They could, in fact, choose not to mention the deceased's role in the war at all. This is a somewhat surprising and disappointing choice for me in my quest to locate information about World War I veterans. As I discussed earlier, local graveyards are a genealogical treasure trove for locating former soldiers relatively efficiently. I always wonder if the families who decided not to mention their relatives' service did so at the man's request, whether they did not place much importance on that service, or whether they were unaware of his service in the Great War.

At the other end of the spectrum, and often coinciding with wartime losses or soldiers who died shortly thereafter, are elaborate graves. One of the most startling examples stands in the Green Hill Cemetery in Augusta County. An elaborately decorated life-sized likeness of Russell Snyder stands "at attention" with his rifle at his side, wearing his uniform, a supply belt, and his helmet. The stone statue stands above a more traditional marble base, which contains the names of other relatives. Russell registered for the Selective Service at age 24 in 1917. He was drafted and sent to Salem, New Jersey, where he served as a private in the Coast Artillery Corps at Fort Mott; he died a little over a year later, on October 8, 1918. Ironically, despite the ornate memorial there is very little surviving documentation of his time in the service or the cause of his death.

Dozens of Virginians died in September and October 1918 during the Meuse Argonne campaign. But none had life-sized statues adorning their gravestones. For example, on my trip to Abingdon I almost walked right by a bland gray granite marker, no higher than a foot off the ground, containing no imagery whatsoever. It didn't even have the subtle cross within a circle commonly found on World War I gravestones. Instead Herbert Ray Hagy's stone provided the dates of his short life, followed by "died … in Tole [Toul] France from wounds received in world war." It was only because of my months researching Base Hospital 45 that I realized Hagy was probably wounded in the Meuse Argonne fighting, sent to the nearby American hospital (where doctors and nurses from Richmond tended to the ailing), and died shortly thereafter.

Other, even more basic inscriptions, assumed the audience would be well aware of the dates of the "world war" and left out the reference altogether. For example, John Lyon's stone at the Blandford Cemetery (Petersburg) simply reads: "1893—In the Argonne—1918."

More expansive epitaphs include the rank of the deceased, his unit, and an inspirational inscription. Back in Abingdon I found David Duncan Burke's stone, which specified that he was a "Lieutenant U.S.A.—A.E.F.," as well as a member of the fraternal society the Woodsmen of the World. And Henry L. Holliday's stone lists his rank as a Private in the U.S. Marine

The gravestone of Russell Snyder (1892–1918) in Green Hill Cemetery, Augusta County (photograph by Nancy Sorrells, 2014).

Corps during "World War I" (he died in 1962, hence the Roman numeral). A lifelong bachelor, he moved frequently after his 1919 discharge from the marines. In 1930 he lived in a boarding house while he worked as an engineer on a steam locomotive in San Antonio[74]; in 1940 he was a mess attendant at a Veterans Administration Facility in Beverly Hills.[75] More than two decades after the end of the war, Holliday was admitted to the U.S. National Home for Disabled Volunteer Soldiers in 1932 for a variety of maladies including bronchitis, arthritis, and lumbago. For me, it is important to (re)locate these inscribed gravestones and record the larger story behind each man's service and sacrifice. Thus, inscriptions that reference a veteran's World War I service is appreciated. I wish that families had thought more often to recognize the wartime efforts of women on their gravestones.

Dedicating a State Memorial

> [The carillon] ... would sound noon, sunset, a goodnight, perhaps ... on Memorial Day it could play the soldiers' old songs: on July Fourth, the National Anthem ... on January 19 the hymn General Lee liked.... The dead would live in the music they loved.
> —*Richmond News Leader*, October 14, 1932

Virginia's official World War I memorial, in the capital city of Richmond, stands in the center of a 287-acre park, better known for its lovely grounds and tennis courts. The carillon is often mistaken as a purely decorative tower, but it holds a set of working bells that, along with a plaque and a flagpole, commemorates the World War I dead from Virginia. A gold star recognizes the efforts of mothers to retrieve their sons' bodies.

This tower was not the original design for the Virginia war memorial. While citizens began to call for a war memorial as early as 1919, the designs for the monument were controversial. The initial suggestions ranged from a utilitarian structure, like a bridge or a library, to a symbolic arch or a neoclassical temple façade. In 1925, a design competition was held and the nationally famous architect Paul P. Cret won with his traditional columnar design. This choice reflected the Richmond committee's effort to follow the guidelines set by the U.S. Commission of Fine Arts: hire professionals to judge a competition and limit the submissions to recognized artists. The competition that Cret won included a budget of no more than $250,000 to complete the monument and a rule that "the equestrian figure be not employed as a dominant motif."[76] Cret, along with two other members of his firm, designed a line of square columns that each stood 60 feet high. This columnar façade rested on top of a platform set within the center of a reflecting pool. The columns were designed to create a dual space: a private area with hedges and a grove for burying the remains of an "unknown soldier" and a second, more public arena for welcoming the living. One of the advisors to the competition believed that "this memorial will soon be recognized throughout the nation as one of the finest in America. Others may be as fine but I do not think any will be finer."[77] And

Virginia World War Memorial Carillon, dedicated in 1932 in Byrd Park, Richmond. The Georgian revival tower was designed by the Boston firm of Ralph Adams Cram in association with Carneal, Johnston, & Wright of Richmond (photograph by Elizabeth O'Leary, 2014).

yet the design was not well received by Richmond residents. To the contrary, they mounted a letter-writing and editorial campaign, hoping to substitute an alternative design.

Disappointed with the "cold stone" of Cret's neoclassical design, dozens of local residents formed the Virginia Citizens Carillon Committee.

With support from several women's organizations these citizens successfully protested the winning design. In March 1926, work on Cret's design was halted by the Virginia General Assembly. He was replaced by a team of Richmond architects who teamed up with another well-known architect, Ralph Adams Cram, to design a tower with a set of 66 bells.[78] This 241-foot-high steel-framed carillon is covered with red bricks that invoke the colonial revival style. Stone accents provide white contrasts against the red façade. Originally there was also a war museum on one of the lower levels of the tower, but it closed in 1964.

Over 15,000 people attended the dedication events in mid–October 1932, which began with a parade through Richmond along Monument Avenue. The parade included seven bands, thousands of veterans, National Guardsmen, Virginia Polytechnic Institute cadets, Virginia Military Institute "keydets," the Richmond Light Infantry Blues, Grays, and the Old Monticello Guard of Charlottesville.[79] The parade started at the George Washington Equestrian Monument in Capitol Square, proceeded along Monument Avenue, and ended three miles away at the new memorial. The inaugural bell concert was played by an internationally known carillonneur named Anton Brees who rang in the new memorial with patriotic songs such as "The Star-Spangled Banner" and "America."[80] Smaller concerts continued each week for a month to showcase the 66 bells.[81] The songs changed each day, but every concert ended with "Carry Me Back to Old Virginny."[82]

An additional feature was added to this site eight years after the dedication of the carillon. In 1940 the Gold Star Mothers contributed a large star, made out of tiles and embedded in the ground near the base of the tower. While the melodic bells comforted Virginians, the star reminded them of the servicemen and women who died during their service. Today, many visitors are unaware of the meaning of the gold star and miss the somewhat subtle inscription on one of the faces of the tower: "Virginia War Memorial 1917–1918." The carillon is just one of dozens of World War I memorials that today has lost some of its meaning for modern audiences.

Interpreting War Memorials

> It is for us to emblazon [the glory of fallen heroes] in imperishable memorials; to engrave their devotion in our hearts and to dedicate ourselves to a perpetuation of the principles for which they fell.
> —Secretary of War Newton Baker, 1920[83]

Dozens of art historians, architects, anthropologists, and historians have weighed in with theories about how and why Americans remember their military dead. At the most basic level, World War I memorials in Virginia help document the deeds and names of men and women who prepared the country for war and, in some cases, who made the "supreme sacrifice." More subtly, these statues reveal a "collective recognition—in short, legitimacy—for the memory deposited there."[84] Because of this important symbolic and emotional value, war memorials reveal fascinating aspects of contemporary social history.

To see how the citizens of Virginia remembered their wartime dead, I set out to locate every World War I memorial in Virginia. After two years, from 2014 to 2016, and over two hundred memorials, I realized that I might never have a complete list. I also recognized that it can be difficult to define what constitutes a "war memorial." I defined it as a physical object created or installed to commemorate one or more individuals involved in or affected by World War I. To keep these parameters manageable, I set aside the gravestones for individuals in a different category for later study. The majority of communal commemorative efforts in Virginia are statues or plaques. They range from traditional statues (often depicting doughboys in their uniforms) to granite blocks (most often with metal plaques attached), from ceremonial arches to allegorical female figures and from functional memorials (such as gymnasiums and bridges) to stained glass windows. These memorials are found on the grounds of courthouses, county office buildings, churches, schools, and public parks. They often commemorate the dead, but some were erected in tribute to soldiers and sailors who returned from the war. And still other memorials honored entire regiments, recognized specific battles, or highlighted the war itself.

Most of these memorials were constructed of cement, stone, or other permanent materials. But in some cases, impermanent materials were deemed most appropriate. In one Norfolk neighborhood, a row of trees was planted to honor World War I veterans; the trees were eventually wiped out by disease, but an accompanying plaque, added to explain the donation, has withstood the test of time. In other cases, commonplace or functional structures were renamed in honor of the war, such as the Memorial Bridge in Roanoke or the Memorial Gymnasium at the University of Virginia. These "living memorials" included the widest range of forms and meaning. On one hand, trees symbolized an arboreal afterlife for the dead, often with individual trees named in honor of specific Virginians. For example, in Winchester they placed small bronze medallions at the base of dozens of trees. Each metal circle contained the name of a local man who died in the war. On the other hand, place and feature names reminded the public about the war, like Pershing Drive in Manassas or Argonne Avenue in Norfolk.

A majority of World War I memorials in Virginia took the form of a statue or a plaque. Most of these designs are limited in their figural and symbolic representations. Most include a list of names, a patriotic symbol (a flag, a shield, or simply stars), and a "mass" (a boulder, obelisk, statue, pillar). A few are spoils of war from Germany, like artillery pieces, and a handful use archways to symbolize the passage from one state to another (be it life to death or peacetime to wartime).

The flag is one of the most common symbols. Today Americans debate about burning or not showing respect for the American flag, but the modern-day association between the flag and a citizen's nationalism is largely a post–1890 phenomenon.[85] In 1916, to solidify its ritual significance and unifying symbolism, President Wilson created Flag Day to commemorate the original adoption of an official United States flag in 1777. On June 14, 1917, many municipalities emphasized the connection between the birth of the "Stars and Stripes" after America successfully won her independence and the wartime efforts of "the Brave" during that wartime summer 140 years later. On Virginia World War I memorials the flag is often draped across the top of plaques, serving the combined function of patriotic banner and mourning shroud.

Eagles often accompany these red, white, and blue banners. After beating out the turkey (Benjamin Franklin's choice), the American bald eagle appears throughout American history on nationalistic images and statues. The bald eagle was selected as the national bird in 1782 based on the perception of its strength, courage, freedom, and incorrectly presumed uniqueness to the American colonies. Symbolically, the eagle is a good choice because of its distinctive profile, consisting of an elongated, hooked beak and a muscular torso which can easily morph into an anthropomorphic figure in cartoons. Many of the plaques on Virginia war memorials contain eagles with outstretched wings, in many cases a conscious parallel to the wings of Horus, a falcon-based god carved across the pediments of ancient Egyptian temples. The meaning of avian arms stretching out across the top of a list of the Virginia dead has clear protective associations. And these birds serve an added compositional advantage of having talons that can clutch flags or other drapery in these memorials.

Not surprisingly, very few of the memorials erected during the 1920s and 1930s recognize the service of women. Instead, they talk about the "men" who served or only list the names of male soldiers and sailors, not female sailors (yeomanettes) or nurses who died in the line of duty. Paradoxically, several pre–World War II war memorials invoke female figures to serve as allegorical symbols of mourning and loss. In other cases, women were depicted as "protected wives and daughters, or mythical figures personifying actions, places and values."[86] In each of these representations, women were used to invoke the protective impulses of men rather than to emphasize the crucial role of women working on behalf of the nation during the war.

This gendered narrative is illustrated on several Virginia statues. The most notable one is "Liberty," designed by architect Charles Keck in 1924. Keck's seated figure is located in the median of a Harrisonburg road whose prewar name, "German Street," was changed to "Liberty." In this statue, a woman sits on a rock wearing a form-clinging dress that hangs to the ground and a pair of Roman sandals just barely visible under the drapes of fabric. Metaphorically she stands for liberty and, as such, she holds a palm frond (symbolizing peace) and an olive branch (also associated with peace). The peaceful elements are balanced with a rifle, sword, breastplate, and helmet, demonstrating her willingness to fight for freedom and American democracy. An anchor around the back of the stone grounds the piece literally and metaphorically. The circular base is inscribed with "They tasted death in youth that liberty might grow old—1917 World War 1918." Here the female form is somewhat ironic: she is ready for war, while women in the flesh were relegated to the sidelines during the Great War.

Another Virginia community selected an image of "liberty" to accompany a list of names of the World War I dead. The Beverly Manor Chapter of the Daughters of the American Revolution (DAR) in Augusta County commissioned a bronze plaque with a bas-relief of a woman. She stands tall with arms outstretched above her head holding a banner that reads, "In Honor of the men and women of Staunton and Augusta County who served their country in the World War, 1914–1918." This is unusual for two reasons: it includes female servicewomen and it refers to the three years of the war prior to America's official involvement. Despite the inclusionary language, only men are listed by name on the memorial even though female nurses from Augusta probably served at home and abroad. But they were not given their due in bronze. Instead, the classically dressed liberty figure welcomes the dead men as she ascends to heaven with her wings, surrounded by a halo of light, and a single star above her head (presumably a reference to the gold stars that signified the death of a family

A memorial to the Great War erected on the side of the Augusta County courthouse (photograph by Nancy Sorrels, 2014).

member in the war). Poetic prose reveals that the names belong to the deceased, "The unreturning brave they give new splendor to the dead," and concludes with a patriotic admonition, "The Right is more precious than peace."

Statues in Virginia, and much of the rest of America, deemphasized the military roles of other groups besides women. One of the most glaring absences is memorials to African American soldiers. As discussed in Chapter 2, black soldiers enlisted in large numbers, far greater than their demographic percentage among Virginia residents. African Americans served as officers, doctors, laborers, stevedores, and soldiers. Several black units served under French command. In gratitude for this service, the French government erected granite markers to honor black regiments: one to the 371st Infantry Regiment, which fought at Hill 188 near the Bussy farm in September and October of 1918, and one for the 372nd Infantry Regiment, which served with the French Army during a grueling nine-day battle in October 1918. Both memorials are located on or near battlefields in France where African American soldiers fought and died.[87] In contrast, there are no individual monuments to African American soldiers on Virginia soil. Instead, the names of black troops are often listed at the bottom of local memorials, in segregated sections commonly prefaced by the once common term "colored."

By the 1920s, hundreds of memorials had been erected to the Virginia men who served during the Great War. The names of white men who gave their lives were listed first, men of color second, and women's wartime service was ignored completely, with rare exceptions, such as the one mentioned earlier and a memorial to Nurses in Arlington National Cemetery (dedicated in 1938). The resulting monuments assigned agency to men's roles, while relegating women to passive roles such as mourners. Abousnnouga and Machin interpreted this emphasis on the actions of men, reflecting the intention to "promote and protect the nation-state."[88] Ironically, men were recognized as the agents behind the nation-state, while the female figure was used to personify abstract concepts such as "the nation."

One surprising element in the word choice on the Virginia memorials is the absence of the words "death," "dying," or "war" (the last is seen only as an identifier such as "World War 1914–1918," not as a noun within the inscription itself). Instead, the most common expression is "In Memory." This term is not unique to war memorials. It became an increasingly popular adage on American gravestones throughout the 19th and early 20th centuries as mourners turned away from the explicit terminology of the colonial era (e.g., "Here Lies Buried"). Originally, "in memory" indicated that the body was located elsewhere (lost at sea or otherwise unrecoverable). But by the beginning of the 20th century this expression was intended to comfort the survivors, emphasizing remembrance rather than a loved one's death (hence, another popular gravestone inscription, "Gone But Not Forgotten").

Other World War I memorial inscriptions laud the dead's "loyalty," "bravery," "service," "splendor," or "honor," and the people and organizations who erected these memorials expressed their "gratitude." These superlatives helped establish what one historian called, the "cult of the fallen soldier," whereby all soldiers were heroes and it became unpatriotic to criticize them or their service.[89]

The announcement of a soldier's passing in a Virginia newspaper provides additional details about public opinion and attitudes toward death. In relating George Parker Thompson's untimely departure, his parents mentioned the "death angel" that visited them after he died from pneumonia at the Naval Training Station at Hampton Roads. Because he had not left American soil, his parents were able to rush to his deathbed to bid a final farewell. Trying to provide comfort for the mourners, the eulogy concluded that despite the most skilled physicians "God loved His Christian Soldier and called him home."[90]

After the war, Norfolk residents remembered the sacrifices of men like Thompson by crafting memorials in their churches, parks, and cemeteries. In the Christ and St. Luke's Church a medieval-inspired stone wall was erected underneath one of the Gothic arches within the church. A World War I soldier in knight's garb along with a medieval maiden flank either side of a large stone tablet. The knight on the left of the tablet is allegedly modeled after the rector of the church in the 1920s, the Rev. Francis C. Steinmetz, and the maiden on the right is modeled after his wife, Mary.[91] Two helmeted angel heads appear below these figures, with carved vines forming a bottom border. Above each figure appears a trellis, which, along with the top edge of the frame, supports a boundary of leafy vines and small coat of arms. An eagle hovers above, carrying an olive branch and arrows, with a cross hanging above it.

These figural representations surround a large rectangular tablet with

Memorial plaque to the Great War in the Christ and St. Luke's Church, Norfolk (photograph by Elijah Palmer, 2015).

five rows of names. The carved text preceding the list of names reads, "In Gratitude to God, This Tablet erected by St. Mary's Guild of Intercession to Honour the Naval Men and Women of this Congregation who served their Country in the Great World War 1917–1918." Because of Norfolk's seaside location, the inscription focuses on sailors. Surprisingly, female sailors are also recognized on the wall. The rank of Yeoman (F), with the "F" identifying the sailor as female, was created during the war to allow a handful of women to serve in the navy, most often in clerical roles. On this memorial, only five of the 108 names are clearly women, reinforcing the rarity of the position.

In communities across the state, high schools and colleges commemorated their students who served and/or died in World War I. As they welcomed home returning veterans who had missed a year or more of classes, these institutions had to work to reintegrate students and recognize the gaps in their rosters. For example, in 1919 Bristol County High School commissioned a plaque to honor six students who died. Two years later, Woodberry Forest Academy, near Madison Mills, placed a plaque in its chapel: A bronze eagle stands on a shield, symbolically protecting the plaque with its wings, while its talons grasp weapons. As with many memorials placed in institutions of learning, there is a section in Latin, *Pro Libertate Humanitatis*, followed by an inscription in English, "This tablet is erected by the Alumni of Woodberry Forest School in honor of their fellows who made the supreme sacrifice in the Great War 1914–1918 waged in behalf of the liberation of mankind and for the preservation of righteousness and justice among men." It was important to recognize the sacrifices of these young adults to encourage the survivors to reenlist in future conflicts.

Designing War Memorials

> The new beauties [the people of the country] see in buildings, monuments and charming landscape features [in Washington, D.C.] are in no respect happy chances, but the consummation of carefully studied plans which have been guided by and submitted to a congressionally appointed board of review in civic art, known as the National Commission of Fine Arts.
> —Editorial, *Washington Sunday Star*, February 25, 1917[92]

In the decades after the Civil War, almost every southern community and many northern communities erected at least one memorial to their veterans. While local citizens usually praised these efforts—most often statues that features horses, generals, and armaments—professional sculptors and artists criticized these designs. In the nation's capital, politicians and planners worried that bad designs would overwhelm the mall and detract from significant buildings such as the capitol itself and newly completed memorials like the one to Lincoln, finished in 1922. After the end of World War I, the National Commission on Fine Arts published pamphlets to try to guide citizens in their selection of new memorials.[93] In its guidelines, *Forms of Memorials and Methods of Obtaining Designers*, the commission encouraged communities to design local memorials for a triple purpose: to "honor our noble fighters, gratify our desire for beauty, and satisfy some of the needs of the community." It stressed that the first step toward these goals would be to "seek the advice of someone trained in the arts."[94] In a similar vein, the American Federation of Arts (also located in Washington, D.C.) published a four-page pamphlet that urged communities to consult with experts, "preferably before the plans are made."[95] Taking into account the thousands of equestrian statues erected between the 1880s and the 1910s, some of these professional groups advised communities to erect "useful community buildings" to honor the Great War soldiers instead of more "stone shafts" topped by horses.[96]

I investigated how this design call was answered in Virginia. Who designed these statues? Who selected the sculptors? Which community members became the arbiters of good design? In many cases, local chapters of the DAR, the American Legion, or the Veterans of Foreign Wars (VFW) led the charge to raise money and select designs for statues and memorials. The names of the artists have often been forgotten, but the sponsors usually included an inscription to showcase their charitable efforts. Dozens of World War I memorials include the distinctive DAR emblem: a spinning wheel in front of a distaff used to hold flax, surrounded by the 13 stars of the original colonies. In Roanoke, the Margaret Lynn Lewis chapter of the DAR dedicated an unusual statue on Armistice Day 1925. The head of a helmeted doughboy is carved into a roughly circular boulder several feet high. The somewhat disconcerting profile was defaced over the next few years. In 1930, the DAR chapter reworked the boulder, adding an additional stone, removing the face, and adding a bronze plaque.[97] The surrounding road was renamed "Argonne Circle" to emphasize the connection to the Great War.

These memorials often share design elements such as rough-hewn stone, an eagle with its wings spread, and flags. A few memorials are unique. A statue on the grounds of the University of Virginia commemorating a Virginia aviator who was shot down a week before American officially entered the war, previously mentioned in Chapter 3, is one of these unusual statues. Designed by Gutzon Borglum, the sculptor of Mount Rushmore, *The Aviator* depicts a lithe male with wings poised on a globe as if he were jumping off a precipice (an allusion to the Greek myth of Icarus, the boy who flew too close to the sun). The man is clad in only his lace-up boots, a belt with a knife sheath, and a fighter pilot helmet.

The memorial was erected by James Rogers McConnell's alma mater, the University of Virginia, in 1919. In 1915, McConnell volunteered for service with the Allies. Like many early American volunteers, he first served in a medical unit, driving ambulances for the American Ambulance Corps, where he had "a glorious experience."[98] He demonstrated courage and dedication to this pursuit, earning the Croix de Guerre for his bravery in rescuing a wounded French soldier under enemy fire. In May 1916, his interest in the still relatively new invention of aeroplanes led him to join the storied Lafayette Escadrille, a fighter squadron consisting of American volunteers. The rudimentary fighter aircraft technology at the time required these pilots to fire and reload the plane's single machine gun with one hand while maneuvering the unsteady craft with the other. On March 19, 1917, McConnell, or "Mac," was flying in a three-plane reconnaissance mission when they were spotted by a German patrol. Mac's Nieuport 11 scout was shot down and hit the ground so hard that it was partially buried.[99] It took several days to access the remains because they were in enemy territory. By the time French troops reached the crash site, McConnell's body was no longer identifiable and his papers had been taken. He died five days after his thirtieth birthday and just over two weeks before America formally entered the war. The French government recommended him for the Croix de Guerre with palm, an honor awarded to either an individual or a military unit whose members performed heroically while fighting the enemy.[100]

Sergeant McConnell's fellow soldiers and local French citizens erected a temporary memorial in Petit Detroit, the site where he crashed and was initially buried. An arched brick tomb was built and French civilians left flowers (despite its hazardous location) and surrounded it with a metal fence. Several years later, his remains were exhumed and reburied at a new memorial built by the French government to honor all of the members of the Lafayette Escadrille.[101]

Meanwhile, at McConnell's prewar residence of Carthage, North

Carolina, citizens decided to erect a traditional war memorial consisting of a marble obelisk. This marker is inscribed, "He fought for Humanity, Liberty and Democracy, lighted the way for his countrymen and showed all men how to dare nobly and to die gloriously." In Charlottesville, the University of Virginia statue reads: "Soaring like an eagle into new heavens of valor and devotion." At each site, the symbolic morphology of the monument helps memorialize "Mac's" name and his deeds. A well-designed war memorial places the person and his or her actions into the mythical arena of immortals. In McConnell's case, his memorials ranged from an Egyptian temple feature, the obelisk, to a mythical Greek character, Icarus. The two designs reveal the American ideology that associated pharaohs with immortality and classical nudes with Greek democracy.[102] In addition to viewing statues, McConnell's family, and the surviving kin of other Virginia veterans, needed rituals to guide their commemorative actions. In the United States the national holiday to commemorate and honor our war dead is Memorial Day.

Remembering the Dead

> Memorial Day will be observed here next Tuesday, when local survivors of the War Between the States will be given dinner at a local hotel, this to be followed by exercises at the Memorial Park.
> —*Richmond Times-Dispatch*, May 11, 1919[103]

Memorial Day encapsulates a long-standing cultural practice of decorating the graves of the departed. Throughout the Civil War grieving family members placed flowers on the graves of dead soldiers.[104] In 1864, multiple communities began to host ceremonies in their respective cemeteries to honor fallen veterans. The head of the Grand Army of the Republic (a Union veterans fraternity) established May 30, 1868, as "Decoration Day," when "every post of the Grand Army should hold suitable exercises and decorate the graves of their dead comrades with flowers."[105] This proclamation formalized a practice that had been occurring for several years, mostly in southern graveyards. Fifty years later, two wars were in local newspaper headlines: "Teutons Advance at Slower Rate" and, on the same page, "Richmond Honors Confederate Dead."[106] A subheading to the latter, mentioned that "Virginians who have died in service in the present war" would also be honored. But each of the Memorial Day celebrations in Richmond that year split their focus between Confederate veterans and men who had died in the recent fighting. The 1918 parade included members Confederate veterans from the Robert E. Lee Camp and soldiers from World War I military organizations, such as the Richmond Howitzers' Association and the 155th Depot Brigade band from Camp Lee. A separate commemorative ceremony was held at Hollywood Cemetery. More than five thousand people gathered that day in Richmond, where Judge Richardson commented, "Creeds and faiths may crumble, worlds may come and go, but not the memory of men who died battling for the truth." As of that spring day, 73 Virginians had lost their lives serving in the current war. The judge shared a grim realization with his audience, reminding them that at the same time they "celebrated the memory of the Confederate fathers ... their sons and grandsons were swelling the casualty list in Picardy [France]."[107]

The first Virginia Memorial Day celebrations after the Great War returned to this southern practice of pairing commemorations of the Civil War and the Great War. In May 1919, survivors of the War between the States were treated to a dinner at a local hotel in Danville; and in Richmond the Hebrew Ladies' Memorial Association held exercises "in honor of Confederate dead" buried in a nearby Jewish Cemetery. One would be forgiven for not realizing that a global war had just ended.[108]

The memorials that Virginians did place on the graves of their dead and erect in the communities where they had lived served many purposes. They recognized the sacrifice of those killed, but they also united mourners and reintegrated the returning veterans back into society. The permanent and living memorials recognized the gallantry, courage, and sacrifice of the veterans. The design elements and word choices on these statues helped elevate the "cult of the fallen soldier" to that of mythical status. Sculptors and community members selected imagery from nature, classical civilizations, and Christianity to illustrate the inevitability of death while reminding the viewer that dying while fighting for one's country qualified the deceased for a special status as a martyred hero and as an admired patriot. Many of these memorials were erected on the lawns of courthouses and other governmental buildings, signifying a political endorsement of the statue and its message. In the end, these monuments revere the sacrifice of the fallen and remind their audience that similar service might be required in the future.

On June 29, 1919, the city of Richmond held a memorial service to honor the "soldier, sailor, marine, and aviator" dead from the war. The Sunday early evening service began with the singing of the "Star-Spangled Banner" and "Onward, Christian Soldiers." Major General Adelbert Cronkhite, whose own son died under mysterious circumstances while in training at Camp Lewis (in Washington), read the names of the dead. If he had access to the final list compiled in 1920 he would have read through the names of over 3700 Virginians. If he limited himself to Richmond residents, he would have read 191 names. None of these men would be returning home. In the next chapter I discuss the fate of those who did.

"The Listening Post," featuring a somber "doughboy." Behind the figure are the names of local units who served and 43 men who died during the war. Designed by Charles Keck and erected in 1924 at the base of Monument Terrace, Lynchburg (photograph John Ramsey, Jr., 2017).

5

Homecomings

> Casino [in Newport News] Crowded With Appreciative Humanity Eager to Do Honor to Living and Dead. Speakers Appeal to Men Who Came Back From War to "Take Up the Quarrel With the Foe" and Keep Country Safe From All Forces of Evil For Sake of Those Who "Sleep in Flanders Field"
> —Newspaper clipping, September 18, 1919[1]

After the Armistice ended the fighting on Monday, November 11, 1918, the AEF began to dismantle its foreign fighting apparatus. On December 19, the first contingent of returning soldiers landed in Virginia—3500 men from the 118th Field Artillery. By the spring of 1919, American troops were arriving back at eastern docks at a regular rate, about 60,000 a week in the busy debarkation port of Newport News alone.[2]

Scores of Virginia units returned through this port. Over the course of two days in May, the following units arrived: the 29th Division (with many Virginians), the 104th Ammunition Train of the 29th Division (including members of the former Richmond Blues), and the 116th Infantry (composed primarily of soldiers from Virginia).[3] There were half a dozen training camps in the vicinity of Newport News, which made it easier to process the release of these men from formal service. Men who joined from out-of-state camps were sent back to their point of entry via trains, and injured men were sent on separate hospital trains for treatment across the country.[4]

Every once in a while, an unexpected passenger debarked from these ships. On December 20, 1918, the *Mercury* docked with hundreds of army casualties, marines, and army officers. But there was also a stowaway: a French boy who had stayed hidden for the first two days of the voyage. When the soldiers discovered him, they dressed him in a uniform and taught him English. Apparently, a captain in the medical corps adopted him.[5]

Even the domestic camps took months to decommission. The cessation of an enlisted men's service required multiple steps, paperwork, and bureaucracy. The Virginia camps weren't completely empty until mid–April 1919, five months after the war ended. That month the last five hundred troops were sent home with little fanfare.[6]

In contrast, when the first boatloads of troops returned from abroad Virginians organized multiple and complex welcome home festivities. In Alexandria, locals raised over $1,500 for a welcome home fund and appointed seven people to manage the money and plan events. When several dozen "Old Alexandria Light Infantry Boys" returned in May 1919, they were greeted by "bells and whistles," "festoons of flags," and relieved "mothers, fathers, wives, and sweethearts." Several bands played, and residents were assured "a hot time in the Old Town."[7] On May 25, 1919, similarly elaborate plans were laid in Hampton Roads for the return of the USS *Virginia*. The ship was met in the harbor by decorated battleships and a balloon from the Hampton Roads naval base that "swooped down" to greet the ship as it neared Old Point.[8] On land, roads were roped off to guide the returning men who were to march in their wartime companies: machine gun, balloon, transportation, etc. Children scattered a "carpet of roses" along the procession route. To help manage the crowds, relatives were instructed to greet each unit at different sites located throughout the city.[9] African American children from Hampton were organized into a "human word" to spell out "welcome" at the Casino Point flagpole.[10]

Businesses took out "Welcome Home" advertisements in hometown newspapers to recognize the servicemen and women. For example, a summer issue of the *Alexandria Gazette* featured expressions of gratitude from merchants like Graham Ogden, who had a "thankful and happy heart" and hoped that the men "never again [had to be] called upon for similar sacrifices." Edison Music Shop greeted the "boys" and "promise[d] to entertain [them] to the best of our ability if you stop and see us." A clothier offered returning men in uniform a 10 percent discount. And the jewelers and opticians, Saunders & Son, extended its thanks for their service and offered them "best wishes for the future."[11] Unfortunately these generous emotional and financial gifts were not continued in the years to come as many Virginia veterans struggled to readjust to civilian life.

Newport News Victory Arch

> Greetings with love to those who return
> A triumph with tears to those who sleep
> —Inscription across the top of
> the Newport News Victory Arch

These words were carved into an "Arch of Welcome and Triumph" built over the course of just two months in Newport News. The author of the quote, who requested anonymity during his lifetime, was prominent Newport News attorney Robert G. Bickford.[12] Inspired by the Arc de Triomphe in Paris, commissioned by Napoleon in honor of an 1806 military victory, the Hampton Roads arch commemorated the return of American troops to Virginia soil. The monument was originally built out of wood with a coat of stucco to create "a fine imitation of marble." Ornamental castings, made out of real marble and stone, were applied at the top of

Newport News Victory Arch (W.M.084.000.Ar, Box 28, Folder 9, Image 5, Virginia War Museum, City of Newport News, VA).

pilaster capitals. On the plinth across the top of the arch the word "Victory" is flanked by the years "1917" and "1918." The arch was designed so that soldiers could pass through it after they debarked from their ships. And nighttime searchlights were employed so that "at night [the arch] will be a thing of beauty that should be a source of pride to citizens of this town."[13]

Unfortunately, ship transport schedules did not always cooperate with the plan for the local civilians to formally welcome returning soldiers home. Many ships returned at night and the soldiers disembarked after dinner, making it impractical to convene a large welcoming committee or to shuttle everyone through the arch. Then there were the casualties, such as the six hundred sick and wounded men who disembarked from the USS *Powhatan* and had to be carried to a nearby hospital in ambulances.[14]

The official dedication ceremony was held on April 13, 1919. No ships were returning that day; instead, civilians and five thousand school children launched their own parade. Virginians of all ages, "from almost every organization of a civic nature in the entire peninsula," joined together to march or ride on floats decorated with flowers and American flags. The review stand was filled with dignitaries, including generals, the city mayor, and other civic leaders. The speeches described the arch "as the guiding light to those who yet are coming here from war, to greet them as they pass on their glorious return." And while one speaker recognized that the arch was "temporary in character" he argued that it represented something "as eternal as the ever lasting hills." The entire event was scheduled to take less than an hour because soldiers had fainted during similar celebrations held in the rising spring heat while clad in their wool uniforms. The event was captured in an aerial photograph taken by Charles C. Epes with a tilted frame-of-reference, suggesting that the pilot was snapping the picture while flying.[15]

As with most Virginia memorials to the Great War, a plaque on the arch listed the names of the local men who died: 32 officers and enlisted men in the army and navy. The plaque was officially unveiled several months later, on September 27, presumably after tabulations could be completed. During that ceremony an American flag was ceremoniously pulled aside by two Boy Scouts whose older brothers had died during the war.[16]

After the triumphant parades and welcome home events, the arch slowly faded into obscurity. Even with its official dedication, this arch had always been temporary in design. The framework of the honorific gateway was wood and brick, with a coating of stucco on the outside to make it appear more permanent. Several decades later, a newspaper reporter described it as "gaunt and deserted" with flaking paint and stucco. This decline was so symbolically charged that in 1962, the community decided to rebuild the gate with more permanent materials.[17]

Segregated Welcome Home Parades

> There was positively nothing the matter with the home-coming celebration in honor of Fluvanna county's world-war colored soldiers … weather was ideal, the crowd was large, the boys in uniform presented a brave appearance, the speaking was fine, the decorations were lovely, refreshments were bounteous and there wasn't a full moment in the day for the celebrants.
> —"Colored Soldiers Get Fine Welcome," Palmyra, 1919[18]

On the face of it, the welcome home events in Virginia recognized the sacrifice of all servicemen. But in truth, almost every welcome parade or event was segregated along racial lines. At the dedication of the Newport News Victory Arch, African American children marched in their own parade, led by an all-black band.[19] When the plaque was installed, the headline read, "Colored People to Have Their Own Exercises." An African American chaplain with the 370th Infantry who passed through Newport News described this town as "a place of a thousand prejudices" with citizens who were "always hateful toward the Negro."[20] The spring and summer issues of the black newspaper the *Richmond Planet* supported this assertion with letters to the editor that complained of racist attitudes in Hampton Roads.[21] This treatment of returning black soldiers was especially galling, as most African American troops had served with distinction during the war under separate and unequal conditions. One of the more egregious examples of poorly treated black troops was in Richmond. A white captain hired out the African American men in the 430th Reserve Labor Battalion to cut wood and dig potatoes. These men were regularly whipped and, if they complained, were threatened with lynching.[22]

Across the commonwealth, many communities planned separate ceremonies to honor their returning white and black veterans. Newport News intended to honor its living and dead along racial lines: "While the white people are acclaiming the living and honoring the memory of the dead, the colored people will be doing likewise at a celebration all their own."[23]

Similarly, the African American community in Harrisonburg planned separate marches (with black soldiers), banquets (served by black members of the Red Cross), and medal ceremonies (in lieu of General Pershing, six local girls pinned the medals on the honorees). The day concluded with "some unusual athelectic [sic] stunts and the best baseball game of the season."[24]

Not surprisingly, the newspaper accounts focused on the positive elements of these welcome home parades. Flag-waving children and weeping women lined the streets, waiting for a glimpse of their returning soldiers. The *Richmond Planet* provided insight into the hearts and minds of some of those veterans. One sardonic cartoon summed up much of the community's frustration, featuring a black solider standing at attention in front of "lady liberty," identified in accompanying text as an allegory for the commonwealth of Virginia. The solider pleads with her, "Your Honor Miss—cutout the flags, and the hurrahs. Abolish the *Jim Crow* laws in your House. Do something of consequence for us."[25] It would be several decades before Virginia made any significant reforms along racial lines.

After the parade decorations were taken down and the celebratory songs faded, the soldiers returned to their peacetime military roles or civilian life with both practical and psychological concerns.

The Wounded

> Clickety clack, went the crutches' tune
> God! How can they be brave so soon!
> Brave, when I can not keep back the tears,
> Thinking ahead of the crippled years.
> —Elizabeth R. Stoner,
> "The Crutches' Tune," 1919[26]

While there are gross calculations of wounded American soldiers, it is hard to pin down the number of nonfatal casualties among Virginians. One contemporary estimate calculated 387 hospitalized veterans in Virginia as of December 1921, three years after the war ended.[27] During the summer of 1919, more than 32,000 sick and wounded men returned to the National Soldiers' Home, General Hospital 43 in Newport News. They had survived their "fight for liberty," but just barely. One article described the casualties as "gassed, armless, legless, many of them wrecks for life." At Camp Stuart Debarkation Hospital, Lieutenant Colonel Leon C. Garcia

The wounded but smiling and envied heroes parading in the cars of the Motor Corps.

Wounded soldiers returning home. A postbellum procession featured "the wounded but smiling and envied heroes parading in the cars of the Motor Corps" (in *Homecoming Celebration: Commemorating the Day When Virginia's Sons of the 29th and 80th Division Returned from the World War*, Virginia Historical Society, call no. D570.3.29th.N2).

assessed each case and assigned these men to hospitals across the country, near their hometowns. While many of these men left Virginia, thousands more remained in Virginia for their care.[28]

At first, the U.S. Public Health service cared for ill and disabled men, but in May 1921 the responsibility for many of these patients was transferred to the War Risk Bureau.[29] The Red Cross volunteered its services, including a Home Service Section to assist the men after they left the hospital.[30] Meanwhile, the federal government balked at building hospitals and, instead, encouraged the states to furnish new facilities.[31] In Virginia, officials worked to calculate just how many of their soldiers were going to require ongoing assistance.[32] One of the fastest-growing medical disciplines during this time was orthopedic surgery, to handle the multitude of muscular-skeletal injuries suffered by many of the soldiers. The growth of this specialization was accompanied by the need for more female "physiotherapy aides," such as occupational therapists and dieticians.[33] Between the new opportunities for female "amputee teams" and the new hospital layouts required for the "curative workshops" and rehabilitation exercises, the federal government hoped that the disabled veterans would require little if any federal assistance after they were discharged.[34] But many of the veterans had suffered debilitating wounds, in some cases losing one or more limbs. Entrepreneurs introduced products designed to "Repair the Shattered Limbs of the War Cripples."[35] However, these rudimentary artificial limbs were not able to provide a full range of motion or grasping possibilities. The state labor commissioner, John Hirschberg, asked manufacturers to come forward and employ "maimed men" when possible.[36] But this was a request, not a requirement. A pharmacist from Alexandria, himself a veteran, concluded that he was "disgusted with the way our government does our disable boys."[37]

The physical wounds from the war were easily noticed and, at least initially, provoked sympathy and accommodation from most civilians. But often the more serious malady was invisible: the psychological trauma suffered by the men and women who had witnessed or participated in the brutal battlefield carnage. At the start of the war, the medical community had just begun studying "war neurosis" or "shell shock." Coined by French doctors in 1915, "shell shock" was originally used to describe soldiers who had been literally "shocked" by the concussion of a shell or, more frequently, had been buried under debris.

When I found a reprint of an article titled "Shell-Shock: A Digest of the English Literature," dated 1917 and stamped with "Library: Surgeon General's Office, April 10, 1918," I figured the medical profession had this tragic condition well within its sights.[38] But after a brief paragraph in which the author, a medical doctor at the Boston Psychopathic Hospital, recognized the prevalence of shell shock, he concurred with a colleague that "the unfit should be checked at the recruiting office and kept at home." In other words, the main concern was not treatment for those suffering, but how to keep men that they believed had "unstable vasomotors" away from the battlefield and other active-duty troops.

Dr. Henry Viets, a first lieutenant in the Medical Service Corps of the U.S. Army, observed that even patients who had "never been within the zone of active warfare" exhibited symptoms. This observation resulted in unfortunate subclassifications of shell shock into cases of "pure exhaustion"; "neuropaths and psychopaths" who were viewed as weak to begin with; "martial misfits," such as dissenters who objected to being drafted in the first place; "concussion cases"; "cortical injury," a separate injury that was sometimes confused with shell shock; and "cases of hysteria."[39] Although the article recognized that many of these men saw "ghastly sights of carnage," many of their symptoms were trivialized as "nervous affections" or "hysteria." Even more disturbingly, the article concluded with a series of treatments that ranged from "the application of strong electricity by the faradic current" to "persuasion," whereby the "patient is convinced by logical argument that his condition is not so serious as he supposes."[40] In Richmond, a report in a postwar newspaper summarized the state of knowledge in 1919 with a story from a London paper titled "'Shell Shock' Is Incorrect." The British physicians felt that "acute nervousness is not [a] product of World War." Instead, they blamed it on an "emotional disorder" that would be "curable by counter suggestion."[41]

The doctors in the Medical Corps of the U.S. Army were optimistic that they could, and should, weed out the "mentally deficient" and "boobs" in their armed forces. This, they felt, would save lives by eliminating "shell-shock patients" from the overseas fighting forces.[42] With this focus on a prophylactic strategy, it was no surprise that many veterans suffering from what, today, we would call post-traumatic stress disorder were placed in asylums where their condition did not receive adequate treatment. Virginia state officials congratulated themselves for seeking federal aid as early as January 1919 to care for these returning soldiers. They planned to use the funds to increase the capacity at two hospitals, Western State Hospital in Staunton and Southwestern State Hospital in Marion. A Petersburg hospital had already been successful in treating several cases of shell shock, but the description of its efforts focused only on how a larger building enabled the hospital to "accommodate more insane people."[43]

At the Southwestern State Hospital in Marion a neuropsychiatric ward was established to house ex-servicemen in 1921, referred to as the Davis Clinic. Dr. E. H. Henderson presided over some of the newest approaches to public health care, including the use of hydrotherapeutic and electrotherapeutic equipment.[44] One patient, who signed himself "one of the boys," wrote to the *Alexandria Gazette* (located more than three hundred miles away) to reassure the public that "we have a wonderful place here" and "the Virginia boys are well looked after and given every courtesy and attention possible."[45] But for many men this care was too little too late. For example, Charles L. Fletcher had served as a second lieutenant in the Second Regiment of the Virginia Volunteers; in World War I he served in Company K. He returned a broken man and the father of an infant son. Soon after his return, he and his wife, Roberta, had a second son. When these boys were 11 and 13, their father died from alcohol poisoning. The coroner estimated that Charles had been drunk for three weeks prior to his death.[46] And in a second instance, just days before the one-year anniversary of the war's end, Lieutenant Samuel H. Staples, from Roanoke, killed himself by "batt[ing] his head against a radiator." He was 32 years old, and the gruesome suicide took place at General Hospital No.

43 in Hampton.[47] His November 4, 1919, death was memorialized on a gravestone in the Fair View Cemetery in Roanoke with the inscription "His name is now on Honors Roll and His Record Rests with God."[48] These cases demonstrate that despite the optimism of doctors and politicians, Virginia hospitals and psychiatric wards had a long way to go before they could provide appropriate care for the returning warriors.

Even Virginia soldiers who returned without the psychological and physically crippling injuries were often angry and maladjusted. The answers from veterans on a four-page War Commission Questionnaire illustrate their postwar frustrations. One high-ranking soldier from Camp Lee summarized his feeling succinctly by channeling a popular quote from Civil War general William T. Sherman: "War is Hell."[49] On the face of it, this comment is nothing more than honest assessment. What makes it remarkable is that the majority of the answers in thousands of state-sponsored questionnaires focused on positive impressions. Like respondents to many employer-sponsored surveys, these soldiers were answering a series of questions knowing that their names were attached to the answers. Moreover, they knew the questionnaires were being compiled "for a permanent record in the Virginia state library where it will be filed as a memorial of the deeds of Virginia soldiers, sailors, and marines of the World War."[50] To increase and encourage participation, Richmond police distributed and attempted to collect 2500 of the questionnaires to "emphasize the importance in making Richmond's war history complete."[51] This material was the foundation for the multivolume series published by A. K. Davis about Virginia's role in the war. Out of roughly one hundred thousand draftees, only 15,000 completed these "military service records."

Given the public and permanent nature of the respondent's opinions, most soldiers emphasized the positive aspects of their service, with only about 15 percent of the respondents expressing negative views. Despite being gassed while serving as a machine gunner, Corporal Otha Lennox Furniss summarized his time in the army as providing him the "great privilege to have given loyal service to the United States."[52] In other cases, soldiers focused on their impending release from service in late May 1919, clearly copied from one another in order to quickly complete the task at hand. A group of more than a dozen soldiers at Camp Lee filled out six questions identically, including the same spelling mistakes such as "nessary."[53] Many respondents stated that their time in the service made them "better" or "stronger" men with a "finer sense of patriotism." If these answers formed part of a private journal, instead of a publicly available survey, one wonders how many soldiers would agree with Major John Woolfolk Burke from Alexandria, who returned with "the confirmation of a personal idea that war is the most idiotic, silly, useless pastime that civilized people can indulge in."[54]

Returning from War

> A fighting soldier is a hero; a returned soldier is a working man out of a job.
> —West Virginia labor journal, January 23, 1919[55]

Most veterans, including the mild to moderately injured, required jobs after they were mustered out of service. After risking their lives for their country, these men expected to return to their prewar jobs. Patriotic editorials and governmental propaganda encouraged employers to take back returning soldiers in their old jobs, but there were no employment laws to force them to do so. Many soldiers found that while they were away their jobs had been given to other workers. Often this replacement was a woman. These female substitutes were so successful during the war that some men had trouble regaining their prewar positions. In Virginia, the head of the Women's Christian Temperance Union urged women to give up their jobs so that returning soldiers could find employment, unless their positions were "essential to earning her own living." Prospective male workers believed that female workers were lowering wages for certain positions.

The War Department worried about the social and economic tensions associated with the release of hundreds of thousands of working men from the armed forces all at once. Initially, it planned to demobilize the troops in measured waves, to allow employers to slowly absorb them back into the workforce. Instead, the families of servicemen pushed the federal government to bring them home as soon as possible. This resulted in large-scale demobilizations where one ship, containing thousands of troops, was mustered out in one day.

The deluge of ex-servicemen looking for work created hardships in many Virginia communities. Fast-growing cities like the ones around the naval shipyards experienced an increased demand for labor (both in shipbuilding and in constructing surrounding homes for the laborers). However, more commonly, the sudden surplus of labor resulted in high unemployment rates, especially in cities such as Petersburg that were located near former training camps and had experienced a rise in laborers during the wartime construction. In Clifton Forge, a local employment bureau was established to help soldiers and citizens find work. A resident observed that this agency, "helped to quell a growing spirit of unrest on the part of those who had been seeking work for some time without results. The soldier's grievance was just, for he had been at the front fighting his country's battles, making property and life more secure, and it was right that upon his return he should not suffer the humiliation of seeking work and finding none."[56] And yet, in other Virginia locales, strikes and riots did occur, after veterans despaired over their destitute circumstances. Some returned from their service with nothing to wear but their uniforms, no money (their military back pay was sometimes delayed), and no jobs.[57]

The federal government introduced several measures to help states employ more of their returning veterans. In 1918 the Smith-Sears Vocational Education Bill appropriated $2 million to start a program to educate and rehabilitate World War I veterans. W. H. Magee was in charge of Virginia, Maryland, West Virginia, and the District of Columbia. While on a visit to Richmond, he assured injured soldiers "that the government stands ready to give them a new start so that there will never be any question of charity."[58] But many ex-soldiers failed to take advantage of this service, either because of the extent of their wounds, mental or physical, or because they had trouble accessing conveniently located vocational classes.[59] A similar federal bill, the Vocational Rehabilitation Act, passed the same year but provided only a small percentage of the men who completed the multiyear training with employment.[60] Across the country, some veterans were reduced to begging on street corners and peddling "welcome home" pennants.[61] In Virginia, entrepreneurs courted veterans in local newspapers, searching for "discharged soldiers and sailors to sell welcome home pennant[s]."[62] Looming economic and employment issues would soon make the situation worse.

By April 1919, the federal director of employment optimistically predicted that the labor market in Virginia was improving.[63] But he failed to see the looming conflict that was emerging in the western Virginia coal mining towns. That fall, striking coal miners took up arms and "guarded" the entrance to the mines to try to prevent scabs from covering their shifts.[64] The local press labeled the strikers as "radical miners" and Governor Westmoreland Davis sent troops to protect miners who crossed the lines to work. Much of the public was not sympathetic to the striking coal miners, since they had been exempted from military service during the war (because of the crucial nature of their jobs). The strikes eventually led to a coal shortage in several Virginia cities, such as Danville. One writer connected the coal shortages to former soldiers freezing to death in their homes and argued that the "miners have gone beyond the limit of anything previously experienced in the history of labor troubles in this country."[65]

Three years after the end of the war, veteran employment and health issues were still unresolved in Virginia. An editorial in the *Alexandria Gazette* observed that "the war risk bureau, the public health service and the board for vocational education all have had a part in taking care of the veterans but they have worked independently and for that reason the desired results have not been obtained."[66] Instead, some Virginia veterans turned to a newly created organization for support: the American Legion.

The American Legion was founded after World War I to assist demobilized soldiers and disabled veterans. After the war ended, American officials observed that the morale of the AEF troops was declining precipitously as they waited abroad in 1919 for many months, desperately wanting to return home. Several officers joined together to create the American Legion. They aimed to decrease restrictive regulations on troop activities while increasing opportunities for recreation, entertainment, and leave. That fall, the American Legion received its national charter from Congress (September 16, 1919). The American Legion's constitution promised to "preserve the memories and incidents of our association in the Great War" and to "consecrate and sanctify our comradeship by devotion to mutual helpfulness." It did this in part by building or buying "clubhouses" across the country to provide spaces for member veterans to socialize.[67]

In Virginia, the Richmond American Legion observed the one-year anniversary of Armistice Day (November 11, 1920) with a "big celebration," a "mass-meeting," and a parade. The legion joined forces with a number of charitable groups: the Red Cross, Knights of Columbus, YWCA and YMCA, Salvation Army, Canteen Workers, and many others. The volunteers marched over a mile from the city auditorium (located at Cary and Linden Streets) to the state capitol. Men from National Guard companies, old home guard organizations (with elderly men), and home defense units participated in the procession. In a departure from previous celebrations in Richmond, the African American veterans were invited to participate in the events.[68] Apparently, there was some disappointment over the number of attendees. To ensure future attendance at legion meetings, the group announced that year that boxing matches would become "a permanent feature of the weekly meetings."[69]

5. Homecomings

The American Legion fought for veteran benefits, albeit sometimes in a more conservative way than its counterpart, the Veterans of Foreign Wars (founded decades earlier in 1899 to serve the needs of U.S. veterans). One of the legion's first achievements was to pressure the Bureau of War Risk Insurance to increase disability payments from $30 a month to $80 a month. These payments were accompanied by a federal pledge to provide veterans with long-term hospitalization, life insurance, and allotments for their families.[70] This federal legislation tried to address the needs of disabled veterans but overlooked a more basic disbursement: a pension for those who had served but did not return as an invalid. When their monthly active-duty salaries ended, the army and navy veterans were removed from the payroll, and many had not yet secured postwar employment.

Between 1920 and 1936, several veterans' organizations joined forces to petition for better economic and social treatments. While the American Legion was a dominant force in these negotiations, several other veterans' groups came to their assistance. For example, in 1920, disabled veterans founded the Disabled American Veterans group. And for more than a decade after the war, two 19th-century organizations were working on veteran issues: the National Home for Disabled Volunteer Soldiers (a carryover from efforts to care for the Civil War veterans) and the Bureau of Pensions of the Interior Department (founded in 1832). In 1930, President Hoover signed an executive order to abolish the former, and the latter became the Veterans Administration. Before this consolidation, these organizations had a monumental task on their dockets: provide adequate pensions to the men who had served in the Great War.

In 1914, after the German empire went to war with the Allied Forces, the U.S. Congress realized that American merchant shipping might be in harm's ways, intentionally or not. It created the War Risk Insurance Bureau, designed to administer insurance for shipping vessels and their passengers during the war. In 1917, Congress passed the War Risk Insurance Act that additionally provided benefits for ex-servicemen in four categories: life insurance, disability payments, long-term hospitalization, and family allotments (for those remaining in the service). Veterans who returned from the war with a disability received $80 a month; if they were blinded they received $180 a month.[71] But as early as 1919, the system that processed these requests had a backlog of over 100,000 claims. The War Risk Insurance Bureau had to turn to other veterans' groups to share the job of caring for injured soldiers and sailors.[72]

Bonus Army

> If our soldiers were red blooded Americans and were fighting for their country they need no bonus, says Miss Gunter in prize winning debate.
> —*Big Stone Gap* (VA) *Post*, July 12, 1922[73]

The largest debate focused on bonus pay for the soldiers. In 1917 and 1918, an American soldier's monthly wages were $30. From this paltry sum they were required to pay a premium for war-risk insurance and for family allotment payments. When compared to the comparable wages of a wartime factory worker back home, this dollar-a-day salary seemed insufficient. After the war ended, veterans and several affiliated organizations began to argue for a retroactive salary raise, or, a postwar bonus (also referred to as adjusted compensation). These arguments were met with resistance as the federal government faced a looming budget deficit, while the public pressured the government to cut taxes. In the quote above, a schoolgirl in Wise County won a local debate contest when she argued that there was no need to pay a soldier for his patriotism and compared returning Great War veterans unfavorably to Civil War soldiers who did not "go to their government and ask for a bonus" when they returned home.[74]

After years of public pressure from more sympathetic citizens and support from the American Legion and its politically connected members, Congress passed the Adjusted Compensation Act of 1924. The bureaucrats who crafted the budget that accompanied this legislation calculated that 4,477,412 American soldiers were entitled to a bonus, based on an average of 398 days' worth of service. After a complicated and often contradictory argument over how much cash the government would have to pay (e.g., deciding that men who served for less than 60 days would receive no pay out at all), Congress passed a bill that would give two billion federal tax dollars to veterans and their dependents.[75] If a veteran was owed less than $50, he was scheduled to receive it as soon as possible, in cash. But if the amount was over $50, the veteran received bonds, in lieu of cash, which would accumulate interest until their maturity in 1945. If the recipient were to die before then, his beneficiaries would receive the payout. The limited utility of this bill led the Veterans of Foreign Wars to refer to this as the "tombstone" bonus.[76]

There were two other provisions to the 1924 Bonus Bill: veterans could take out a loan (a percentage of what they were eventually owed) and, in 1925, the range of qualifying disabilities was increased (to include illnesses like tuberculosis or neuropsychological disorders). While the Bonus Bill did not satisfy all of the veterans' requests, it was a start. But then the stock market crashed and many veterans fell on hard times. On October 29, 1929, Virginia papers shared articles from the Associated Press with headlines that warned "Huge Selling Wave" and "All Stock Sales Records Broken on Market Today."[77] In the years that followed, the Great Depression added to the financial woes of World War veterans. In response, the American Legion sponsored employment drives for ex-servicemen, and the VFW called on President Hoover to encourage businesses to hire veterans.[78]

In 1931, Congress increased the amount that veterans could borrow from their future bonuses, but many felt that they should be awarded the full amount remaining on their bonds and used the terminology from a decade earlier, their "bonus," to broadcast their demands. In the spring of 1932, tens of thousands of veterans from all over the country, including several hundred from Richmond, Petersburg, and Fredericksburg, began arriving at the capitol in Washington to encourage the passage of the Patman Bonus Bill.[79] This act was designed to pay the veterans their due immediately and in cash.[80] On April 8, Virginians woke up to headlines that read, "Veterans Swarm into Washington Demanding Bonus." These ex-servicemen called themselves the "Bonus Expeditionary Forces" (paralleling the name of the AEF that they once served in). Organizers said that they had collected over 2.5 million signatures in support of a cash bonus.[81] It took 20 packing cases and a truck to deliver the petitions to members of Congress.

Despite this public spectacle and broad-based support, a little over two months later, on June 17, the U.S. Senate defeated the Patman Bill. About 20,000 veterans, along with their families, were waiting in makeshift camps in and around the capitol while the Senate debated the bill. When the exhausted and frustrated men in the Bonus March (also referred to as the Bonus Army) heard the bad news, many refused to leave, threatening to wait until they received their bonuses, even if that wasn't until 1945 (the original payout date). On July 28, 1932, the army, under the orders of the chief of staff, General Douglas MacArthur, and Major Dwight Eisenhower, violently cleared out the "Bonus Army" camps. Both men had themselves served in the Great War: MacArthur fought abroad and received the Medal of Honor, while Eisenhower commanded a post of the Tank Corps in Pennsylvania. Another World War I veteran, Major George S. Patton, Jr., also participated in this effort to remove the ex-servicemen. The veterans of the Great War finally received their cash bonuses in 1936, nine years earlier than the original payout date. That same month, January 1936, Virginia newspapers reported that economic relief cases in Virginia had dropped by 50 percent in November and December. The New Deal–era Works Progress Administration was also slowly making headway in providing jobs and welfare payments to suffering families.[82] Twelve years after the end of the first war and just four years before the start of the second, Virginia veterans were getting their economic and health needs adequately met.

Inevitably, while soldiers had been away at training camps and fighting abroad there had been major and minor lasting societal changes: clean-shaven men (required to get a good fit for a gas mask); men wearing wristwatches (earlier they carried pocket watches, while women wore wrist timepieces); and the introduction of bras (corsets required too many metal stays, which were in short supply as rationing increased). And new federal policies had recently emerged, including the implementation of daylight saving time to save on electricity, Social Security, and Prohibition. This last one, temperance, was not well received in Virginia, one of whose counties, Franklin, was labeled the "Moonshine Capital of the World."[83]

Temperance

> Likeable Young Man Pays the Freight: Bootlegger was Fine Solider and Meddled in Nobody's Business
> —*Big Stone Gap* (VA) *Post*, November 29, 1922

Throughout the 19th century, religious revivalism and "perfectionist" movements had encouraged the passage of laws to restrict the consumption of intoxicating drinks. In Virginia, the Woman's Christian Temperance Union (WCTU) and the Anti-Saloon League had a particularly strong presence. The WCTU supported temperance because its members believed that alcohol destroyed marriages and families. And some industrialists wanted to decrease alcohol consumption in order to increase efficiency in their factories. On March 10, 1916, the governor of Virginia signed the Mapp Prohibition Act into law and appointed a prohibition commissioner, J. Sidney Peters. By the outbreak of the World War in Europe, temperance societies were common in American communities. During the war, President Wilson supported a temporary ban on alcohol production to save grain as part of his "wheatless" campaign.

The year America entered the Great War, this "temperance coalition" of interests led 18 additional states to adopt prohibition. Influenced by these groups, the War Department banned the sale of liquor in the vicinity of training camps and forbade men in uniform from purchasing drinks.[84] Two years later, the 18th Amendment was ratified (January 16, 1919) and when it took effect the next year (January 16, 1920), the legislation made it illegal to produce, transport, or sell alcohol. Although technically the consumption of liquor was permissible, for the next 13 years, until the amendment was repealed, federal agents struggled to prevent the manufacture and sale of intoxicating liquors in the United States.

In Virginia, as elsewhere in the United States, the populace responded to national prohibition by producing their own alcoholic beverages ("moonshine") and creating illegal bars ("speakeasies"). A criminal element filled the void of manufacturing, transporting, and selling alcohol ("bootlegging"), leading to an explosion in organized crime. The Loudoun County court records reveal a fair amount of alcohol production and its transport, as well as a spike in licenses to pharmacists to sell alcohol for "medicinal" purposes. In response to violators, other Loudoun County residents chartered a community association in 1918 to pursue the goals of an earlier Prohibition and Evangelical Association. These individuals also held grand temperance bush meetings (akin to outdoor revivals) in support of temperance.[85] The Virginia women who endorsed prohibition used that platform to support several wartime efforts. For example, members of the Virginia WCTU appealed to its members to donate foodstuffs and books and magazines to the "boys in the camps."[86] In Jeffersonville WCTU members raised money to buy an ambulance and send it to France.[87] Virginians who opposed prohibition were labeled "bolshevists" and "anarchists," in part because President Wilson hoped to conserve grain for soldier rations rather than alcoholic beverages.[88]

Efforts to enforce prohibition inevitably led to violence. In 1919, four Virginia prohibition agents killed two alleged bootleggers, Lawrence Hudson and Raymond Shackelford, on the Valley Turnpike when they resisted arrest. In turn, a Shenandoah County attorney and the adjutant general, Joseph Lane Stern, called for federal troops to oversee the trial and ensure that there was no public disturbance.[89] As the *Charlottesville Daily Progress* explained, "feeling against the [prohibition] officers is said to be high."[90] Federal officers in Virginia went to great lengths to prosecute bootleggers. In one instance, officers opened a Norton man's coffin in an effort to locate illegally transported liquor. The deceased's uncle pressed charges for this "unusual, disgraceful, and unwarranted" act.[91] One month later, in the same small town, two deputy collectors were wounded when they raided an illegal still.[92] Returning veterans were also punished if they violated the federal restrictions on alcohol possession and consumption. In 1922, John Shepherd, a "fine looking solider [and] a hard worker" during the war was accosted by officers as he left his still "with a keg of moonshine liquor on his shoulder." His military service did not exempt him from paying a $266 fine.[93]

While many civilians and soldiers in Virginia sought ways to evade the restrictions, in some cases Prohibition provided women with a political platform that they had never had previously. For example, Sarah Haines Smith (identified only as "Mrs. Howard M. Hoge" in the newspaper), from Lincoln, vigorously chaired the state Women's Christian Temperance Union. In recognition of her service, Governor Stuart gave her the ceremonial pen that he had used to sign the state prohibition bill on November 1, 1916. Throughout her long life she devoted herself to the cause of temperance, as president of the Virginia WCTU for 40 years and editor of a WCTU publication called *Virginia Call*. Upon her death, at age 72 in 1939, her Loudoun County neighbor former governor Westmoreland Davis "pronounced her a figure in Virginia of whom all woman hood might well feel proud."[94] Simultaneously, other Virginia women had their political sights set on another agenda: female suffrage.

Suffrage for Women

> Mrs. C. M. Ferrell, a leader of the anti-suffrage ranks [in Virginia], said, "I think it is a shame and a calamity [that Tennessee ratified the 19th Amendment]. Dog-gone-it. I hope Tennessee burns up."
> —*Richmond Times-Dispatch*, August 19, 1920

Prohibition efforts and women's suffrage movements had existed throughout the 19th century. The broad brushstrokes behind the passage of the historic 19th Amendment are well known. In 1848, a group of women, and a handful of men, met in Seneca Falls to edit Thomas Jefferson's "self-evident" truth that "all men are created equal." Espousing the then radical belief that women were not simply wives or daughters, they began a 72-year battle to achieve political autonomy for women that culminated with the 19th Amendment almost two years after the end of the Great War and 18 months after the start of prohibition. The capstone came on August 18, 1920, when the 19th Amendment to the Constitution was finally ratified. Virginia had several surprising roles to play in this fundamental expansion of citizenship rights in America.

The commonwealth framed female suffrage in terms of states' right, invoking parallels with the South's 19th-century "war of secession." Virginians who supported "anti-suffrage" legislation were upset that two-thirds of the states could, in effect, enact federal legislation. Unlike their peers in Idaho and Utah (which had given women the right to vote in the late 19th century), some Virginians opposed any and all efforts to give women an opportunity to cast ballots. An editorial in the *Richmond Times-Dispatch* directly opposed President Wilson's plea to the Virginia General Assembly in which he urged the assembly to ratify the federal amendment of 1919. The author of the article complained bitterly that the president was trying to interfere with the state's right to determine the eligibility of women to vote, asserting that he demonstrated "not a drop of Southern, much less Virginia blood in his veins." The angry missive concluded with the observation that "women suffrage" was "the most stupendous and insidious evil now confronting civilization."[95] These sentiments were shared by many members of the Virginia General Assembly. Five years earlier the assembly had defeated a proposal for women's suffrage by a vote of 75 to 13. A local paper reported, "The result was not unexpected, but the suffrage advocates were disappointed at the small size of the vote cast in its favor."[96] Many Virginia newspaper cartoons and propaganda placards supported this decision, arguing that "a woman's place is in her home," and featured pictures of sobbing babies accompanied by the caption "Mummy's a Suffragette." These contemporary posters found a sympathetic audience despite the later wartime contributions of thousands of Virginia women in charitable organizations, on farms, and in the military.

To pressure the reluctant General Assembly, local chapters of suffragist organizations formed across the commonwealth. In Loudoun County, Jane Lee Powell chaired the Equal Suffrage League.[97] The woman's suffrage group held its 1913 statewide convention in Lynchburg. On the eve of the meeting, delegates were greeted by a newspaper editorial whose authors were "profoundly convinced that the cause will never prevail in Virginia and does not deserve to prevail."[98] As late as September 3, 1919 (months after the summer passage of the 19th Amendment but before it was officially ratified), pro-suffrage forces sponsored a half-page announcement in a Richmond newspaper that featured a "victory map" to illustrate "why Congress passed the Federal suffrage amendment." They argued forcibly, often in all caps, that Thomas Jefferson himself would have wanted the Virginia General Assembly to "keep pace" with the passage of federal amendments and concluded that it was too late for a state referendum (to nullify the national act). They concluded, "This amendment, enfranchising womanhood in America, must inevitably succeed."[99] In this postwar milieu, female suffragists argued that a woman had earned the right to participate in the democratic process and that every woman should receive additional education to make her "the best possible citizen and patriot."[100]

A third, and more surprising, role that Virginia played in the women's voting movement was a horrific one: the imprisonment and torture of suffragists in the Occoquan Workhouse in Lorton. In the early 20th century the American penal system included "workhouses," prisons where petty offenders were expected to work. The U.S. government purchased a 3200-acre tract of land in Lorton, along the banks of the Occoquan River, to establish an "industrial farm." By a perverse logic, the prisoners were supposed to rehabilitate themselves by constructing their own stockades and dormitories. Two years later, in 1910, a separate workhouse was built to house women. These prisoners were expected to do laundry, make clothes for male and female prisoners, and tend gardens to produce food.[101]

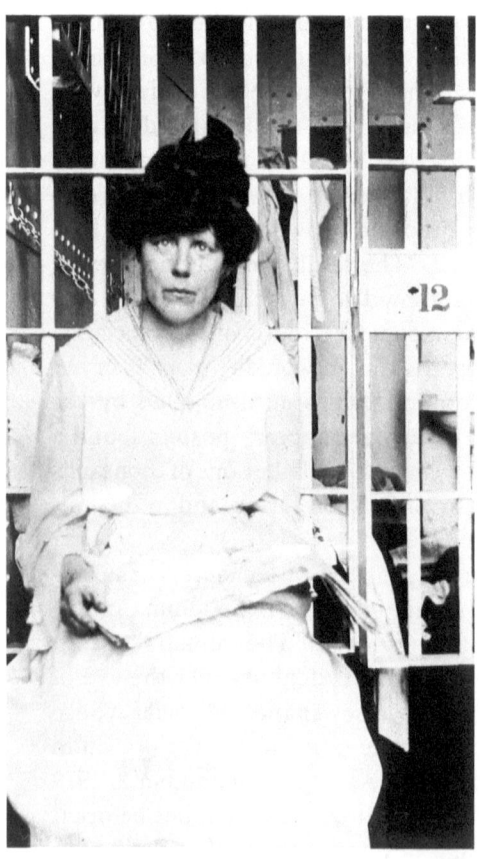

Lucy Burns imprisoned at the Lorton Workhouse in Northern Virginia (photograph by Harris & Ewing, Washington, D.C., November 1917. Library of Congress, Digital ID: http://hdl.loc.gov/loc.mss/mnwp.274009).

On August 28, 1917, as the World War raged abroad, several dozen suffragists were arrested for protesting in front of the White House. On November 14, 1917, 31 picketers arrived at the Occoquan Workhouse to serve out their two-month sentences, all for the temerity of wanting to vote. In the weeks that followed, a sadistic superintendent and his wardens beat them and, when they went on a hunger strike, force-fed the women through a tube.¹⁰² Superintendent W. H. Whittaker subjected the women to solitary confinement, restrained them with shackles, and even gagged them.¹⁰³ With help from lawyers, the suffragists were finally released from prison at the end of November, two weeks into their initial two-month sentence. Afterwards, some of these women toured the country on a "Prison Special" railroad car, continuing to fight for their cause. A year later President Wilson spoke in favor of female suffrage, concluding that "we have made partners of the women in this war; shall we admit them only to a partnership of suffering ... not to a partnership of privilege and right."¹⁰⁴

Finally, on August 18, 1920, Tennessee ratified the 19th Amendment, becoming the 36th state to do so and meeting the three-quarters' requirement to pass the legislation (there were 48 states at that time). So although the Virginia General Assembly did not vote in favor of the amendment, the state would be required to adhere to the national legislation. Accordingly, the Equal Suffrage League of Virginia became the Virginia League of Women Voters and set to work at once to register and educate female voters in time for the upcoming presidential election between Warren G. Harding and James M. Cox on November 2, 1920.¹⁰⁵ The thousands of Virginia nurses, along with their less numerous colleagues, ambulance drivers, camouflage painters, fingerprinting scientists, and yeomanettes, finally had a say in shaping American democracy.

Returning African American Soldiers

> Every time a white man insults a Negro, every time he conveys by his conduct an overweening sense of his race superiority to a Negro, he contributes to the cause out of which these race riots have come.
> —*Richmond Planet*, August 16, 1919

The reception that some African American soldiers received upon their return to Virginia was diametrically opposite to the generally peaceful, albeit sometimes resentful, acceptance of female voters. The Virginia that black veterans experienced in the years after their return was a violent and unsavory one marred by lynchings, the second incarnation of the Ku Klux Klan, economic insecurity, segregated housing and businesses, along with daily racism and prejudice. Dozens of black Virginians were lynched. In 1920, Dave Hunt, a 25-year-old man from Wise, was hung from a bridge for allegedly assaulting an elderly woman, and later the same community lynched a black boy.¹⁰⁶ Virginia did not pass an antilynching law, to specify that it was a state crime, until 1928. Throughout the 1920s, returning black veterans and their families were threatened by bloodthirsty mobs and the KKK. Some African Americans feared that these violent threats were part of an effort "to keep the negro soldier in his place."[107] Between April and November 1919, racially motivated riots and lynchings broke out across the country. This tumultuous period would later come to be known as the "Red Summer."[108]

During this tense year, minor public disagreements often escalated quickly. For example, toward the end of the war, on October 4, 1918, an

Sardonic cartoon featured in Richmond's African American newspaper titled "Under Many Flags." The piece of paper on the ground reads, "Let him who is without sin cast the first stone. Bible," and the caption for the United States reads, "Lynching Negro for 50 Years. 58 in 1918." Drawn by George H. Ben Johnson (*Richmond Plant*, February 8, 1919, 2).

African American waitress in Hopewell argued with a man identified only as "a Spaniard named Gomez." After some type of altercation—the details are hazy in the newspaper accounts—the waitress was struck and appealed to her friends for help. Within hours a large crowd of African American workers from the nearby DuPont plant gathered, and shots rang out.[109] The *Richmond Planet* claimed that several hundred shots were exchanged between police and the rioters; in the end, three black men were shot, one of whom died.[110] A white newspaper reporter described this as a "race riot" and agreed with the mayor's decision to send out two companies of infantrymen from nearby Camp Lee to restore order.[111] Almost two months later, on November 29, another fight broke out in an African American theater in the nearby community of Petersburg. Authorities labeled this a "near riot."[112] In the prejudicial reporting from white newspapers, disputes in black communities were quickly labeled "riots," whereas similar outbreaks of violence in white neighborhoods were attributed to more specific causes. As a result, it is sometimes hard to understand the underlying causes of these disturbances. But it was not surprising to read one black commentator conclude, "The retired Negro soldier, used to arms, returning from the war environment resenting the ingratitude he sees in all of this, is prompted to 'direct' action to remedy his wrongs."[113] These black ex-servicemen of Hopewell, like John Lenwood Brown (1885–1985), had to make difficult decisions about what was best for their families.

Due to racial injustices and poor pay, thousands of African Americans from rural areas throughout the south, including Virginia, fled to the North, most often to cities like Washington, D.C., or Chicago. One white commentator in Hopewell claimed that "a thousand or more" black residents left the city the day after the October incident in 1918.[114] Southern blacks were "induced by the prospect of very high wages" in the North while dismayed by "discrimination in educational facilities and in the administration of justice" in the South.[115] African American Virginians who remained, like Mr. Brown who worked as a laborer at the DuPont brickyard, faced daily racist restrictions in Jim Crow Virginia.

I was surprised to uncover the origins of segregated federal public housing in the Virginia war efforts. In Chapter 3, I discuss how the federal government teamed up with a Newport News shipping company to create a federally subsidized housing development called Hilton Village. This community was named after an antebellum farm that relied on slave labor. Following emancipation, freed African American men and women settled near the former plantation, along the peninsula. This community was forcibly removed when a developer purchased land there in 1880 to create the Old Dominion Land Company. Decades later, a new community was built there and marketed exclusively to whites. Hilton Village was the first federally supported housing development that was restricted by race in the United States.

Segregated communities were also planned in another seaside community: in Portsmouth at a site counterintuitively named after a white naval hero, Thomas Truxtun. Truxtun was the first wartime housing project constructed by the federal government solely for African Americans in the United States.[116] One of the architects, Rossel Edward Mitchell, wrote that his plans for the Portsmouth community of Truxtun represented a "significant advance in homes for colored workers." If you compare the basic, five-room clapboard houses in Truxtun to the dozen or more ornamental designs found in the Newport News community of Hilton Village, the differences in "separate but equal" are readily apparent.[117] And while Truxtun's architects used a decorative colonial revival style for their homes, the original plan did not include curbs for the streets or gutters for the homes. When the Truxtun development was officially unveiled on May 25, 1919, there were 250 structures, most of which were residential, with a couple dozen businesses. The plan also called for a school, church, theater, and car garage, but only the school was completed.[118] Residents of the neighborhood included returning veterans, like Pitt Hawkins (1881–1960), who worked for the Norfolk Naval Yard after completing their wartime service.

The all-white counterpart to Truxtun was the nearby Cradock development. Built to house white laborers who worked at the Norfolk Naval Shipyard, it contained over 1200 houses. Two bridges were necessary to connect this creek-filled farming land to the naval yard and nearby Portsmouth. The family homes in this development contained five or six rooms and were adjacent to a business district.[119] World War I veterans lived in both Truxtun and Cradock. Some of these men were required to register two decades later for World War II, although it is unlikely that any of them were called up because of their advancing age. In the years after their initial service, society gradually forgot their sacrifice, spending annual holidays like Memorial Day or Armistice Day focused more on football games and picnics than on military parades and dinners honoring veterans.

6

Commemorations

> The "increasing enthusiasm" with which Americans join in the annual observance of Armistice Day, the President suggests, "enforces the conclusion that it is destined to be one of the notable anniversaries in our calendar ... an occasion for appraisal of our relationship to and participation in those wider concerns which involve the welfare of all mankind."
> —*The Washington Herald*, November 11, 1922[1]

The Great War ended, Virginians came home, communities welcomed them back, and then the one-year anniversary of the Armistice arrived. Today Veterans Day honors veterans from all wars, but it originated with the decision to commemorate the recently concluded, catastrophically deadly First World War. After helping to negotiate the Treaty of Versailles, President Wilson proclaimed November 11, 1919, the first Armistice Day. He hoped that on this day Americans would "be filled with solemn pride in the heroism of those who died in the country's service and with gratitude for the victory, both because of the thing from which it has freed us and because of the opportunity it has given America to show her sympathy with peace and justice in the councils of the nations."[2] It would be a day of parades, public meetings, and a brief halt to any and all business at 11:00 a.m., when the original ceasefire took place.

Congress, however, did not officially recognize this anniversary until 1926 when it passed a resolution that called for "thanksgiving and prayer and exercises designed to perpetuate peace through good will and mutual understanding between nations." How local celebrations might improve communications with foreign powers was not specified. The resolution's final clause called for municipalities to display the flag on all government buildings, "inviting the people of the United States to observe the day in

"Peace Day parade," November 11, 1918. Note the horse-drawn fire truck, the exceptionally long ladder, and the troops following alongside (Holsinger Studio Collection, X06955GB, Special Collections, University of Virginia Library, Charlottesville).

schools and churches, or other suitable places, with appropriate ceremonies of friendly relations with all other peoples."[3]

November 11 was not made a legal holiday until 1938 when Congress declared Armistice Day a legal holiday and dedicated the day to the lofty goal of maintaining "world peace."[4] The term "Armistice" was replaced with "Veterans" in 1954 when President Eisenhower signed a proclamation to broaden the holiday to recognize Americans who served in other wars.[5]

Curious to see how that bittersweet anniversary was first recognized in Virginia, I turned to local newspapers. I didn't have a clear image of what the "parades and public meetings" would entail, but I certainly hadn't imagined a "gentleman from Texas" riding in a car and pulling ten floats, containing dozens of women, by his neck. And yet, there it was, as part of a full-page advertisement welcoming "boys," the returning soldiers, to "Virginia's Armistice Celebration 'World's-War.'"[6]

A more traditional parade was scheduled for Armistice Day eve, on

Monday, November 10. This event featured floats from the Red Cross and "floral" entries. A nearby exposition hall featured exhibits from marines, army, and navy units, alongside 50 "working exhibits," band concerts, and four "stupendous attractions." The announcement, or more accurately, paid advertisement, was sponsored by a car distributer, Markel, Inc., that used the dubious tagline "Our Service Is Sworn By—Not Sworn At."[7]

Intrigued, I decided to hunt down the "stupendous" acts considered appropriate for a one-year anniversary of the end to a global catastrophe. At first I couldn't find any mention of them, though I did learn that Richmonders agreed to open up their homes to three hundred out-of-town guests (thousands came), to sell souvenir programs to raise money for a permanent memorial, and to provide free tickets for each veteran as long as they registered in advance. The parade was scheduled to depart from the "Stuart Monument" (the 1919 readership would have known that this was the memorial to Civil War general J. E. B. Stuart) and head east, toward the state capitol. The ceremonies included the requisite flag ritual: one given by a French delegation to the State of Virginia and one presented to Governor Davis by a "ladies' committee" to honor those who made the "supreme sacrifice."[8] As with the postwar statuary, women were initially associated with mourning and caring for the dead. On that fall day, relatives of dead soldiers were presented with bronze medals embossed with a gold star, a reference to the symbol that families hung in their windows if they lost a loved one. The household flag contained a single gold star on a black background, representing the men from Richmond who didn't make it home.[9]

I was expecting a solemn tone to the parade preparations, something similar to modern-day Veterans Day observances: maybe a moment of silence at 11:00 a.m. on the 11th day of the 11th month, or perhaps a poetry reading or a recitation of the names of the dead. Instead, thousands of visitors were treated to a "week of jollity, frolic, with here and there a solemn observance in remembrance of those men who today are buried in foreign soil in order that their ideals of democracy might prevail."[10] In my experience, solemnity and jollity do not co-occur naturally. Then again, I learned that the "armistice strong man" mentioned earlier was going to pull one hundred Red Cross nurses with a two-inch rope around his neck; that sounded like a recipe for comic disaster.[11] And that was just the beginning: the Gray's Armory was being turned into a "hippodrome society circus," the royal Italian band was going to play in Byrd Park (the future home of the Virginia war memorial), and troops were going to be fed free meals.

They were not, however, going to be in the parade. Instead, they would be the "spectators," observing and, it was hoped, appreciating, "those who labored at home for them while they fought abroad or prepared themselves for foreign service in this country."[12] I was glad to see that the home-front activities were getting their time in the spotlight.

Every wartime organization that I have previously discussed in this book participated in the parade. There were the obvious groups: the Red Cross, the Knights of Columbus, and the Jewish Welfare Board, but there was also the War Camp Community Service and Federation of Mothers Clubs.[13] Women and African Americans were, as always, held to a different standard. In the case of the former, parade organizers were worried that the "fair sex" would tire easily. So they selected a short route for the female contingents, with "three rest periods of two minutes each."[14] Richmond's African American residents were forced to plan their own "colored homecoming celebration," which was an "entirely separate and distinct demonstration" of patriotism, held in another location with different performers.[15] Even the newspaper's announcement of this segregated event was on page six, rather than with the front-page discussion of the whites-only celebration.

As for the four amazing acts, on November 10, the newspaper reported that the "carnival attractions" were late in arriving. A tightrope walker planned to walk across a 50-foot-high wire at nine o'clock that night. The paddle wheel spinner was, alas, arrested by the commonwealth attorney for betting. Apparently, the "booths and carnival shows" included illegal gambling.[16] The day itself, November 11, featured more emotional contrasts, where the "note of thanksgiving for the cessation of hostilities" was added to "the much louder note of festivity and merrymaking which [rang] throughout the city."[17] Although the newspaper did not dwell on it, I assume that at 11:00 a.m. businesses closed for a short period of time and Americans paused what they were doing to honor the dead.

In a poignant juxtaposition, a short, 14-line story at the bottom of the newspaper's front page promoting the upcoming "continuous entertainment," announced that the first of the American corpses were due to arrive at New York harbor on November 9, 1919. The transport ship *Lake Daraga* returned the bodies of more than one hundred soldiers who died while fighting in Russia.[18] On November 13, a funeral was held in their home state of Michigan, where American government officials, local politicians, and an attaché from the Russian embassy attended the ceremony in Detroit.[19]

A Half Century of Armistice Day Celebrations in Virginia

> This is only the second anniversary of Armistice Day—a day destined, if we will, to keep company with the immortals of the calendar that mark great moments of history that shall never die.
> —*Richmond Times-Dispatch*, November 11, 1920[20]

In subsequent years, the Armistice Day ceremonies reflected a more nuanced balance between celebrations and remembrance. At 10:59, 1920, the day began with "one sacred minute of silence" when "every head will bow, every wheel will stop, industry will come to a standstill, pleasure will cease." Somewhat jarringly, that brief moment of silence and genuflection was followed by the burst of "a hundred whistles, sirens, [and] bells" to symbolize "the joy of peace ... overwhelming the sorrow of war."[21]

For decades, these parades and ceremonies incorporated ex-servicemen, until they passed away from their wounds, sicknesses, or old age. Through the 1920s, most Virginia Armistice Day and Fourth of July parades featured veterans from three wars: Confederate soldiers, men who fought in the Spanish-American War, and Great War veterans. In 1920, 55 years after his war ended, one determined ex-confederate rode over 50 miles on his war horse from his home in Caroline County to the state capitol to participate in the November 11 ceremonies.[22] The veterans who attended these ceremonies were often awarded medals or distinguished service crosses. These ceremonies gave civilians a chance to learn additional details about the service of their fellow Virginians. For example, on November 11, 1920, Lieutenant John Campbell Boggs (Second Machine-Gun Company) was awarded a medal for his actions near Soissons on July 21, 1918, when he "took charge of a machine-gun crew and protected an exposed flank and defeated a counterattack of the enemy."[23] After he returned from the war he married Mattie Walton Epes and lived until age 85 in 1981.

Communities throughout Virginia hosted these annual events to commemorate the war's end and honor those who had served. In Fredericksburg, the mayor issued a proclamation in 1920 requesting that businesses and homes display American flags and churches toll their bells. He also asked citizens to observe a moment of silence at 11:00 a.m. and briefly suspend their activities.[24] In Alexandria, the YMCA hosted an "Armistice Supper" that offered baked beans and creamed oysters, among other delicacies, while two local football teams competed in a special match, which pitted the "Dreadnaughts" versus the "Seamen Gunners."[25]

Most of the news coverage focused on the ex-servicemen. Women usually marched after the all-male units passed by, representing the thousands of Virginians who worked with the Salvation Army, the Red Cross, and other domestic groups. Children marched as well, representing organizations such as the Boy Scouts and Girl Scouts and YWCA and YMCA. Most of these honorific parades were organized by the American Legion as part of its efforts to increase morale among ex-servicemen and to support their transition back into civilian life.

Gradually, these epic multiday festivities faded in intensity and focus. As early as 1922, a football game, instead of an Armistice Day parade, provided the headline for the Richmond paper: "V.M.I.-Carolina Gridiron Battle Climax of Holiday." A smaller article noted that the accompanying parade, supposedly focused on the Armistice celebration, was expected to be the largest of its kind due to the number of out-of-town visitors on hand for the game. In another trend that would increase over the decades, retail stores were to stay open that November 11 because it was a Saturday—"the most important day to trade" for the "buying public." Businesses did agree, however, to close for three minutes at 11:00 a.m.[26]

To see how Armistice Day was honored as the World War I veterans aged and the public memory faded, I took a sample of one community's newspaper articles on this anniversary from issues in 1929, 1939, 1949, and 1959. I selected my hometown, Charlottesville, and its local paper, the *Daily Progress*. By 1929, new terms were being used to describe the "Great War" as it became a conflict associated with the "misery of the 'War of wars.'" Businesses still observed a moment of silence and the community hosted a parade, mostly composed of civic organizations and clubs. Confederate veterans, now in their seventies or eighties, continued to march alongside those from the world war.[27]

A decade later, in 1939, the Charlottesville newspaper headline read, "Armistice Day Quietly Observed Here along with Rest of Nation." A second European war had begun less than three months earlier, causing the reporter to observe that on that 21st anniversary of the Great War's end, conditions in Europe were more reminiscent of November 11, 1914 (near the war's beginning) than November 11, 1918 (at its end). Post offices and banks in Charlottesville observed holiday hours on November 11, 1939, but grocery stores kept their regular hours. The American Legion had taken over most of the holiday planning, which was limited to a dinner program. Meanwhile, in Northern Virginia, political dignitaries and President Roosevelt visited the Tomb of the Unknown Solider at Arlington National Cemetery.[28]

Thirty-one years after the end of the war, in 1949, every time World War I was mentioned on the Charlottesville front page, it was accompanied by a reference to World War II—effectively blaming the settlement of the first war for the onset of the second. Tucked inside on the ninth page of the newspaper, an article with a New York byline bemoaned World War I as the "most stupendous war mankind had known"—a significant description seeing as World War II had just ended. The rest of the short article contained quotes related to war and peace, but no mention of parades or even dinners.[29] The only local references to Armistice Day were paid advertisements: The local American Legion Post 74 featured a man standing in front of the number "11" on a calendar and expressing the sentiment, "We'll be remembering with mixed emotions of pride and sorrow, the contributions made by our buddies in the First World War."[30] The local Citizens Bank took out a separate advertisement that focused on their hopes for peace and reminded the public that "a minute of reverent silence" was expected at 11:00 a.m. on November 11.[31] Gone were the exuberant communitywide parades or the long speeches over dinners honoring the veterans of the Great War.

By 1959, specific reference to the World War I "Armistice" had disappeared from articles about the annual observance. In 1954, President Dwight Eisenhower had officially changed the name to "Veterans Day" to include those who had served in World War II and the Korean conflict. In the November 11, 1959, Charlottesville paper World War I veterans were passed over except for one sad caption that summed up their fate. It accompanied a picture of Alvin York, the famous American soldier who singlehandedly took 132 Germans prisoner and was one of the most decorated soldiers during the First World War. The caption read, "Just another day for Sgt. Alvin York." The short summary concluded, "The 71-year-old veteran, ill and partly blind, said Veterans Day is nothing special to him—'every war is to end wars and we've still got 'em going on or coming up.'"[32]

In the early years after the war, Memorial Day and Armistice Day were not the only time that World War I soldiers were honored and remembered. Even religious holidays, such as Christmas, were used to remember community members who had passed or to raise money for social causes, like relief for poor children or "the needy" during the winter season. The annual anniversary of the nation's independence from Great Britain was another such holiday where veterans were recognized for their service.

Fourth of July Celebrations and the Great War

> Never has Independence Day meant so much to so many people as it will this year with the signing of peace and the home coming of nearly two million men from overseas.
> —*Richmond Times-Dispatch*, July 1, 1919[33]

Before I had children, I hadn't been to a parade in almost two decades. At the 2016 Independence Day parade in the small Virginia town of Crozet most of the paradegoers alongside me appeared to be in the company of children as well. From this family-fun perspective, it's easy to trivialize these events as an out-of-season Halloween candy giveaway. But nearly a hundred years ago, during and directly after World War I, the long line of citizens of all ages carrying flags, waving at troops, and wearing red, white, and blue served many other crucial functions, namely reintegrating the returning soldiers into society, albeit superficially, and demonstrating the support of the home front for their overseas efforts.

First, the World War I–era parades recognized veterans by inviting them to participate in the processions and to end their day with free meals and awards ceremonies. Second, boys were introduced to the importance of military service and saw, firsthand, the accolades that might accompany this work. Boy Scouts and Girl Scouts were often included in the parade lineup. And third, the day's festivities drew the community together, one potluck and celebratory event at a time. In the case of July 4, 1919, these communal events helped Virginians heal from their loses, offer their gratitude to the armed forces, and promote a strong sense of nationalism.

Because it took many months to demobilize and transport tens of thousands of troops back home, Virginians turned the Fourth of July 1919 into a combined Welcome Home Day and celebration of our independence. In Washington County, soldiers and sailors were given a "bountiful lunch" by the local Red Cross and "handsomely decorated cars" drove in the parade.[34] The president of the Norton Athletic Association traveled as far as Cincinnati in May to "secure the greatest attractions that can possibly be had" for the summertime festivities.[35] Pulaski County promised an event to "eclipse anything of the character which has been held here [in the past]."[36] Tazewell County, worried about the dozens of competing celebrations, decided to hold its "monster" event on July 5. To honor their veterans, both "those who have been overseas and those who have served in the camps," the local Women's Christian Temperance Union created a memorial picture using formal photographs of each local man who "sleeps in France."[37]

As the fourth day of July dawned in 1919, Richmonder Mrs. M. W. Wilson recommended gathering family and friends for a picnic or "lawn fete." She encouraged families that had lost a loved one not to mourn but instead to "gather a few of his comrades" and invite them to the house party. She instructed the menfolk to prepare a campfire for making coffee and roasting potatoes and provided a dozen recipes for the women to make, including an "edible cannon cracker recipe."[38]

In addition to these "Welcome Home" events, Virginia communities celebrated Independence Day in a variety of other ways. The popular Richmond department store Miller & Rhoads, took out a large advertisement on the "most glorious Fourth" and admonished its audience, "No one should be too busy or too occupied to unfurl the Stars and Stripes."[39] Other Virginians celebrated a little too much. On the eve of the holiday, two of Pittsylvania's "prominent farmers" were arrested, along with two others, for operating an illicit liquor establishment. Federal authorities poured out 1500 gallons of beer and light wine.[40]

At the state level, the governor of Virginia had a more practical goal for the Fourth of July holiday. Using powers vested in him by a February 20, 1918, act of the General Assembly, he declared a second public holiday: "Good Roads Day." On July 4 and 5, 1919, Virginians were urged to gather their neighbors and discuss the best ways of securing "good roads." The proclamation explained, "The building of good roads will make possible the proper economic and social development of the Commonwealth." Governor Davis hoped that these citizens would bring "their teams, tools, and materials" to these meetings and jump right in to make the work days a success.[41]

At the national level, July 4, 1919, went down in the history books for another reason: it was the day that Congress approved the 19th Amendment. Six weeks later it would be ratified, giving women the right to vote— just one of the many social changes ushered in after the Great War.

Almost one hundred years later, Abingdon, Virginia, that far southwestern town that I toured with my children, promoted an "All-American Independence Day Extravaganza." The 2016 festivities included family-friendly events, food, music, and fireworks. That year, the Abingdon Fife and Drum Corps was invited to celebrate Abingdon's Revolutionary War history. World War I was knocked out of the public spotlight again. And, in a final irony, the local food spectacle (a watermelon eating contest) was accompanied by a German-inspired "beer garden."

Flag Day

> I should call your attention to the approach of the anniversary of the day upon which the flag of the United States was adopted by the Congress as the emblem of the Union, and to suggest to you that it should this year and in the years to come be given special significance as a day of renewal and reminder, a day upon which we should direct our minds with a special desire of renewal to thoughts of the ideals and principles of which we have sought to make our great Government the embodiment.
>
> —President Woodrow Wilson, May 30, 1916[42]

President Wilson penned these words in 1916 when he established the Fourth of July's lesser-known cousin, "Flag Day." He felt that Americans should symbolically refocus their attention on their "thoughtful love of America" by honoring the flag each year on June 14. It was no accident that the president was concerned about the nation's "united hearts" and "mission of truth and justice" in the midst of a global catastrophe that the United States was only narrowly avoiding that year.

The flag itself was a powerful symbol of what Americans fought for in the First World War. The "stars and stripes" had been adopted as the official flag in 1777, during the American War of Independence. At the Continental Congress held the previous summer, a committee was formed to create a seal for the burgeoning "United States of America." The flag borrowed colors from this design, the now famous red, white, and blue. The 18th-century designers intended red to signify "hardiness and valour," white to represent "purity and innocence," and blue as "the color of the Chief" (a.k.a., the not yet created position of the president of the country; in 1777 there was only a president of the Congress) to represent his "vigilance, perseverance, & justice."[43]

During World War I, the American flag contained 48 stars but otherwise was identical to today's "stars and stripes." A separate "Naval Jack" flag was flown on ships, made up of a blue background with 48 white stars (minus the white and red stripes). In a military context flags have always held an important meaning: symbolizing the various nations at war and thus, holding special value if captured. Standard-bearers were appointed to carry the flag, and they in turn signaled where the unit was at any given moment. Often the flag-bearer stood or fought near the leader of the unit. Thus, if the flag fell, it quite likely signaled the fall of the unit itself. By World War I army companies carried a guidon, a small rectangular flag often with a triangle-shaped piece removed from its end, which represented the unit and its commanding officer.

Two months after the United States entered World War I, the National Propaganda Department released a Flag Day poster reminding its audience that 1917 was the 140th anniversary our flag's creation. The artists, and the governmental agency behind the poster, highlighted the parallels between the 18th-century and 20th-century fights for freedom, equating the colonists' fight for independence to American citizens' fight to "make the world safe for democracy." The poster depicted two revolutionary soldiers raising a large furled flag up a flagpole with a cannon at its base and an eagle hovering above, intently supervising, or perhaps blessing, the proceedings. Given the challenges facing the country in the summer of 1917, I mentally added a modern-day slogan to the bottom of the poster: "What would George Washington do?"

Days before President Wilson signed the declaration of war in April 1917, Richmonders were urged to "Buy a Flag To-Day." Women at "100 or more stations scattered over the city" were selling American flags; they planned to donate the proceeds to a war-relief fund to assist hospitals. The *Richmond Times-Dispatch*

Celebrating Flag Day on June 14, 1917. Note the implicit 140th celebration of America's Independence in 1777 (Call No. POS–World War I–US, no. 412, Library of Congress Prints and Photographs Division Washington, D.C.).

announced to its readers in no uncertain terms that "every loyal American should take pride in showing his country's colors" given the precipitous political circumstances. And in case that message wasn't clear, the front-page article concluded, "Every man, woman, and child whose heart is with the President in this national crisis should have a flag before nightfall."[44]

Throughout the Great War, Virginia women made and donated honorific flags to units in which their sons, husbands, and sweethearts served. For example, the Roanoke Women's Auxiliary made a "solidly and handsomely" embroidered flag, valued at more than one hundred dollars, for the Jo Lane Stern Battalion of Infantry, a group of volunteers named after a former adjutant general from Virginia. The women who presented the troops with this flag hoped no less than to "render aid and encouragement to the men of the battalion in their social and military affairs, and to stimulate their activities generally."[45]

When the troops finally returned home from their duties abroad, they were greeted with a sea of flags. During a June 1919 "Welcome Home" event in Norfolk, "practically everybody who saw the parade had some kind of a flag, large or small."[46] These early 20th-century Virginians viewed the flag as "an emblem of liberty and freedom" that combined "individual independence" with "a united and closely bonded people."[47] And yet these welcome home celebrations were segregated and, initially, women did not have the right to vote for the elected officials who represented American democracy. Following closely upon the peace celebrations was the national holiday especially oriented to women's expected role in the kitchen: Thanksgiving.

Thanksgiving

> With blue skies and one of the greatest holiday crowds in her history, Thanksgiving Day broke joyously over Richmond yesterday. And not only was there a happy beginning, but that happiness continued throughout. All day long the huge throngs surged along the streets, made merry in the hotel lobbies and in the cafes, guessed at the score of the great football game ... and celebrated in various ways.
> —*Richmond Times-Dispatch*, November 26, 1915[48]

While the origins of Thanksgiving are shrouded in uncertainty, by the early 20th century the holiday had morphed into its modern-day traditions: a day focused on eating a feast with family, watching football, and retail sales and parties and dances for the wealthier Virginians.[49] Most households adhered to socially accepted gender divisions. One Tazewell County newspaper advertisement summarized the holiday as "the time of all times when every housewife sets a fine table, and how well she knows that an abundance of delicate china enhances the beauty of the Thanksgiving dinner table."[50] And while the families of today that sit around a television watching football are using a modern convenience not yet invented in World War I, newspaper reporters even then explicitly linked their celebrations to "pigskin and gridiron." Virginians closely followed the games, which were "inseparably associated with the last Thursday in November."[51] On that autumnal day, Americans were also asked to give thanks for their own "blessings" and to donate money or foodstuffs to those less fortunate.[52] After multiple European nations went to war in 1914, some Virginia communities turned their November charitable efforts toward needy countries abroad. For example, the Needlework Guild in Alexandria sent $14 to "the Belgians" in addition to their donation of 420 garments to local charities closer to home.[53]

Woodrow Wilson's 1915 Thanksgiving address to the nation focused on national defense without "breaching" America's friendship with both sides in the conflict. After recognizing that "another year of peace has been vouchsafed us," Wilson concluded his address by inviting Americans to "cease from their wonted occupations and in their several homes and places of worship render thanks to Almighty God."[54]

In sharp contrast, the November after America entered the war, Wilson's Thanksgiving Day Proclamation talked about the "immeasurable disaster" that had shaken the world and left it in "sorrow and great peril." He referenced another American holiday, the Fourth of July, in drawing parallels between American colonists "taking up arms against a tyranny" in the 1770s and Americans "defend[ing] the rights of free men throughout the world" in 1917.[55] As a core American holiday, Thanksgiving became an ideal platform for wartime propaganda.

The Thanksgiving holiday of 1918 fell a little over two weeks after the end of hostilities. Alongside football and feasting, newspaper editors predicted that a "deeper reverence" would mark the day, since "families of rich and poor … will combine in thankfulness for the knowledge that their loved ones are returning." The Retail Merchants Association decided that Richmond businesses, with the exception of clothing stores, would close for the day to mark the "deeper significance" of a postwar Thanksgiving. On that November day, some soldiers would be arriving in Richmond from camps and bases in Newport News and Norfolk; local citizens were asked to host a solider, or two, for dinner.[56] Richmond churches hosted sermons with titles like "When the Boys Come Home" and, simply, "Thanksgiving." And the Beth Ahabah Synagogue sponsored a lecture optimistically titled "A Permanent Peace."

Nearby the Westhampton College for women entertained male student colleagues from its parent institution, Richmond College, who served in the SATC. A four-piece orchestra provided music for dancing while "guests were served ice cream and cake arranged to represent khaki tents." And with no sense of irony, the Richmond Howitzers Women's Auxiliary hosted a "peace ball" at the Howitzers Armory—which housed the artillery that not long before wreaked devastation on enemy troops entrenched along the western front.[57]

By 1919, pleas for charitable assistance on the "day of thanks" turned to postwar needs. In Alexandria, the local hospital—after "two years of the most severe trials" and "the trying days of the scourge of the Flu"—begged for donations to finance exterior painting, a new "X-Ray plant," new laundry machinery, and an ambulance. Similarly, an Alexandria children's home asked that the "little ones be remembered" during the holidays.[58]

Echoing the formality of the American president's annual Thanksgiving proclamation, in 1919 the governor of Virginia tailored his official proclamation in thanks "for the return of our sons from overseas," while recognizing that other thoughts would "turn in grateful memory to our immortal dead who sleep on the battle fields of France."[59]

Christmas in Wartime

> The Christmas which we experienced in the Base Hospital at Camp Lee, Virginia, in the year 1918, will not be forgotten. It is my earnest wish that we all might "carry on" our memories of that Christmas as we knew it here.
> —*Lest We Forget*, Base Hospital, Camp Lee 1919[60]

During the two-year war, Christmas served as the catalyst and focus of thousands of Virginia knitters. As part of the holiday's giving spirit, in 1917, Richmond women shipped 450 Christmas stockings to their sons and husbands serving abroad in the Richmond Light Infantry Blues.[61] Most Virginia communities sent dozens if not hundreds of "Christmas boxes" to the troops abroad.[62] The "housewives" of Goochland County put so much effort into their gifts for soldiers that they planned to exhibit samples at the Virginia state fair. Unfortunately, the fair was canceled that year due to the influenza epidemic.[63] In Bruton Parish Church, located in

Williamsburg, the local children gave up their own tree and sweets so that the money could be sent to a "fund for the suffering children of Europe."[64]

Soldiers in the trenches and front line hospital wards also celebrated the December holiday. At Richmond's own Base Hospital 45, established in Toul, France, nurses and patients hung streamers and flags, placed candles, erected trees, and even put up electric lights. Creatively placed clocks and curtains helped make the medical setting feel more like home. In one scrapbook photograph, an anemic pine tree is laden with tinsel or popcorn and a handful of ornaments, while an American flag is placed within a series of individual boughs that were attached to the wall. An unidentified object sits at the end of a bed; it looks like a toy drum but, given the setting, I could not help but wonder if it were a decorated chamber pot.[65] These decorations were not left to chance. The head of the hospital, Richmond native Lieutenant Colonel Stuart McGuire, ordered each of the 85 wards to erect a tree and promised a prize to the best-decorated one.[66] On December 24, 1917, nurses at the hospital filled 1600 pairs of woolen

A Christmas card featuring seasonal decorations at a Base Hospital No. 45 Ward in Toul, France, December 1918. Most of the medical personnel at this hospital were from Richmond (Virginia Historical Society, Mss1.B6696a25).

socks with cookies, candy, and cigarettes, and distributed them to their military patients. Some of these treats were sent by the Equal Suffrage League of Richmond.[67] The hospital also hosted parties on Christmas Eve and provided a turkey dinner the next day.[68]

One year later, more than a month after the Armistice, in nearby Cusy, France, the 305th Detachment enjoyed a lavish feast even while they impatiently waited to go home. It included both a turkey and a chicken as well as sides (mashed potatoes, olives, bread, and peas), fruits (grapes, apples, and mandarins), American dessert (nut fudge), and a traditional French dessert (Roquefort and Swiss cheese). The meal was accompanied by a choice of beverages (coffee, white wine, red wine) and concluded with cigars or cigarettes.[69]

Virginians back home, at Camp Lee, were still in active service in December 1918. In an effort to "bring Yuletide cheer" in order to "make the boys forget for the moment the monotony of life in a military camp" domestic welfare workers decorated the camp's base hospital in holiday adornment.[70] A Christmas tree was erected in the building of the Jewish Welfare Board, oddly enough, while the hospital mess officer dressed up as Santa Claus and a "trio of vaudeville funsters" sang for a large crowd of troops and patients.[71]

After the war ended, Christmas became an important catalyst for reaching out to World War I veterans. In December 1921, the American Legion Auxiliary (the women's branch of the group), gave holiday gifts to all 387 hospitalized veterans in Virginia.[72] Their Christmas dinner included local delicacies, like oyster stew and oysterettes, as well as mincemeat pie and raisin cake. As a nod of appreciation to our Gallic ally they included "French peas" and "French Fruit salad" on the menu.[73]

Memorial Day

> Memorial Day was established to bring to our minds afresh each year the heroic dead to whom the preservation of the Union was due. We add to it now [1919] the memory of the heroic dead of an undivided country who laid down their lives for liberty and righteousness.
> —Secretary of War Newton D. Baker, May 30, 1919[74]

There is one last, obvious, American holiday that honored World War I veterans: Memorial Day. Originating after the end of the Civil War and first referred to as "Decoration Day," this May holiday honors the veterans who lost their lives serving their country. On May 26, 1919, Richmond

Memorial Service

to the

Soldier, Sailor, Marine and Aviator

DEAD

of the

CITY OF RICHMOND

Committee on the Service

REV. J. J. GRAVATT, D. D., *Chairman*
President of the Ministerial Union

RABBI E. N. CALISCH, PH. D.
Rabbi of Beth Ahabah

RT. REV. D. J. O'CONNELL, D. D.
Bishop Catholic Diocese of Virginia

CITY AUDITORIUM
JUNE 29, 1919
4:30 P. M.

WHITTET & SHEPPERSON, PRINTERS, RICHMOND, VA.

Program from Memorial Day services in Richmond, June 1919 (Virginia Historical Society, D609.U6.R55.1919).

organized a "Jubilee Week" to welcome home "the men in gray" who fought in the Great War. In a "roll call" of the dead at the historic Hollywood Cemetery, Lieutenant Colonel Stuart McGuire read the names of the several thousand Virginia soldiers who had perished during the war.

Of course, few if any of the bodies of the Virginians who died in the World War were present. The process of returning them home involved a complicated logistical effort to exhume, identify, and ship bodies back home across the Atlantic. The veteran corpses on hand were, instead, those of the Confederate dead. Accordingly, McGuire assured his audience that the "18,000 heroes of the Confederacy who sleep in [the cemetery]" were not forgotten. During the ceremony, the grandchildren of these Confederate veterans placed a wreath on the pyramid that stood to mark the unidentified southern dead in the Civil War section.[75]

The focus on the Civil War dead during post–World War I Memorial Day celebrations set Virginia apart from many of the other American states after the Great War. In the decades after the end of the Civil War, women in various ladies' memorial associations played a large role in creating and supporting the myth of "The Lost Cause." These women's groups along with surviving veterans, recast the southern effort as a fight for secession and states' rights rather than to defend slavery. According to the calculations of Virginians, the South lost because of the Union's better access to resources and manpower.[76] In 1915, as Europe's intensive four-year war was just beginning, Virginia military personnel and civilians were commemorating the 50th anniversary of the end of the Civil War. In the South it was a bittersweet moment. Memorial associations and veterans crafted an interesting spin on their defeat. In their view, Confederate soldiers were doomed saviors and their wives were tragic martyrs. Thus it was only natural in Virginia that these aging local heroes would serve as inspirations for men heading off to fight in the "Great War." In 1916 an Alexandria reporter argued that although the ongoing world war was ruining European economies, they were not yet as hard hit as southerners during the American Civil War. The writer concluded that despite two years of deadly fighting and $50 billion worth of damage, "the sacrifices made thus far by European belligerents are only about half as great as those we [Confederates] made half a century ago."[77]

In the weeks immediately after America's entry into the European war, memories of the Civil War stood out prominently in the minds of Virginians. Many veterans were still alive (albeit elderly) and many of the middle-aged men in positions of authority had been children during the war, deeply influenced by their interactions with veterans.[78] With the amnesia of the passage of time, the veterans viewed war as an adventurous and romantic undertaking. Henry May called this older generation of warriors "the beleaguered defenders of nineteenth-century tradition ... the professional custodians of culture."[79] Judging from some contemporary accounts, it was as if Virginia sent two contingents to war in 1917: the future veterans of '17 and the old-school veterans of '61 (an expression used in Virginia newspapers to emphasize the year that their soldiers went to war, versus '65, the year that they surrendered).

6. Commemorations

The shared courage of soldiers from both wars was emphasized. On June 4, 1917, Richmond residents memorialized Jefferson Davis during an exercise hosted annually by the United Daughters of the Confederacy at the Davis Monument on Monument Avenue in Richmond. This front-page news item was accompanied by stories that threatened draft dodgers from the current war with prosecution and mentioned a visit to Arlington National Cemetery by President and Mrs. Wilson to decorate Confederate graves. In Virginia, these Confederate soldiers were placed on a metaphorical pedestal alongside their contemporary comrades.[80]

The linkages expanded greatly after the Armistice of the Great War. In a section of a World War I report from the mid-1920s titled "Service Flag," Goochland County began its overview with an account of the unveiling of a "handsome shaft erected by the United Daughters of the Confederacy (UDC) in memory of the heroes of 1861–1865." That same day, June 22, 1918, the members of the UDC presented a large service flag to four community members dressed symbolically as a Red Cross nurse, a soldier, a sailor, and a woman who personified America itself. The narrator of these wartime events commented with wonder that this event was "the first time in the history of the county [that] the white and colored races met together to celebrate with the same feeling of patriotism the honor done to their solider boys." I had to wonder whether the white author of this comment was on the same page as her African American neighbors when I read further and learned that the speaker that day was the grandson of Robert E. Lee (the commander of the Army of Northern Virginia) and that the grandchildren of other Confederate officers served as guests of honor.[81]

Similarly, the Hollywood Memorial Association in Richmond dedicated a section within its historic cemetery to Confederate officers in October 1918. This prominent spot, located several hundred yards past the entrance to this large, 135-acre burial ground, contains an ornate concrete arch adorned with an urn, the bore of a cannon, and a pole for one of the Confederate battle flags. About a dozen Civil War–era gravestones lie beyond the arch. It is worth remembering that Virginians were still fighting and dying in a horrific, global war that month.

Veterans Associations

> Fifty-five years ago we embarked on our duties as members of the A.E.F.... The loyalty to 45 is what has made this one of the few veterans' association that have met continuously. We ask those that can

> come, do so! And, those not able to attend, we ask God's blessing on them.
> —Commander J. Albert Hill, 1974.[82]

Virginia veterans of the Great War returned home from the war with uncertain futures. The modern-day complement of social services did not yet exist and many were without jobs. To cope with reentry into civilian life and continue their wartime friendships, World War I veterans began organizing annual reunions of their military units.

One active group was the doctors, nurses, and staff members who worked abroad at Base Hospital 45 in Toul, France. On January 18, 1919, the officers received orders to return home, the nurses sailed home on March 3, and the remainder of the staff left France on April 9.[83] The entire unit was officially discharged on April 19, 1919.[84] Within two years, some of the former staff members suggested the idea of a veterans' association, and a reunion was arranged for February 28, 1921. The surviving members of the unit held a banquet at the Hotel Richmond (a stately hotel built in 1904, today used as an office building), at which they decided to form a permanent association.[85]

Dr. McGuire, the former head of the hospital, was appointed the honorary commander of the association for life by his former staff. One member accurately predicted, "As the years go by the association will mean more and more to each of its members, for in it are friendships, formed during the stress of war, which can never be replaced."[86] Over the next five decades, the Base Hospital 45 Veterans' Association met annually. Initially, their large reunions were held in fancy hotels with lavish dinners and memorial events in nearby cemeteries. The lectures that accompanied the meals focused on the work and legacy of the very successful hospital. Dr. McGuire and his wife, Ruth Robertson, who was the head nurse at the hospital, led the commemorative events until poor health forced him to pass the baton to a colleague. Of course, by the 1950s, the veterans were aging: Dr. McGuire had passed in 1948, and the annual speeches drifted further and further away from the hospital itself. In 1956, a particularly off-topic and long-winded speaker shared a rambling historic overview about "Anglo Saxon ideals" that began with 16th-century Spaniards and only made it, chronologically, up to a late-18th-century French academy before briefly referring to a Richmond doctor who may have inspired the creation of the Medical College of Virginia.[87] These last years of the formal veterans' association were drastically different from the original focus that converted an abandoned French infantry barracks in Toul into a 2300-bed, 85-ward modern hospital, complete with an X-ray department, laboratory, three operating rooms, and a morgue. The last entry in the guest book used during the annual reunions, filled with hundreds of previous signatures, is dated February 27, 1961, with an illegible line that looks like the shaky handwriting of a very elderly visitor.[88] The last signatory was also most probably the donor of the guest book to the Virginia Historical Society, preserving the paper trail of a once very active group.

Besides the active veterans of Base Hospital 45, other former units reconstituted themselves back home in Virginia to a lesser degree. The 80th Infantry Division created many homecoming events. Organized on August 5, 1917, at Camp Lee, the 80th Division consisted of men from Virginia as well as Pennsylvania and West Virginia. Nicknamed the "Blue Ridge Division," it adopted an insignia with three blue mountain peaks (symbolizing each of the states) and the Latin motto *Vis Montium* (Strength of the Mountains). The 80th Division shipped out to France, with 23,000 soldiers, on June 8, 1918, and returned a little over a year later, on June 26, 1919. During the fall of 1918 it participated in the Somme and Meuse Argonne offensives.[89] Men such as Sergeant Hurshel Tilson Chesser, from Scott County, fought in multiple battles that helped turned the tide of the war. Sergeant Chesser served in Company K, 317th Infantry Regiment in the Meuse Argonne offensive and the Battle of Saint-Mihiel. He served in one of four infantry regiments within the 80th, each part of a different brigade. The brigades (such as the 155th, 159th, and 160th) were supported by a remount depot, a field signal battalion, an engineers regiment, field artillery, and division trains (which provided supplies, military police, trucks, engineers, and sanitation equipment).[90] This complex order of battle indicates the complexity of an army division's structure and the final challenges of demobilizing tens of thousands of soldiers.

Two decades later, a Virginian, Major General George Hairston Jamerson, of Martinsville, was elected national commander of the 80th Division Veterans' Association (1936–1938). During the war he had commanded the 317th Regiment and, later, was promoted to the rank of brigadier general and commanded the 159th Infantry Brigade. After the war he remained in the army for decades until he retired in 1933 and moved to Richmond.

As veterans of all ranks and divisions aged, their numbers slowly declined. After World War II, new members joined the veterans groups of historic units such as the 80th. The last surviving American "doughboy," Frank Buckles, from West Virginia, died in 2011, thereby breaking the first-person connection to men and women who served in the Great War.

Centennial Celebrations

> [The people who lived under the shadow of war] "construct[ed] a mythic version of the events of 1914–18 from a complex mixture of fact, wishful thinking, half-truth, and outright invention, and express[ed] that version in novel and play, in bronze and stone, in reunion and commemoration, in song and advertisement."
> —Jonathan L. Vance, *Death So Noble*, 2001[91]

On the one hundredth anniversary of World War I, Americans—including Virginians—continue to organize commemorative events to return the conflict to the attention of a modern-day audience. At the beginning of 2013, President Obama established the World War I Centennial Commission, "a commission to ensure a suitable observance of the centennial of World War, to provide for the designation of memorials to the service members of the United States Armed Forces in World War I, and for other purposes."[92] One of the goals was to construct an official World War I memorial in Washington, D.C. Eventually it was decided to remodel Pershing Park, a war memorial created in 1981 to honor General John J. Pershing's role in World War I. The national World War I Centennial Commission hopes to raise $35 million to install a newly designed landscape to be titled "The Weight of Sacrifice."[93]

As the war's centennial began Virginia was just starting to contemplate ways to commemorate the Great War. In 2014, the commonwealth organized a World War I committee, which was tasked with exploring commemorative options and serving as a clearinghouse for the collection and dissemination of information about events commemorating the centennial of the World War.[94] I joined this statewide committee in 2015 and promptly volunteered to curate Virginia's World War I pages on the national centennial commission website (www.worldwar1centennial.org).[95] As part of this effort, I created a map of "sites to visit," and over the next year I visited each of them. They ranged from libraries (The Woodrow Wilson Presidential Library) to traditional military museums (The Virginia War Memorial, which designed several exhibit cases dedicated to World War I between 2014 and 2018) and from active military bases (Fort Lee in Petersburg) to outdoor sites (the Carillon, the state's official World War I memorial). Virginians living near these sites were probably well aware of their region's contributions to World War I. Despite this plethora of historic sites, I wondered how many local stories about sacrifice and service during the Great War had been forgotten.

In 2014 I began a multiyear quest to locate memorials to the Great

War in communities across the state. With the help of many individuals, I began to build a model of Virginia's diverse contributions, one town or city at a time. Alongside my memorial hunt, I visited museums and historical societies that were displaying artifacts used by and sharing stories about local residents during the war. Some of these exhibit sites were expected: museums dedicated to the history of warfare or individuals who served large roles (such as the Woodrow Wilson Museum and Library in Staunton, Virginia) or institutions that hosted exhibitions and lectures about the Great War (such as the MacArthur Memorial in Norfolk). Several Virginia military organizations planned events at which honor guards paid tribute to the long-dead veterans and speeches recognized the recipients of medals of honor from the conflict. But I also found intriguing commemorative remnants from unexpected quarters: A high school student in Abingdon donned an all-white suit to depict Hubert Hagy, who had died in France after he was wounded in battle, in a midsummer "spirit

Local high school student Kanin Clark portraying Washington County veteran Hubert R. Hagy at his gravesite in 2016. The Historical Society of Washington County conducts a living history tour of Abingdon's historic Sinking Spring Cemetery each summer, with volunteer reenactors portraying "spirits" of various persons buried there (photograph by Charlie Barnette).

walk" in a local cemetery. Another unexpected commemorative celebration was the Virginia International Tattoo, an annual music festival held in Norfolk that features military bands. A "tattoo" is an historic Dutch term that means "turn off the taps" and centuries ago signaled the end of an evening of drinking for soldiers.[96] In 2017, the theme of the 21st season of the Virginia International Tattoo was "Over There: 100 Years of America and Its Allies." The performers also performed a special tribute in honor of the one hundredth anniversary of the founding of Naval Station Norfolk.[97]

Dozens of localities across Virginia have similarly interesting ceremonies planned to mark the anniversary of the start (April 6, 2017) and end (November 11, 2018) of the global hostilities. This book went to press just as Virginia commemorated the anniversary of President Wilson's war resolution on April 6, 1917. The event, held exactly one century later, featured political dignitaries including Governor Terry McAuliffe, Major General Timothy P. Williams (Virginia's adjutant general), and Jaime Areizaga-Soto (deputy secretary of veterans and defense affairs). I was selected as the keynote speaker and focused on what Virginians were doing during that crucial week, Sunday, April 1, through Saturday, April 6, 1917. Over 150 people attended the ceremony at the cavernous base of Virginia's official World War I memorial, the Carillon. The master of ceremonies was Delegate Kirk Cox, the chair of the official Virginia World War I and World War II Commemoration Commission.[98] An important corollary to the speeches was a variety of exhibitions hosted that morning in the Carillon, including a student art contest sponsored by the Virginia War Memorial, artifacts displayed by descendants of World War I veterans, and replica artifacts created by a 3-D printer at the Virginia Commonwealth University Virtual Curation Laboratory. The curation of existing and production of new forms of commemorative artifacts from the war are important steps in remembering the role of Virginians in the Great War. Parked outside that day was a more portable exhibition, housed in a trailer that toured throughout the state. Titled "Profiles of Honor," the mobile exhibition featured additional artifacts, biographical vignettes, and a small recording studio and scanner so that descendants could share memories and copies of papers from their relatives' World War I service.

This symbolic event, held at the official state memorial and overseen by the political leader of the state, was one of dozens of commemorative ceremonies that spring. The Newman Library at Virginia Tech, hosted an exhibition titled "Stories from the Great War: VPI Men in Service of Their Country, 1917–1918." This display focused on the lives of nine (out of over a thousand) alumni who fought on the western front.⁹⁹ This brick-and-mortar exhibit was accompanied by a broader initiative created by E. Thomas Ewing (professor of history, Virginia Tech) that focused on "VPI in World War One" and revolved around an online database containing biographies of many of the thousand-plus Virginia Tech alumni who served in the war.¹⁰⁰

At other college campuses, senior seminars and advanced methodological courses focused on the history of the World War. In the spring of 2016, I visited a history class taught by Professor Warren Hofstra, a colleague at Shenandoah University. In honor of the upcoming centennial he instructed his students to pick a war-related topic and investigate the local efforts on that subject. Similar to the goal of this book, he wanted to teach broader themes—such as women's roles in early 20th-century America and economic trends—from a grassroots perspective. Taken together, the local activities that his students uncovered—ranging from the sale of Liberty Bonds to help finance the war to the initiatives of junior Red Cross nurses who sponsored wellness campaigns—contributed to Virginia's wartime efforts. Dozens of other faculty at Virginia colleges and universities, such as Old Dominion University and the University of Richmond, offered seminars that narrowed in on America's role in the war.

Other Virginia colleges and universities hosted blogs and websites to increase understanding of the state's role in the war. For example, Norfolk State University (NSU) created a blog called "World War I in Norfolk, Va.," which took a holistic approach to studying the impact of the Great War on the local community. Professor Stephanie Richmond worked with her students in History 380: U.S. Military History to post historical narratives, photographs, and biographies about civilian workers and Norfolk servicemen during the war.¹⁰¹ As with many of these exhibitions, digital and concrete, local libraries were integral to their success. In the case of the NSU project, the Slover Library and Norfolk Public Libraries provided assistance. A year earlier I came across a fascinating project hosted by the Handley Regional Library in Winchester.

Led by Gene Schultz, a local historian who was investigating Winchester's role during the war and his own family history, the Winchester Library began a project to relocate dozens of bronze medallions that were cast in the 1920s to honor Winchester soldiers. On Armistice Day 1924, 49 circular markers had been placed at the base of red oaks trees and dedicated to a Winchester or Frederick County soldier who died in the war.¹⁰² In a move copied by dozens of Virginia communities, a local street was renamed "Memorial Avenue" and served as the symbolic site for the tree planting. The plaques were embedded in the sidewalk just below each tree. Unfortunately, this curb-level placement led to car damage and loss over the years, and today none of the markers remain in place and only about a dozen have been relocated.

More than nine decades later, Schultz, a board member at the local historical society, set out to learn more about each of the 49 men memorialized. One was Solomon Johnson, a soldier in the 369th Infantry Regiment, an African American unit under French command that earned the moniker "Harlem Hellfighters." Johnson lost his life on October 2, 1918. He probably died of wounds that he received at the fight at Bellvue Signal Ridge or near Les Rosiers.[103] He was likely the first Winchester casualty of the war. Shultz also tracked down the descendants of Clifton A. Nelson, born in the South River section of Warren County. Nelson had been drafted at age 22 left his job as a teamster to join an African American unit led by a white officer. Remarkably, just days after his descendants visited the Handley Library in 2016 searching for information, Nelson's badly dented medallion was recovered. At some point it had been painted yellow to try to prevent car damage. The medallion included a star (symbolizing the gold star banner that families who lost a soldier hung in their homes), two olive branches (denoting peace), and the acronym "ALA" (American Library Association). Private Nelson died from disease while training at Camp Lee on October 10, 1918. His grand-nephew, Ronald Nelson, came to see and photograph the memorial. He served in the Vietnam War, continuing a multigenerational commitment by his family to serve in the U.S. military.[104]

The Virginia National Guard has also been very active in commemorating the one hundredth anniversary of its role in the war. Many of these actions revolve around obtaining or promoting pieces of material culture that were used during the conflict by the guard. Alexander F. Barnes, a retired guardsman and Virginia National Guard command historian, led the effort to recover World War I–era war trophy German cannons given to the United States by France in the 1920s—though you might not think that there would be a lot of century-old cannons lying around.

In 2016, however, just after the Fourth of July, Virginia National Guard soldiers recovered a German *Minenwerfer* ("mine thrower") that was given to the U.S. government by the French government in gratitude for the 29th Division's sacrifices in the Meuse Argonne offensive. The trench mortar had been displayed in front of the Petersburg National Guard armory for four decades. When the armory closed in the 1960s and later was renovated as a business, the mortar was lost. It turned up again at a local auction house, with no explanation for its whereabouts during the intervening decades. In 2016, a local law firm, the auction house, the U.S. Army Center of Military History, and some Virginia National Guard soldiers teamed up to retrieve, refurbish, and display the mortar. It was moved to the Virginia National Guard's Joint Force Headquarters in Staunton, where it will serve as a memorial. As retired guardsman Al Barnes explained to me, "It started as a 'National Guard' search but it morphed into a RAIDERS OF THE LOST ARTillery crusade—I want to see how many of the 43 I can either locate or determine were destroyed ... sort of a Cannon Quest."[105] In addition to these outdoor museums containing artifacts from the Great War, more formal exhibitions of material culture are planned in Virginia over the next few years.

The Library of Virginia plans to host an exhibition about the local effects of influenza, which hit Richmond and nearby Camp Lee hard in the winter of 1918. And in the spring of 2016 the MacArthur Memorial in

Virginia National Guardsmen recovering a German *Minenwerfer* near Petersburg on July 7, 2016. It was originally part of a two-cannon display at the Petersburg Armory, along with a German 105mm Howitzer that the Guard had previously recovered. It is scheduled for inclusion in a diorama at the National U.S. Army Museum near Fort Belvoir (photograph by Alexander F. Barnes).

Norfolk opened a more broadly focused exhibit titled "Over Here, Over There." This exhibit focused on the training of and campaigns fought by American soldiers as well as home front activities, including a look at local efforts in Hampton Roads and the founding of the Norfolk Naval Base.[106] The artifacts in this exhibit range from nationally distributed propaganda posters to a photograph of soldiers sterilizing uniforms of the 166th Infantry to remove pests and poison gas residues. Some of the artifacts on display at the Quartermaster Museum on the grounds of Fort Lee highlight the home-front actions during the war, such as women sewing commemorative pillowcases with red, white, and blue trim or embroidered handkerchiefs with poems about Camp Lee. Viewing these collections provides yet another layer of understanding of this chronologically distant yet important conflict.

Dozens of local historical societies have mounted smaller displays. For example, the city of Lynchburg focused on the role of its citizens during the war with the Lynchburg Museum System's exhibition titled "It Was My Privilege and My Duty: Lynchburg in World War I." Some of my favorite memorials are vitrine cases containing items of daily life from the period between 1917 and the early 1920s. These wartime objects were saved by grieving parents, love-sick soldiers, professional nurses, and other Virginians. Many of these objects include "trench art," keepsakes crafted by bored or recuperating soldiers consisting of bullets or artillery shells carved into jewelry or vases. Other treasures include personal belongings such as helmets and uniforms, often adorned with patches that tell the story of the soldier's duties and honors; embroidered handkerchiefs (sometimes with heart-wrenching lines like "remember me"); and photographs of soldiers in clean and well-pressed uniforms, clearly taken before they saw combat. For most Virginians, these are the objects that still matter today, the tangible remnants of their ancestors' service and their love for family and country.

To help locate these widely distributed exhibitions, a retired National Guardsman and World War I historian, Alexander Barnes, developed a driving tour of World War I–related sites in the Old Dominion. His brochure guides drivers over hundreds of miles, from the Woodrow Wilson Presidential Library Foundation in Staunton to the U.S. Marine Corps Museum in Quantico. It includes small-scale museums that have First World War exhibits, like one for the 116th Infantry in Verona, and large-scale ones like the Virginia War Museum in Newport News.

Since I am writing this book in the age of the Internet, my discussion of commemorative events would be incomplete if I did not discuss efforts to promote the centennial on social media. Several researchers have realized that "the materiality of the medium [the Internet] exercises a profound impact on the collective image of the Great War."[107] These "desktop historians" are heavily involved in curating modern memories of the war. In 2014, several members of Virginia's then informal World War I Committee created a Facebook page to share their ideas with a broader audience. Within a year there were over five hundred likes and regular comments and feedback on popular posts. Later, when the World War I Committee joined with the World War II Commission in 2016, some of the original committee members branched off and created a second "Virginia in the Great War" Facebook page. That page quickly attained over one hundred likes.

Throughout 2017 and 2018 I will leverage the power of social media to share information about Virginians in the Great War with a broader audience. As mentioned earlier, in 2014 I had established a website to share information about the World War I memorials found in almost every city or county in the commonwealth (http://www.lynnrainville.org/ww1-memorials/index). Many online audiences no longer browse websites directly, so I will disseminate photographs and research about the monuments via Facebook and Pinterest (a board titled "World War I Memorials in Virginia"). A decade from now, these "apps" might be obsolete, but for now they serve the purpose of attracting attention to a more permanent website.

Outreach through social media and exhibitions may not reach one of the most important audiences: young adults and children. In Virginia schools, World War I gets short shrift in the state-mandated Standards of Learning (SOL). The Virginia SOLs establish minimum expectations for what students should know at each grade level in a wide range of subjects. The "History & Social Science" category covers topics related to history, geography, civics, and economics. The end goal is to "prepare students for informed participation in shaping the nation's future."[108] The Great War and its repercussions are required reading at only a handful of points in the public school curriculum. One example is students being asked to demonstrate the ability to "evaluate United States involvement in World War I, including Wilson's Fourteen Points, the Treaty of Versailles, and the national debate over treaty ratification and the League of Nations."[109] In Virginia, middle-school students are expected to "explain the reasons for the United States' involvement in World War I and its international leadership role at the conclusion of the war."[110] Finally, in world geography, Virginia students have to demonstrate the worldwide impact of the war. However, none of the issues relate specifically to events in the United States.[111] None of these "standards" relate to home-front activities or, unfortunately, any of the major American battles fought along the western front.

The goal of integrating world affairs into the classroom is always challenging, but ideally it should not occur at the expense of forgetting local contributions. Since the end of the Great War, teachers have worked to explain the event to their students. In Alexandria, the second Armistice Day, November 11, 1920, was observed with "special exercises."[112] Other postwar teachers struggled to interpret the changed European geography with outdated maps. These educators warned, that they could not explain to their students "the failure of Gallipoli campaign ... [or] the reason for the location Verdun" until they received updated maps.[113] We cannot expect 21st-century students to care much about the subject if it is introduced in fourth grade and then not mentioned again until a short lecture in world geography class years later. Nor can we expect students to remain interested in the topic of the Great War if their parents and neighbors don't reinforce the topic. Well-written and engaging children's books can also help inspire young readers to want to visit historic sites to learn more about a topic. So far I have located only two books for children that focus on Virginia's role in the war. One focuses on Edith Wilson and the herd of sheep that she put to work on the White House lawn to raise money for the war effort. The other is an independently published book called *Jad and Old Ananias*. While the title may seem a bit misleading, the short story features Jad, a boy from Westmoreland County Virginia, who likes to explore a nearby beach. There he meets "Old Ananias," an African American veteran from World War I who tells the boy about his time in the French trenches. Jad decides to mount a publicity campaign to share Ananias's story far and wide. At one point his friends develop a rhyming song about the veteran, set to the beat of a double Dutch jump rope tune. In the book, the veteran's story successfully reaches a wide audience, even leading to an appearance on the Oprah Show. Some of the details suggested that this was based on a true story so I excitedly looked into a black World War I veteran named Ananias from Virginia. The tale was based on a true story, but the real-life inspiration was local World War II veteran Willie Thompson.[114]

In fact, this book reminded me of another glaring gap in our understanding of World War I: that of the contributions of African American soldiers and the segregated conditions at every step of their service. When I started this research, I knew that the American military was segregated up until 1948, but I had not fully realized that these racial separations occurred at all levels and all times: during training camp, on ships traveling to and from Europe, in separate units on the battlefield, different hospital wards for the injured, and in the welcome home parades, celebrations, and memorials upon their return. When they crafted mortuary memorials for the soldiers who did not come back, most Virginia towns placed the names of black soldiers at the bottom of an otherwise alphabetical list of the dead. Frequently this section is captioned "colored."

As the centennial approached, some southern communities began to question this century-old practice of segregating the names of the dead on World War I memorials. This led to a series of controversies over

A children's book that discusses the wartime contributions of the First Lady, Edith Wilson, and the White House's herd of sheep. Mrs. Wilson was born and raised in Wytheville, Virginia.

whether to recast the metal plaques (combining black and white names into one alphabetical list), to add explanatory language elsewhere on the memorial (to call out the racism inherent in the Jim Crow South), or to erect separate memorials to African American troops. In 2016, community members in Arlington raised the question of what to do with their memorial, located in the Clarendon neighborhood. Their bronze plaque lists ten names of army and navy personnel who died during the war and then, at the bottom after a small space, the names of two African American soldiers. Both the NAACP and some local officials agree that a new plaque should be commissioned to integrate the list of names.[115] But there is a surprising road block: a Virginia law that prevents changes to war memorials after they are erected.[116] The differing public opinions about this statute in communities throughout the state do not provide any clear resolutions.

Just as it did a century ago, the Commonwealth of Virginia has created a bureaucracy to manage the commemoration of the Great War. In the 1920s, the governor appointed Arthur Kyle Davis to head up the Virginia War History Commission. Davis was given a monthly budget, and with those funds he hired dozens of personnel and recruited over a hundred commission chairs from many of Virginia's cities and counties. He published seven volumes in an effort to summarize these findings. In 2014, the Virginia General Assembly authorized a World War I Centennial Committee.[117] I was on an early version of this committee, accompanied by legislators, museum professionals, college professors, and representatives from the national World War I Commission. We arranged ourselves into specialized subcommittees with jurisdictions from educational programming to public events and from marketing to fund-raising. I was placed in charge of the Virginia page on the national World War I centennial website (a year later this page was taken down and folded into the Virginia tourism site). Over the next two years we met quarterly and began to compile suggestions for raising awareness about the upcoming centennial and appropriate ways to commemorate Virginia's role in the war. In 2016, on the eve of commemorative dates (such as April 6, 2017), the committee was combined with a preexisting World War II Commission. The latter was created in 2014 to honor the 75th anniversary, in 2016, of the United States' entry into that conflict. The rationale for combining the two global wars included explanations such as "World War I is a forgotten war, yet it was really the first of two chapters, World War II being the second" and that by combining the two the group members could merge resources and avoid an overlap in fund-raising.

I was disappointed that World War I could not stand on its own legislative-supported legs as the basis for a free-standing commission. I learned belatedly that committees are mostly honorific and lack budgets, whereas commissions are provided funding and staff support. After two years of working with an all-volunteer group trying to organize large-scale commemorative events, several of us welcomed the commission status but regretted the necessity of combining two distinct wars. With two important events to focus on, the commission established a new set of objectives, and some of the original committee members splintered off into a separate group to focus more narrowly on sharing historic information about Virginia's role in the Great War.[118] Several of these individuals also served a nonprofit corporation called "Virginia World War One Commemoration Foundation," incorporated on August 25, 2015. The all-volunteer World War I Committee merged with this more formal, and funded, commission in 2016.

Despite all of the 21st-century commemorative efforts discussed here—exhibitions, online databases, reinstalled statues, and academic courses—the success or failure of raising awareness in Virginia about the role of its citizens in the Great War may hinge on other events. I am reminded of the 1990s, when film adaptations from books such as Thomas Keneally's *Schindler's Ark* (which was met with critical acclaim on the big screen as *Schindler's List*, directed by Steven Spielberg, based on the screenplay by Steven Zaillian) and Stephen Ambrose's *Band of Brothers* (made into an HBO TV series) introduced a new generation to the historic efforts of World War II veterans. And while the First World War has been memorialized in American films, few of these once-popular titles remain well known today: *The Big Parade* (1925), *All Quiet on the Western Front* (winner of the 1930 Academy Awards for Best Director and Outstanding Production), and *Sergeant York* (featuring Gary Cooper, whose performance won him the award for Best Actor). As this book goes to press there are a handful of potential World War I blockbusters set to hit theaters in 2017–2018: *Sgt. Stubby: An American Hero* (an animated film about a stray dog who befriends an American doughboy during the war) and *Wonder Woman* (which places the eponymous heroine in World War I, helping an American pilot to end the war). PBS also produced a series titled *The Great War*, which aired in three parts in April 2017.[119] Whether these films are well received and result in greater awareness and interest in the war remains to be seen.

Epilogue

War Commission Series (1920s)

If I had realized the fate of the seven-volume book series about Virginia and its role in World War I, I might never have begun this project. Just years after that war ended, when I would have expected interest to be at its apex, the governor of Virginia formed a War History Commission to document the history of Virginians at war. However, even at such a timely moment, the head of the commission, Arthur Kyle Davis, had a difficult time getting ex-servicemen to fill out a four-page questionnaire about their time in the war. To efficiently retrieve information from a wide variety of servicemen, Davis encouraged individual counties and cities to appoint commissioners to oversee the survey efforts locally.

Davis had great difficulty finding individuals willing to serve, and those who did contribute to the effort encountered low participation rates within their communities. In tallying the statewide results, Davis concluded that "Practically nothing has been done in Amherst," while other county-based officers gave up "in discouragement" after failing to find support or cooperation for their efforts.[1] In Charlotte County, the War Commission report concluded that the local chair was "on the defensive, interpreting every suggestion from this office as an insult, either to his intelligence or to his ability as a chairman." The end result was that "nothing is being done" and the commissioner expressed the hope that the chair be removed from office.[2]

This Book (2017)

My hope is that this book will serve as a reminder of the contributions of Virginians to all aspects of wartime service. When I first became involved in a World War I cemetery project in 2014, I realized that I knew very little about the war and even less about Virginia's role in it. The more I looked, the more roles I found in which Virginia and Virginians were involved during the Great War. I wanted to increase awareness about events and people quickly being forgotten. Every public lecture that I have given so far on this topic encourages at least one, and usually several, members of the audience to come up to me afterwards with their family or hometown story of a World War I veteran. As a historian with decades of experience working in museums and designing exhibitions, I encourage these memory keepers to donate copies of their family photographs or letters to local historical societies or state-level repositories. By making this material more widely accessible, the stories of the Virginia men, women, and children during the Great War can be passed down to future generations.

This approach won't help a fifth grader in Virginia pass his or her SOL test (which requires knowledge of more esoteric, synthetic, and internationally focused facts), but it may be more enticing and, in the end, engender a greater passion about the connection between local and national history. One historian observed that today Americans know less and less about "history" (defined as dates and facts about worldwide events and people), but they know more about multiple generations within their own families than ever before. This change has come about, in part, because of online databases that provide relatively easy and inexpensive access to genealogical information. In the past decade several companies have expanded exponentially to meet the desire of many Americans to learn more about their family trees (Ancestry.com, FamilyHistorySearch.com, FindMyPast.com) or their ancestors, final resting places (BillionGraves.com, FindAGrave.com). Finding out about a relative's military service (which can be found on Fold3.com, or Militaryindexes.com) should be an important part of this quest.

At the very least, all residents of Virginia can take a moment to locate their nearest World War I memorial. As my multiyear project has demonstrated, there are hundreds of these statues, plaques, and memorial buildings in the Old Dominion. Some are hidden in plain sight, like the Roanoke Memorial Bridge that thousands of cars drive over each day. But I doubt many drivers stop to view the ornate iron plaques that are mounted on several of the concrete pillars. One begins with the dates 1917 and 1918 and continues with the eloquent homage, "They have crossed the river. Now they rest in the shade of the trees." Below this quote, a variation on Thomas J. "Stonewall" Jackson's last words, is a list of Virginians who died during the war. The City of Roanoke added its seal at the top and decorated the edges of the curved plaque with a beautiful array of flowers, stars, geometric designs, and even snakes. To balance the Civil War–era quote at the top, the city included a Woodrow Wilson quote at the bottom: "In a righteous cause they have won immortal glory, and have nobly served their nation in serving mankind."

A "farmerette" reenactor, Anna Kiefer, standing next to the Charles Keck statue *Liberty*. This Harrisonburg memorial reads, "They tasted death in youth that liberty might grow old" (photograph by Carole Nash, 2016).

To further such a possible trend, I organized an event to call attention to these forgotten memorials in the heavily biased Civil War landscape of the Old Dominion. On a Saturday in September 2016, I asked six World War I reenactors to stand guard at memorials throughout the state. I included male soldiers as well as female farmerettes. One woman stood at the base of the *Liberty* statue in Staunton, dressed in an authentic (and hot) woolen overshirt, pants, and carrying an old hoe. She represented the thousands of Virginia women who worked in the fields while their fathers, husbands, and brothers were sent off to train in the Virginia camps and then fight abroad. At the official state memorial, the Byrd Park Carillon, a soldier in his "kit" worn by a member of the AEF infantry, carrying a faux rifle, was joined by a Red Cross nurse. Other obelisks and historic markers were "guarded" by modern-day Virginians wearing replica uniforms. Many passersby honked, waved, and some stopped to pick up flyers that encouraged them to locate additional memorials in their communities and learn more about the local men and women who served. It is my hope that through efforts like this World War I, and Virginia's significant role in it, will not remain forgotten much longer.

Chapter Notes

Preface

1. "Assassins Murder Heir to Austrian Throne: His Wife Also Slain," *Richmond Times-Dispatch*, June 29, 1914, 1–2.
2. "Sad Case of the Minister to Austria," *Richmond Times*, August 6, 1899, 7; "The Malediction that Promised Wreckage of the Hapsburg Imperial Dynasty," *Richmond Times*, July 26, 1914, 48; "News and Gossip from Foreign Courts and Capitals," *Richmond Times*, October 19, 1902, 21–30. The German-language *Richmonder Anzeiger* had been published since at least 1858.
3. John Lewis-Stempel, "The Killing of Franz Ferdinand: A Single Shot That Unleashed Hell on Earth," *Express*, March 16, 2014, www.express.co.uk/news/world-war-1/465127/The-killing-of-Franz-Ferdinand-The-single-shot-that-unleashed-hell-on-earth.
4. *Alexandria Gazette*, June 29, June 30; *Richmond Times-Dispatch* June 29 and June 30.
5. While there is no agreement among historians as to the definition of the term "total war," here I borrow from definitions by Förster and Nagler in *On the Road to Total War* and by Maureen Healy in *Vienna and the Fall of the Habsburg Empire*. In his article "Total War," Imlay discusses the lack of consensus on the use of the term.

Chapter 1

1. "Defense Council to Aid Sale of Liberty Bonds," *Richmond Times-Dispatch*, May 17, 1917, 3.
2. Peter T. Kilborn, "U.S. Turns into Debtor Nation," *New York Times*, September 17, 1985. See also Sharrer, "Let's Celebrate," 1.
3. *Hamilton Enterprise*, August 7, 1914. See also Terry Sharrer, "Loudoun Chronology," unpublished MS.
4. Bennett, "Wheat and War," 82.
5. "Blacksburg," *Richmond Times-Dispatch*, June 8, 1913, 11.
6. Sharrer, "Let's Celebrate," 2.
7. *Loudoun Mirror*, 1917, quoted in Sharrer, "Let's Celebrate," 1.
8. U.S. Department of Agriculture, *Usual Planting and Harvesting Dates*, 5.
9. A. K. Davis, "Loudoun County," in *Virginia Communities in War Time*, 7:87.
10. Terry Sharrer notes, Extension Reports.
11. A. K. Davis, "Newport News," in *Virginia Communities in War Time*, 7:149. The Newport News cannery was located at 39th and Washington Streets.
12. "Virginia Asks for Aid in Maintaining Roads," *Richmond Times-Dispatch*, July 22, 1918, 3.
13. Sharrer, "Loudoun Chronology." Different countries modified these lyrics. For example, an Australian soldier cited other parts of the Kaiser's anatomy. Gammage, *The Broken Years*, 25.
14. "Defense Council to Aid Sale of Liberty Bonds," *Richmond Times-Dispatch*, May 17, 1917, 1, 3.
15. April 18, 1917, photograph by Rufus W. Holsinger, University of Virginia Library, Holsinger Studio Collection Call no. MSS 9862, negative X05030B1.
16. Lucy Ashton Faulkner of Boydton to her son, Rev. Thomas Green Faulkner, Faulkner Papers, Virginia Historical Society (hereafter VHS), Mss 1 F2735 b, section 3, folder 8, files 101–12.

215

17. "President Wilson Asks That Every School Will Have a Regiment of Boys and Girls in the U.S. Volunteer War-Garden Army," *Moderator-Topics*, March 9, 1918, 3.
18. National Emergency Food Garden Commission, press release, VHS, Mss1W22960 4,472–4481, section 27, Ware Family Papers.
19. Lokke, "The Food Administration Papers for the State of Virginia in the National Archives," 221.
20. "School Children Will Help in Garden Work," *Richmond Times-Dispatch*, March 19, 1918, 10.
21. "School Garden Armies: A Word to the Richmond Recruits, What the Army Means Now and Hereafter," *Richmond Times-Dispatch*, May 13, 1918, 5.
22. "Daylight," National Emergency Food Garden Commission press release, VHS, Mss1W22960 4,472–4481, section 27, Ware Family Papers.
23. *Richmond Times-Dispatch*, June 20, 1918, 6.
24. Lucy Ashton Faulkner to her daughter, February 15, 1918, Faulkner Papers, VHS, Mss 1 F2735 b, section 3, folder 8, files 101–12.
25. U.S. Department of Agriculture, U.S. Food Administration, "Have You Eaten Your Pound of Potatoes Today? Save Wheat By Eating Potatoes," Special Collections, USDA National Agricultural Library, https://www.nal.usda.gov/exhibits/speccoll/items/show/230.
26. *Clinch Valley News*, December 20, 1918, 3. Such messages were commonly found in newspapers across the country, e.g., *St. Martinsville Weekly Messenger*, July 6, 1918, 2.
27. Janney and Janney, *A Medieval Virginia Town, 1914–1918*. Cornwell's was a grocery in Purcellville.
28. Poster created by Cushman Parker in 1917, Library of Congress, http://www.loc.gov/pictures/item/2002712335.
29. U.S. Department of Agriculture, "Eat More Cottage Cheese," Special Collections, USDA National Agricultural Library, https://www.nal.usda.gov/exhibits/speccoll/items/show/221.
30. Warrenton Garden Club Receipts, VHS, call no. TX 715 W26.
31. *Richmond Times-Dispatch*, December 10, 1917, 6.
32. "Meatless Meal Plan Has Disadvantages," *Richmond Times-Dispatch*, July 1, 1919, 1.
33. Faulkner Papers, VHS, Mss IF 2735b, files 101–12.
34. Eggleston, "Supplement to Food Administration Papers."
35. "Lunchburg Popular," *Evening World*, August 29, 1918, 12.
36. A. K. Davis, "Lynchburg," in *Virginia Communities in War Time*, 7:122–23.
37. *Ibid.*, 121.
38. *Ibid.*, 124.
39. *Ibid.*, 125.
40. "Why Uncle Sam Selected Warren for Horse Raising," *Richmond Times-Dispatch*, March 11, 1917, 26.
41. *Equidae* is the taxonomic family that includes horses, mules, donkeys, and zebras. The term "equid" can be used to refer to any members of this family and will be used in this book on occasion instead of the more awkward term "horses and mules." Mules are produced when a male donkey is bred to a female horse and are often unable to reproduce.
42. Mark St. John Erickson, "World War I Horses," *Newport News Daily Press*, November 29, 2014.
43. Parker, "U.S. Cavalry Remount Program," 7.
44. "Henry of Navarre," National Museum of Racing and Hall of Fame, https://www.racingmuseum.org/hall-of-fame/henry-navarre.
45. "Horses to Be Improved," *New York Times*, June 8, 1919, 1.
46. "Horses for War Zone Are Uniformly Dark," *Charlottesville Daily Progress*, January 4, 1915.
47. Schwarzkopf, "The Changed Status of the Horse in War," 61.
48. Mark St. John Erickson, "Newport News Became a Springboard for WWI War Horses," *Newport News Daily Press*, December 4, 2016; Koenig, *The Fourth Horseman*.
49. A note in the Front Royal Remount Station file indicates that the stones had been sent to the Fort Robinson Museum in Nebraska. When I emailed the curator in the summer of 2016 about their fate she could find no evidence of their existence in the collection.
50. Catherine Christen, environmental historian, Smithsonian-Mason School of Conservation, personal communication with author, May 5, 2016.
51. Waterfront Lumber company supplied the wood.
52. Mark St. John Erickson, "World

War I Horses," *Newport News Daily Press,* November 29, 2014.

53. Bate, "Buying British Remounts in America," 27.

54. Koenig, *The Fourth Horseman,* 101.

55. *Ibid.,* 1–35.

56. *Ibid.,* 80–82.

57. *Ibid.,* 123.

58. *Ibid.,* 115–16.

59. *Ibid.,* 264–66.

60. Quoted in MacDonald, "Guncotton in France," 106.

61. W. Williams, *History of the Manufacture of Explosives,* 18–19.

62. *Ibid.,* 9.

63. Molineux, "Penniman and the Powder Plant Boom," 63.

64. *Ibid.,* 63.

65. *Newport News Daily Press,* cited in Molineux, "Penniman and the Powder Plant," 65.

66. Molineux, "Penniman and the Powder Plant Boom," 68.

67. "Wilmington Women Risked All in Ammunition Factory," StarNews Online, August 3, 2014, http://www.starnewsonline.com/news/20140803/wilmington-women-risked-all-in-ammunition-factory.

68. "Virginia Complimented on Its Work for Women," *Richmond Times-Dispatch,* November 8, 1918, 9; Molineux, "Penniman and the Powder Plant Boom," 66.

69. R. Thornton, *The Houses That Sears Built.* In March 2016, I located a Sears home from Penniman in Norfolk. "That Rascally Haskell," Sears Modern Homes, http://www.searshomes.org/index.php/tag/penniman-virginia/.

70. Sears Archives, http://www.searsarchives.com/homes/bydate.htm.

71. "Civic Movement for Better Homes," *Richmond Times-Dispatch,* July 9, 1922, 14.

72. Andre, *Draft Environmental Impact Statement,* 39.

73. *Hampton Roads Virginian Pilot,* December 21, 1922.

74. *Newport News Daily Press,* December 22, 1922.

75. Rosemary Thornton, Sears Modern Homes blog post, March 6, 2016, http://www.searshomes.org/index.php/2016/03/06/pottstown-and-penniman-and-more/.

76. *Richmond Times-Dispatch,* June 1938.

77. Crowell, *A History of the 313th Field Artillery,* 1–2.

78. *Ibid.,* 4.

79. *Ibid.,* 5.

80. *Ibid.,* 10–11.

81. *Ibid.,* 5.

82. "E. R. Wheatley," *University of Virginia Alumni News* 7, no. 1 (September 1918): 10–11.

83. Crouch, *First Flight,* 86.

84. Hennessy, "Men and Planes of World War I," 22.

85. J. McConnell, *Flying for France,* 54–55.

86. Kiffin Yates Rockwell memorial page on findagrave.com, http://www.findagrave.com/cgi-bin/fg.cgi?page=gr&GRid=7593262.

87. Mark St. John Erickson, "Aviation History Unfolded at Curtiss Flying School," December 29, 2013, *Newport News Daily Press,* http://articles.dailypress.com/2013-12-29/features/dp-nws-evg-curtiss-flying-school-20131229_1_glenn-curtiss-hampton-roads-newport-news-point.

88. Mark St. John Erickson, "Langley Field Founders Envisioned an Air Power Center Like No Other," *Newport News Daily Press,* April 18, 2016, http://www.dailypress.com/news/military/langley100/dp-langley-centennial-founding-20160417-story.html.

89. Quarstein, *World War I on the Virginia Peninsula,* 44.

90. Joe Cooper to his mother, Mrs. C. S. Cooper, in Malvern, Arkansas, September 27, 1918, Butler Center for Arkansas Studies, Central Arkansas Library System, BC.MSS.99.31.

91. Widely attributed to Collis P. Huntington and inscribed on a stone memorial at Newport News Shipbuilding Yard.

92. The first *Kearsarge* was built during the Civil War and destroyed in 1894. *Indianapolis Journal,* February 9, 1894, 1.

93. Quarstein, *World War I on the Virginia Peninsula,* 17.

94. Gordon Smith, "World War 1 at Sea: United States Navy," Naval History Homepage, http://www.naval-history.net/WW1NavyUS.htm.

95. *Journal of the American Society of Naval Engineers* 11 (1899), unpaginated advertisement location 1135 in a scanned version available through Hathi Trust.

96. U.S. Senate, *Naval Investigation,* 1634–42.

97. *Ibid.*

98. Paul Bean, "Profile of the USS Virginia," unpublished research, for the Virginia Historical Society webpage.

99. "Camilla Rickmers SS (1914–1917) Ticonderoga USS (+1918)," Wreck Site, http://wrecksite.eu/wreck.aspx?156893.

100. His next of kin was his sister, Mrs. Cashti Craft, who lived at 1344 43rd Street, Norfolk. McHenry, *U.S. World War I Naval Deaths, 1917–1919*.
101. 1900 U.S. Federal Census, Norfolk, Tanners Creek, District 0038, Household 769/875, roll 1719, 47a.
102. Quartermaster log, April 21, 1918, VHS, Mss 3M 4435a1 (Maui).
103. Quartermaster log, April 26, 1918, VHS, Mss 3M 4435a1 (Maui).
104. "Troops Reach 'Home,'" *Ogden Standard*, December 17, 1918, 8.
105. "Doggoned Determination," *Ocala Evening Star*, December 18, 1918, 1.
106. Mark St. John Erickson, "Daring German Sea Raiders Bring World War I to Hampton Roads," *Newport News Daily Press*, April 25, 2015, http://www.dailypress.com/features/history/dp-nws-world-war-1-german-sea-raiders-20150425-story.html.
107. Phyllis A. Hall, "The German Village at the Portsmouth Naval Shipyard," *Olde Times*, 5–7.
108. History of Naval Station Norfolk, Naval Station Norfolk, 1917–2017: 100 Years, http://www.nsnbg.com/editorial-content/history/.
109. "New U-Boat Foes Slide Down Ways," *Ocala Evening Star*, July 4, 1918, 2.
110. Ibid.
111. Ramsay, *Lusitania*, 169.
112. "Mr. Albert Lloyd Hopkins," The Lusitania Resource, http://www.rmslusitania.info/people/saloon/albert-hopkins/.
113. *Richmond Times-Dispatch*, August 13, 1915, 10.
114. Ibid.
115. *Richmond Times-Dispatch*, May 7, 1915, 6.

Chapter 2

1. Cramer, *Newton D. Baker*, 95.
2. Crowder, *Operations of the Selective Service System*, appendix, 396, table A.
3. *Richmond Times-Dispatch*, March 19, 1917, 1.
4. *Richmond Times-Dispatch*, March 27, 1917, 1.
5. *Richmond Times-Dispatch*, April 2, 1917, 1.
6. *Richmond Times-Dispatch*, April 4, 1917, 1.
7. *Richmond Times-Dispatch*, April 6, 1917, 1.
8. *Richmond Times-Dispatch*, April 7, 1917, 1.
9. A. K. Davis, "Scott County," in *Virginia Communities in War Time*, 7:503–5.
10. "President Calls America to Arms," *Richmond Times-Dispatch*, April 3, 1918, 2.
11. "Resolution Is Adopted by Congress," *Clinch Valley News*, April 6, 1917, 1.
12. Chambers, *To Raise an Army*, 129–131.
13. "Virginia Called on to Furnish 18,000 Men," *Richmond Times-Dispatch*, April 3, 1917, 5.
14. *Richmond Times-Dispatch*, July 20, 1917, 1.
15. Report of the Adjutant-General of Virginia, 1918, Part II: The Selective Service, VHS Collections, 6–7.
16. A. K. Davis, "Petersburg City, History," in *Virginia Communities in War Time*, 7:170–72.
17. *Richmond Times-Dispatch*, April 6, 1917, 3.
18. Selective Service Act, 65th Congress, first sess., Ch. 15, 1917, 76–83, available at http://www.legisworks.org/congress/65/publaw-12.pdf.
19. "U.S., World War I Draft Registration Cards, 1917–1918," ancestry.com, http://search.ancestry.com/search/db.aspx?dbid=6482.
20. "Five Myths about World War I," *Washington Post*, April 6, 2017.
21. Thanks to Dr. Terry Sharrer for the lead about Isaiah Ashby.
22. *Richmond Times-Dispatch*, August 16, 1918, 1.
23. Crowder, *Operations of the Selective Service System*, 212.
24. *Richmond Times-Dispatch*, April 7, 1917, 1.
25. Virginia War Commission Questionnaire, December 26, 1922, Library of Virginia, http://image.lva.virginia.gov/WWI/pages/001/0166.html. Private Isdell entered the 318th Infantry at Camp Lee on September 24, 1917. Before and after the war he worked as a fisherman.
26. Kennedy, *Over Here*, 168.
27. Newport News is not discussed in either Wilson, *New York and the First World War*, or Kennedy, *Over Here*.
28. Quarstein, *World War I on the Virginia Peninsula*, 8.
29. "Retreat, Hell! We Just Got Here," The American Legion, https://www.legion.org/stories/other/retreat-hell-we-just-got-here.

30. A. K. Davis, "Giles County," in *Virginia Communities in War Time*, 7:179.
31. Private McKnight T. Hudson, March 5, 1923, Virginia War Commission Questionnaire, Library of Virginia, http://image.lva.virginia.gov/WWI/pages/001/0161.html.
32. *Ibid.*
33. Harter, "A Soldier of Song in World War I," 103–5. This unit became the Virginia National Guard after 1916.
34. *Ibid.*, 106.
35. *Ibid.*, 107.
36. Sheet music in VHS Collections. Each was published in Virginia: "Come Boys..." in Richmond, "Soldier Boy" in Gladys "Somewhere in France..." in Roanoke. Entire books would be necessary to convey the musical history of African American jazz musicians during and after World War I.
37. Harter, "A Soldier of Song in World War I," 109–10.
38. *Ibid.*, 110.
39. *Ibid.*, 112–13.
40. Wayland, *Men of Mark and Representative Citizens*, 303.
41. "Rockingham County Virginia Tombstones by Cemetery," Heritage Museum, Harrisonburg-Rockingham Historical Society, http://www.heritagecenter.com/cemeteries/cem/cem221.html.
42. Percy Holladay diary, handwritten notes in a small booklet titled "Memorandum," VHS, Mss1 H7185h105, section 5.
43. Ferrell, *Collapse at Meuse-Argonne*.
44. I located Eugene Ragland's gravestone in St. Johns' Baptist Church Cemetery, Gordonsville.
45. "The University of Virginia and the World War," *Alumni Bulletin of the University of Virginia* 15, no. 1 (1922): 48.
46. *Richmond Times-Dispatch*, December 2, 1917, 8.
47. *Richmond Times-Dispatch*, April 7, 1917, 6.
48. University of Virginia *Alumni News*, September 1918.
49. *Alexandria Gazette*, October 3, 1917, 2.
50. A. K. Davis, "Rockbridge County History," in *Virginia Communities in War Time*, 7:378–81.
51. *Alexandria Gazette*, "Another Canadian Officer for Institute," August 12, 1917, 15.
52. A. K. Davis, "Rockbridge County History," in *Virginia War History in Newspaper Clippings*, 2:381.
53. *Ibid.*, 2:378.
54. *Ibid.*, 2:381.
55. A. K. Davis, "Richmond City History," in *Virginia Communities in War Time*, 7:277.
56. A. K. Davis, "Roanoke City History," in *Virginia Communities in War Time*, 6:464.
57. *Ibid.*
58. *Ibid.*, 6: 445.
59. Bristow, *American Pandemic*, 54.
60. Poster designed by Lawrence Wilbur, ca. 1917, Library of Congress, http://www.loc.gov/pictures/item/93502235.
61. *Students' Army Training Corp Regulations*, Special Regulations no. 103.
62. *Ibid.*, 12.
63. "Union University Unit," *Richmond Times-Dispatch*, September 18, 1918, 4.
64. "Student Army Training Corps," *Richmond Planet*, September 28, 1918, 5.
65. *Nashville Globe*, October 11, 1918, 7.
66. "Colored People Join Preparedness Campaign," *Richmond Times-Dispatch*, April 9, 1917, 5.
67. "School for Negro Soldiers," *Richmond Times-Dispatch*, January 6, 1917, 8.
68. Lauranett Lee, "Giles B. Jackson," http://www.EncyclopediaVirginia.org/Jackson_Giles_B_1853–1924.
69. *Richmond Times-Dispatch*, "For 'Negro West Point,'" January 10, 1917, 3.
70. This figure comes from the online database of "Virginia's Military Dead" (created by the Library of Virginia); 582 (or about 16 percent) of the dead were listed as "negro" or "colored." Library of Virginia, http://www.lva.virginia.gov/public/guides/vmd/vmdintro.htm#wwi. More than 37 percent of the database listings lack an entry for "race," so the number of African Americans Virginians who died during World War I is certainly higher. The number of African Americans in Virginia who were drafted comes from Crowder, *Operations of the Selective Service System*, 458, table 71-A.
71. *El Paso Herald*, "17 are Dead at Houston after Negro Troop Riot," August 24, 1917, 1.
72. Lentz-Smith, *Freedom Struggles*, 111.
73. C. Williams, *Torchbearers of Democracy*, 122–23, 146–47, 164.
74. Lentz-Smith, *Freedom Struggles*, 126.
75. Barbeau and Henri, *The Unknown Soldiers*, 169–73.
76. Fisher and Buckley, "Urbane Francis Bass," in *African American Doctors of World War I*, 29.

77. Virginia Foundation for the Humanities, *Fayette Street*, 24.
78. "Lieut. Urbane F. Bass Killed in Action in France," *Richmond Planet*, November 9, 1918, 2.
79. His gravestone lists his date of death as October 7, 1918.
80. "Distinguished Service Cross, World War I," U.S. Army Medical Department, http://ameddregiment.amedd.army.mil/dsc/wwi/wwi_ad.html.
81. Medical College of Virginia, Base Hospital No. 45 newsletter, vol. 1, November 6, 1917, 1; "U.S. Army Base Hospital No. 45, Scrapbook History, vol. 1," VHS, Mss3 Un328a.
82. "Miss Robertson to Be Chief Nurse of Hospital after All," Medical College of Virginia, *Base Hospital No. 45*, 1, no. 1 (November 5, 1917): 1, VHS, Mss3 Un328a.
83. Virginia War Commission Questionnaire, Library of Virginia, http://image.lva.virginia.gov/WWI/pages/060/0098.html; "Nursing News and Announcements," *American Journal of Nursing* 19, no. 1 (1918): 60.
84. Brian McNeill, "Exhibit Shines Light on MCV Unit of Doctors, Nurses in World War I," *VCU News*, https://pubapps.vcu.edu/news2013/article/Exhibit_shines_light_on_MCV_unit_of_doctors_nurses_in_World_War.
85. Lake, "The Epidemic," 3.
86. *Loudoun Mirror*, October 8, 1918.
87. Lake, "The Epidemic," 2.
88. *Ibid.*
89. "Mrs. Patterson Tells of Woman's Land Army," *Richmond Times-Dispatch*, April 12, 1918, 5.
90. Arnold Bennett, International News Bureau, "Sir Auckland Geddes's Speech Is Criticized," *Richmond Times-Dispatch*, November 17, 1918, 5.
91. A. K. Davis, "Lynchburg City History," in *Virginia War History in Newspaper Clippings*, 2:106.
92. *Ibid.*, 2:108.
93. "Will Organize Great Army of Women Workers," *Richmond Times-Dispatch*, March 24, 1918, 4.
94. "Advisory Committee," *Richmond Times-Dispatch*, April 6, 1919, 9; birth name Juanita "Neta" Massie from of marriage certificate. *Virginia: Select Marriages, 1785–1940* (database), Ancestry.com.
95. Sharrer, "Let's Celebrate," 2
96. *Richmond Times-Dispatch*, July 18, 1918, 5. Thanks to Dr. Terry Sharrer for this lead.
97. "Gather Peach Pits for 40 Gas Masks," *Washington Times*, September 20, 1918, 10. In Newport News school children collected thousands of peach stones and nut shells to be used by the Red Cross in making the carbon for the gas masks. A. K. Davis, "Newport News City History," in *Virginia Communities in War Time*, 7:143.
98. "Land Army Is Rewarded," *Richmond Times-Dispatch*, September 5, 1918, 3.
99. Brent Witt, "Society," *Richmond Times-Dispatch*, August, 25, 1918, 1.
100. *Richmond Times-Dispatch*, July 18, 1918, 5.
101. A. K. Davis, *Virginia Communities in War Time*, 6:xliv.
102. A. K. Davis, "Brunswick," in *Virginia Communities in War Time*, 6:42.
103. A. K. Davis, "Appomattox," in *Virginia Communities in War Time*, 6:24.
104. A. K. Davis, "Fauquier," in *Virginia Communities in War Time*, 6:125.
105. A. K. Davis, "Clifton Forge," in *Virginia Communities in War Time*, 6:65.
106. A. K. Davis, "Accomac County's Red Cross," in *Virginia Communities in War Time*, 6:3.
107. Orwig, "Persuading the Home Front," 19.
108. Court testimony cited by Capozzola, *Uncle Sam Wants You*, 84–85.
109. A. K. Davis, "Chesterfield," in *Virginia Communities in War Time*, 6:55.
110. A. K. Davis, "Clifton Forge Red Cross," in *Virginia Communities in War Time*, 6:67.
111. A. K. Davis, "Appomattox," and "Chesterfield," in *Virginia Communities in War Time*, 6:20–21 and 6:54–55.
112. A. K. Davis, "Goochland County," in *Virginia Communities in War Time*, 6:187.
113. A. K. Davis, "Montgomery," in *Virginia Communities in War Time*, 6:287.
114. A. K. Davis, "Richmond City History" in *Virginia Communities in War Time*, 7:258.
115. *Ibid.*, 7:249.
116. "'Greasy Jobs' Profitable," *Richmond Times-Dispatch*, November 11, 1918, 3.
117. *Richmond Times-Dispatch*, December 1, 1918, 4.
118. Elson, *Lynchburg, Virginia*, 288, citing local newspaper, June 21, 1918 and June 26, 1918.
119. Rosemary Thornton, "Wilmington Women Risked All in Ammunition Factory," *Wilmington (DE) Starline News*, August 3, 2014, http://www.starnewsonline.

com/news/20140803/wilmington-women-risked-all-in-ammunition-factory.
120. "Women Still Flocking into Munition Reserve," *Richmond Times-Dispatch*, August 27, 1918, 10.
121. A. K. Davis, "Suffolk and Nansemond County History," in *Virginia Communities in War Time*, 6:539.
122. A. K. Davis, "Richmond City History," in *Virginia Communities in War Time*, 7:270.
123. Foxwell, *In Their Own Words*, 161–62.
124. "No. of WWI Navy Women, by State," Navy Press release, July 30, 1942, American Women in World War I, https://americanwomeninwwi.wordpress.com/tag/military-women/.
125. McDaid, "Virginia Women and World War I," 117–18.
126. Bekers, De Meyer, and Strobbe, "Shape Recognition for Ships," 158.
127. "School for Camoufleurs," *Monroe (NC) Journal* September 17, 1918, 2.
128. "Painting of Ships—New Development," *Richmond Times-Dispatch*, August 25, 1918, 1, 10.
129. Hewitt, *Women Marines in World War I*, 77.
130. McDaid, "Virginia Women and World War I," 117.
131. *Ibid.*, 117.
132. *Ibid.*, 115.
133. *Ibid.*, 117.
134. "Address of President Wilson Delivered at Mount Vernon, July 4, 1918."
135. United States Census 2010, http://www.census.gov/2010census/.
136. Historical Census Browser, Library of Virginia, http://mapserver.lib.virginia.edu/. This calculation is complicated by changing variables from the 1910 Federal Census to the calculations included in the 1920 Federal Census. In 1920 the category was "native white males 21 years of age and over of foreign or mixed parentage."
137. "An Act to Authorize the Secretary of the Interior to Issue Certificates of Citizenship to Indians," chapter 233, http://legisworks.org/congress/68/publaw-175.pdf. See Rountree, *Pocahontas's People*, 213 for variability in the draftability and volunteerism among Virginia Indians.
138. Sterba, *Good Americans*, 83–130.
139. 1910 U.S. Federal Census.
140. A. K. Davis, "Lynchburg City History," *Virginia Communities in War Time*, 7:111.
141. Alexander F. Barnes, personal communication with author.
142. "To Speak at Mount Vernon," *Alexandria Gazette*, June 26, 1918, 4.
143. "The Draft Numbers," *Alexandria Gazette*, June 28, 1918, 1.
144. *Richmond Times-Dispatch*, "National Food Problem and Possible Solution," April 22, 1917, 48.
145. *Big Stone Gap (VA) Post*, May 8, 1918, 1.
146. "Ho for the Hoe!," *Richmond Times-Dispatch*, June 13, 1917.
147. *Alexandria Gazette*, February 4, 1918, 1.
148. A. K. Davis, "Richmond City History," in *Virginia Communities in War Time*, 7:272.
149. *Ibid.*
150. *Richmond Times-Dispatch*, July 20, 1917, 3.
151. A. K. Davis, "Portsmouth," in *Virginia Communities in War Time*, 7:212.
152. A. K. Davis, "Richmond City History," in *Virginia Communities in War Time*, 7:308.
153. Nationwide, the first "loan" was April 24, 1917, which issued $5 billion in bonds at 3.5 percent interest; a second loan was authorized on October 1 of the same year for $3 billion at 3 percent interest; on April 5, 1918, the third Liberty Loan offered another $3 billion in bonds at 4.5 percent interest; and, finally, on September 28, 1918, the fourth and last loan offered $6 billion in bonds at 4.25 percent.
154. "Posters: World War I Posters," Library of Congress Propaganda Poster Collection, http://www.loc.gov/pictures/collection/wwipos/.
155. *Richmond Times-Dispatch*, October 20, 1917, 1.
156. "Fifth's District Total Reaches $175,741,740," *Richmond Times-Dispatch*, October 31, 1917, 10.
157. Located in the 1910 Federal Census, Richmond, Marshall Ward, Desmond Wray, son of Luther and Minnie Wray born in 1906. Roll T624_1645, 14A, Enumeration district 0128, FHL microfilm 1375658.
158. *Richmond Times-Dispatch*, July 14, 1918, 7.
159. A. K. Davis, "Richmond City History," in *Virginia Communities in War Time*, 7:302.
160. *Ibid.*, 7:271.
161. *Richmond Times-Dispatch*, January 4, 1918, 10.

162. *Clinch Valley News*, February 1, 1918, 4.
163. Quarstein, *World War I on the Virginia Peninsula*, 91.
164. A. K. Davis, "Petersburg City History," in *Virginia Communities in War Time*, 7:183.
165. A. K. Davis, "Richmond City History," in *Virginia Communities in War Time*, 7:308.
166. *Ibid.*, 7:307.
167. A. K. Davis, *Virginia War Agencies, Selective Service and Volunteer*, 4:3–4.
168. *Ibid.*, 4:14–15.
169. *Ibid.*, 4:19–20.
170. Walters, "General William T. Sherman and Total War," 476.
171. Inaugural address of prime minister Clemenceau to the National Assembly on November 20, 1917. Quoted in Ferro, *The Great War, 1914–1918*, 199.
172. Förster and Nagler, *On the Road to Total War*, 1–28.
173. W. Davis, *Address of Governor Westmoreland Davis*.
174. Commanding officer of the Lynchburg State Guard to the adjutant general of Virginia, February 2, 1918, Virginia Home Guard and Virginia Volunteers organizational status reports, 1917–1919, Virginia National Guard Archives, Joint Force Headquarters, Sandston, Virginia. Alexander F. Barnes, personal communication with author.
175. Company Order no. 24, Second Company, Richmond Grays, October 27, 1919, Virginia Home Guard and Virginia Volunteers organizational status reports 1917–1919, Virginia National Guard Archives, Joint Force Headquarters, Sandston, Virginia;, Alexander F. Barnes, personal communication with author.
176. Commanding officer, First Company Richmond Grays to the Adjutant General of Virginia, February 2, 1918, Virginia National Guard Archives, Joint Force Headquarters, Sandston, Virginia; Alexander F. Barnes, personal communication with author.
177. Major Jos. LeMasurier, Q.M.C. (Quartermaster Corps), Virginia National Guard, to the Adjutant General of Virginia, October 16, 1918, Virginia National Guard Archives, Joint Force Headquarters, Sandston, Virginia; Alexander F. Barnes, personal communication with author.
178. A. K. Davis, *Virginia War Agencies, Selective Service and Volunteer*, 4:305–8.

179. "Captain" to "Our Contributing Members and Friends," "Lynchburg State Guard" letterhead, April 21, 1919, Virginia National Guard Archives, Joint Force Headquarters, Sandston, Virginia.
180. Virginia Defense Force home page, http://www.vdf.virginia.gov/.
181. *Richmond Times-Dispatch*, "Chaplain Tells of His Fort Myer Experiences," July 30, 1917, 1.
182. *Richmond Times-Dispatch*, July 23, 1917, 7.
183. *Richmond Times-Dispatch*, May 14, 1917, 2.
184. *Ibid.*
185. Shepherd, "No 'Summer Holiday,'" 281–82.
186. *Richmond Times-Dispatch*, July 30, 1917, 8.
187. For example, "Venereal Disease at Camp Lee Is Serious," *Richmond Times-Dispatch*, June 11, 1918, 10; and "State Authorities are Determined to Improve Conditions in Virginia Generally, and Especially in Territory Adjacent to Camps," *Richmond Times-Dispatch*, May 22, 1918, 14. The latter article discusses venereal disease, prostitution, and vagrancy.
188. *Richmond Times-Dispatch*, June 3, 1918, 3.
189. A. K. Davis, "Winchester," in *Virginia Communities in War Time*, 6:629–57.
190. A. K. Davis, "Portsmouth City History," in *Virginia Communities in War Time*, 7:211.
191. A. K. Davis, *Virginians of Distinguished Service*, 1:24.
192. *Petersburg Progress-Index*, June 25, 2011, "Virginia Guard Chaplain Thomas Bulla Honored at Fort Pickett," http://www.progress-index.com/progress-index/news/1.1166106/archive.
193. *Richmond Times-Dispatch*, September 9, 1917, 5.

Chapter 3

1. *William and Mary Quarterly*, review "Publications of the Virginia War History Commission, by Arthur Kyle Davis, *William and Mary Quarterly*, 2nd ser., 6, no. 3 (July 1926): 268.
2. I am indebted to the archivists and librarians at the Library of Virginia for their assistance and stewardship of this material.
3. Inspirational card in the papers of a National Guard 29th Division soldier's pa-

pers, in A. Barnes, *Let's Go! The History of the 29th Division*, 30.

4. David Maurer, "I have learned much writing about our area's history," *Daily Progress*, April 30, 2017, section C, 2.

5. Hobart Clements's biographical information compiled from his gravestone in Mount Olivet Cemetery, the Charlottesville telephone book, his World War I draft card, and *USDA Employee Newsletter* 26, no. 16 (1967): 3.

6. Information obtained from cemeteries in Esmont and Alberene and World War I draft cards.

7. *Richmond Times-Dispatch*, June 23, 1918, 9.

8. *Richmond Times-Dispatch*, January 1, 1917, 10.

9. *Richmond Times-Dispatch*, May 25, 1919, 5.

10. *Virginia, Death Records, 1912–2014*, Ancestry.com. Tapscott's wife requested a military headstone for her husband three years after his death, in 1950.

11. National Register of Historic Places Inventory—Nomination Form, "Virginia War Memorial Carillon," File #127–387, 1984; Ellen K. Turner, "A Carillon Reminds," *Richmond News Leader*, October 24, 1925, 8.

12. Hollywood Cemetery "Notables" page, http://www.hollywoodcemetery.org/about/notable-people.

13. Harry Kollatz, Jr., "Richmond's Most Obstinate Man," *Richmond Magazine*, August 5, 2016, http://richmondmagazine.com/news/richmond-history/richmonds-most-obstinate-man/.

14. War Department, General Order, no. 49 (1922).

15. As documented in "U.S. Army Base Hospital No. 45 Scrapbook History," vol. 2, VHS, Mss 3Un328a1..

16. Ireland, *The Medical Department of the United States in the World War: Administration American Expeditionary Forces*, vol. 2, chapter 23.

17. Newspaper clipping dated January 10, 1919, *U.S. Army Base Hospital 45 Records*, 1917–1952, Scrapbook. Mss 3Un328a1 VHS.

18. Newspaper clipping dated 1941,*U.S. Army Base Hospital 45 Records*, 1917–1952, Scrapbook. Mss 3Un328a1 VHS.

19. McNeill, Brian "Exhibit shines light on MCV unit of doctors, nurses in World War I," November 7, 2014. https://news.vcu.edu/article/Exhibit_shines_light_on_MCV_unit_of_doctors_nurses_in_World_War.

20. VCU online archives, Base Hospital No. 45 Collection, https://gallery.library.vcu.edu/items/browse?collection=95.

21. "Exhibit Shines Light on MCV and the Practice of Medicine, in the Field and on the Homefront during World War I," VCU Libraries, http://www.library.vcu.edu/about/news/2014/exhibit-shines-light-on-mcv-and-the-practice-of-medicine-in-the-field-and-on-the-homefront-during-world-war-i.html.

22. Beth Ahabah Synagogue History, https://bethahabah.org.

23. A. K. Davis, "Richmond City History," in *Virginia Communities in War Time*, 7:259.

24. *Ibid.*, 7:253.

25. "Magic Transformation about Cantonment Site," *Richmond Times-Dispatch*, September 30, 1917, 12.

26. "The Western Front Today—Lochnager Crater," firstworldwar.com, http://www.firstworldwar.com/today/lochnagar.htm.

27. Engelbrecht and Hanighen, *Merchants of Death*, 174.

28. O'Gorman and Anders, *Fort Lee*, 23.

29. *Richmond Times-Dispatch*, September 30, 1917, 12.

30. *Ibid.*

31. Crowell, *A History of the 313th Field Artillery*, 3–4.

32. 2010 Census.

33. Dr. Steve Anders, newsletter article, Army Quartermaster Foundation, Fort Lee, Virginia, http://old.qmfound.com/DavisHouse.htm.

34. A. K. Davis, "Petersburg City History," in *Virginia Communities in War Time*, 7:166.

35. *Richmond Times-Dispatch*, "Impressive Parade," May 22, 1918, 2.

36. A. K. Davis, "Petersburg City History," in *Virginia Communities in War Time*, 7:170.

37. "The Spirit of the American Doughboy," E. M. Viquesney Doughboy Database, http://doughboysearcher.weebly.com/the-spirit-of-the-american-doughboy.html

38. "From the Capital by Rail Direct to Newport News," *Richmond Times-Dispatch*, June 30, 1918, 11.

39. Order of Battle of the United States Land Forces in the World War, *Zone of the Interior: Territorial Departments, Tactical Divisions Organized in 1918, Posts, Camps, and Stations* 3, part 2 (1918): 519.

40. Quarstein, *World War I on the Virginia Peninsula*, 61.

41. *Alexandria Gazette*, January 22, 1919, 3.
42. *Richmond Times-Dispatch*, December 14, 1918, 6.
43. *Alexandria Gazette*, December 9, 1918, 2.
44. *Richmond Times-Dispatch*, January 11, 1919, 2.
45. "Newport News Shipbuilding Facts," Huntington Ingalls Industries website, http://newsroom.huntingtoningalls.com/presskits/newport-news-shipbuilding-facts.
46. Order of Battle of the United States Land Forces in the World War, *Zone of the Interior: Organization and Activities of the War Department*, 3, part 1, 522.
47. *Ibid.*, 187, 520.
48. Quoted in Quarstein, *World War I on the Virginia Peninsula*, 95.
49. Yarsinske, *Lost Norfolk*, 91.
50. Quarstein, *World War I on the Virginia Peninsula*, 97.
51. *Ibid.*
52. *Ibid.*, 29.
53. U.S. Federal Census: 1910, 26,246 vs. 1920, 47,013.
54. 1919 municipal survey, cited in Quarstein, *World War I on the Virginia Peninsula*, 103.
55. Quarstein, *World War I on the Virginia Peninsula*, 103.
56. National Register of Historic Places Inventory—Nomination Form "Hilton Village," Virginia Historic Register, 3.
57. *Ibid.*
58. Hubbard and Joannes, "The First War Emergency Government Towns II," 333, 336.
59. National Register of Historic Places Inventory—Nomination Form "Hilton Village," Virginia Historic Register, 3.
60. *Ibid.*, Item no 7, 1 (a continuation sheet).
61. "Newspaper Men Invade Dismal Swamp and Secure Pictures," *Richmond Times-Dispatch*, November 4, 1906, 29.
62. Traylor, *The Great Dismal Swamp in Myth and Legend*, 152.
63. Claimed in 1942.
64. "Suffolk Cemetery Reopens but Few Know about It," *Hampton Roads Virginian-Pilot*, January 25, 2007.
65. A. K. Davis, "Suffolk and Nansemond County History," in *Virginia Communities in War Time*, 6:540.
66. *Ibid.*
67. *Ibid.*
68. A. K. Davis, "Shenandoah County History," in *Virginia Communities in War Time*, 7: 386.
69. A. K. Davis, "Loudoun County," in *Virginia Communities in War Time*, 7:90.
70. As evidenced in summaries found in A. K. Davis's multivolume War History Commission series.
71. A. K. Davis, "Nottoway County," in *Virginia Communities in War Time*, 6:391.
72. *Ibid.*
73. Vogt, "To Whom It May Concern," Library of Virginia.
74. A. K. Davis, "Giles County," in *Virginia Communities in War Time*, 6: 175–181.
75. A. K. Davis, "Clifton Forge," in *Virginia Communities in War Time*, 6: 61.
76. Elson, *Lynchburg, Virginia*, 288.
77. A. K. Davis, "Albemarle County," in *Virginia Communities in War Time*, 6: 684.
78. "The Martha Washington Inn," Haunted Places to Go.com, http://www.haunted-places-to-go.com/martha-washington-inn.html; "The Martha Washington Inn," http://theshadowlands.net/famous/martha.htm.
79. The modern-day seal was redesigned in 1963.
80. A. K. Davis, "Washington County," in *Virginia Communities in War Time*, 6:579.
81. *Ibid.*, 6:583.
82. Columbia University Roll of Honor, http://www.warmemorial.columbia.edu/harry-clay-williams.
83. Accession no. 08551, Washington County Historical Society.
84. "John Jesse Henderson, Dingus/McConnell Family Tree," https://www.ancestry.com/family-tree/person/tree/22883403/person/1353659802/facts
85. "State Not Issuing Service Medals," *Richmond Times-Dispatch*, July 8, 1919, 6.
86. A. K. Davis, "Washington County," in *Virginia Communities in War Time*, 6:585.
87. "*Ibid.*, 6:584–86.
88. "Historic Sites: Sinking Spring Cemetery," http://www.virginia.org/listings/HistoricSites/SinkingSpringCemetery/.
89. Carroll, *First Ladies*, 150.

Chapter 4

1. Vera Mary Brittain, *Roundel: "Died of Wounds," Verses of a VAD* (1918) https://www.poetryfoundation.org/poems/57312/roundel.

2. "Academy of Medicine Discusses Influenza," *Richmond Times-Dispatch*, September 7, 1920 12.
3. DeBruyne and Leland, *American War and Military Operations Casualties*, 2.
4. Numbers taken from "Equitable Distribution of Captured War Devices and Trophies," Congressional Report no. 171, 3. A second contemporary source puts Virginia's manpower contribution at 73,062 and Tennessee's at 75,825. In contrast, New York sent the largest number of men, 367,864 (or almost 10 percent of the total American troops). Ayres, *The War with Germany*, 21.
5. *Richmond Times-Dispatch*, November 27, 1918, 8.
6. This analysis was calculated from a list of 2,771 fatal casualties provided by the Library of Virginia.
7. *Newport News Daily Press*, August 6, 1919, 1.
8. *Ibid.*
9. Margaret Thornton to Jessie Thornton, July 8, 1918, in M. Thornton, *Letters from Edgar's Trunk*, 7. Margaret Thornton to Jessie Thornton, July 8, 1918.
10. Bristow, *American Pandemic*, 44.
11. Crosby, *America's Forgotten Pandemic*, 18, 21–25.
12. Bristow, *American Pandemic*, 44.
13. *Richmond Times-Dispatch*, November 27, 1918, 8.
14. Bowen, *The Medical Department of the United States Army in the World War*, 388.
15. Informational poster signed by John Dill Robertson, commissioner of health.
16. *Richmond Times-Dispatch*, "Army Tents for Men in Richmond College," September 30, 1918, 10.
17. *Richmond Times-Dispatch*, "Influenza Epidemic Spreads to Richmond," October 1, 1918, 1.
18. "Influenza Situation Is Considered Grave," *Richmond Times-Dispatch*, October 5, 1918, 10.
19. Bristow, *American Pandemic*, 50.
20. *Richmond Times-Dispatch*, October 8, 1918, 7.
21. "Influenza Safeguards Taken by Dr. Flannagan," *Richmond Times-Dispatch*, October 2, 1918, 14.
22. *Richmond Times-Dispatch*, October 22, 1918, 4.
23. *Richmond Times-Dispatch*, November 5, 1918, 1.
24. *Richmond News-Leader*, October 11, 1918, 1; *Richmond Times-Dispatch*, October 8, 1918, 10.
25. U.S. Army Medical Department, Office of Medical History, "Port of Embarkation: Newport News, Va.," http://history.amedd.army.mil/booksdocs/wwi/wwivoliv/chapter7.htm.
26. Crowder, *Operations of the Selective Service System*, 167–68.
27. Kennedy, *Over Here*, 186.
28. U.S. Army Medical Department, Office of Medical History, "Port of Embarkation: Newport News, Va.," http://history.amedd.army.mil/booksdocs/wwi/wwivoliv/chapter7.htm.
29. Local newspaper clipping in a World War I scrapbook, undated, Library of Virginia Accession no. 37219, box 141, scrapbook 33, Virginia War History Commission Series X.
30. Clayton Yerby to his "dear Aunt Affie," August 13, 1917, VHS, Mss1 H7185h 9–16.
31. Undated letter addressed "My precious boy," from "devotedly Mother," *ibid.*.
32. Graham, *The Gold Star Mother Pilgrimages of the 1930s*, 57–58.
33. Letter from Percy Holladay to his parents, Affie and William Holladay, August 26, 1918. VHS, Accession no. Mss1 H7185h 45–104.
34. Holladay Papers, VHS, Mss1 H718h 45–104.
35. *Richmond Times-Dispatch*, June 22, 1918, 3.
36. A. K. Davis, "Danville," in *Virginia Communities in War Time*, 7:46.
37. Holladay Papers. VHS, Mss1 H7185 h 45–104, section 4.
38. *Washington Times*, December 13, 1918, 16.
39. Order of Battle of the United States Land Forces in the World War. *Zone of the Interior: Territorial Departments, Tactical Divisions Organized in 1918, Posts, Camps, and Stations* 3, part 2, 1:67.
40. *Ibid.*, 1: 251, "Preparation for Further Attack," Souilly, October 11, 1918–21h.
41. *Ibid.*, 1:252–53.
42. Faust, *This Republic of Suffering*, 239–45.
43. Hodgkinson, "Clearing the Dead," WWI Resource Centre, http://www.vlib.us/wwi/resources/clearingthedead.html.
44. Barbeau and Henri, *The Unknown Soldiers*, 99.
45. I found Eugene Ragland's gravestone in the St. John's Baptist Church Cemetery in Cobham, where his regimental affiliation

was indicated. He survived the war and died in 1958.

46. *Return of the 807th Pioneer Regiment.*
47. Barbeau and Henri, *The Unknown Soldier,* 104.
48. *Ibid.,* 165–66.
49. Quoted in Lengel, *To Conquer Hell,* 102.
50. *Ibid.,* 103.
51. Hodgkinson, "Clearing the Dead."
52. Ford, "Creation of Aluminum Identification Tags," in *Details of Military Medical Administration,* 26.
53. Budreau, *Bodies of War,* 22.
54. *Ibid.,* 21.
55. *Ibid.,* 111–12.
56. Moore, "New Plans for Arlington National Cemetery," 494.
57. American Battle Monuments Commission Annual Report, 4.
58. Meuse Argonne Cemetery, plot E, row 43, grave 13.
59. Newspaper clipping, "Capt. Conrad Killed," in Library of Virginia Scrapbook 4, p. 60.
60. A. K. Davis, entry for Robert Young Conrad, in *Virginians of Distinguished Service in the World War,* 1:33.
61. Rainville, "Memorials from the Great War," 13–14.
62. A. K. Davis, *Virginians of Distinguished Service in the World War,* 1:158.
63. "Flanders Field" brochure, 2, American Battle Monuments Commission website, https://www.abmc.gov/search/node/Flanders%20Field.
64. Reed and Roland, *The Camel Drivers*; Gorrell, *History of the American Expeditionary Forces Air Service, 1917–1919,* series E (special thanks to Steve Miller for the reference); Clapp, *A History of the Aero Squadron,* 25 (quote).
65. "Pvt. Franklin Leslie Dawson," Find a Grave, http://www.findagrave.com/cgi-bin/fg.cgi?page=gr&GRid=19377400&ref=acom.
66. *Washington Post,* October 10, 1920, 3.
67. "Harding Places Floral Tribute on Hero's Tomb," *New York Tribune,* November 12, 1922, 2.
68. Dodge, *Arlington National Cemetery,* 73.
69. Timothy L. Frank, Arlington National Cemetery historian, personal communication with author, April 13, 2017.
70. "Frank Nelson Lewis," Arlington Cemetery website, http://www.arlingtoncemetery.net/fnlewis.htm.
71. Gravestone located on Find a Grave website which includes a lengthy inscription, https://www.findagrave.com/cgi-bin/fg.cgi?page=gr&GRid=57193510; supplementary obituary from the *Richmond Times-Dispatch,* November 7, 1918, 7.
72. "Captain Myron H. Peck," 2nd Division—Second to None website, http://2nd-division.com/images/men/peck.myron.htm.
73. U.S. Department of Veterans Affairs, National Cemetery Administration, "Headstones, Markers and Medallions," http://www.cem.va.gov/hmm/index.asp.
74. 1930 Federal Census, San Antonio, TX. roll 2296, p. 1B enumeration district 0108.
75. 1940 Federal Census, Beverly Hills, CA, roll T627_222, p. 46B, enumeration district 19–5.
76. Kern, *Virginia's World War I Memorial,* 26.
77. *Ibid.,* 28.
78. National Register of Historic Places Inventory—Nomination Form, "Virginia War Memorial Carillon," 1984, continuation page 2.
79. "State's Singing Tower of Bells to be Dedicated as Memorial for World War Dead Today," and "Martial Strains of 7 Bands to Enliven Parade," *Richmond Times-Dispatch,* 15 October 1932, 3.
80. "15,000 Bow to War Dead at Dedication of Memorial," *Richmond Times-Dispatch,* October 16, 1932, 1.
81. *Richmond Times-Dispatch,* October 16, 1932, 1; Carillon dedication program, 5–12, "Virginia War Memorial Commission," Library of Virginia, call no. D675.R5 A3 1932.
82. Carillon Dedication Program, 11.
83. Quoted in *Richmond Times-Dispatch,* November 11, 1920, 1.
84. Levinson, *Written in Stone,* 63.
85. S. McConnell, "Reading the Flag," 110.
86. Abousnnouga and Machin, *The Language of War Monuments,* 163.
87. Rainville, "Memorials to the Fallen," 60.
88. *Ibid.,* 169.
89. Mosse, "National Cemeteries and National Revival," 2; Mosse, *Fallen Soldiers.*
90. "In Memory of Geo. Parker Thompson," Virginia War History Commission, Series X. Scrapbook 32, section 14, Library of Virginia, Accession no. 37219, box 140.
91. Elijah Palmer, paper for an inde-

pendent study in the Old Dominion University History Department, unpublished MS 2016.
92. "The National Commission of Fine Arts and Its Works," *Washington Sunday Star*, February 25, 1917, 4.
93. *War Memorials*.
94. "War Memorials—Suggestions for Their Treatment"
95. *Ibid*.
96. Jackson, *Community Building as Soldiers' Memorials*, cited in "War Memorials—Suggestions for Their Treatment."
97. Sallie S. Holsinger, regent of the Margaret Lynn Lewis chapter, DAR, personal communication with author, September 12, 2016.
98. James Rogers McConnell to a friend, 1915, Documenting the American South Papers.
99. McConnell, *Flying for France*. Details of his death are from an afterword to the 1917 edition, which contains letters written by his fellow pilots after his death.
100. McConnell, *Flying for France*, 70.
101. "James Rogers McConnell," American Field Service website, http://www.ourstory.info/2/c/Mac.html.
102. Rainville, "Memorials to the Fallen," 51–62.
103. "Will Observe Memorial Day," *Richmond Times-Dispatch*, May 11, 1919, 15.
104. Bellware and Gardiner, *The Genesis of the Memorial Day Holiday in America*, 16.
105. Hazeltine, *Anniversaries and Holidays*, 77.
106. *Richmond Times-Dispatch*, Friday, May 31, 1918, 1.
107. *Richmond Times-Dispatch*, May 31, 1918, 1. The article references the 122nd Depot Brigade band but the official list of units at Camp Lee does include this unit; instead, it might have been the 155th Depot Brigade.
108. "Give Thanks for Living at Confederate Service," *Richmond Times-Dispatch*, May 15, 1919, 3.

Chapter 5

1. Newspaper clipping, September 18, 1919, W.M.084.000.AR, Virginia War Museum, box 29, folder 4.
2. *Newport News Daily Press*, December 17, 1918.
3. *Newport News Daily Press*, May 21, 1919, 1.
4. *Newport News Daily Press*, April 11, 1919, 1.
5. *Newport News Daily Press*, December 20, 1918.
6. *Newport News Daily Press, Newport News*, April 11, 1919, 16.
7. "Heroes Home Tonight," *Alexandria Gazette*, May 27, 1919, 1.
8. *Newport News Daily Press*, May 20, 1919, 1.
9. *Newport News Daily Press*, May 20, 1919, 1.
10. *Newport News Daily Press*, May 25, 1919, 1.
11. *Richmond Times-Dispatch*, June 10, 1919, 5.
12. Undated article, published 37 years "later," in War Memorial Files.
13. "Returning Troops to be Given Rousing Welcome by This City," *Newport News Daily Press*, March 11, 1919, 8.
14. "Two Transports on Heels of Matsonia," *Newport News Daily Press*, May 21, 1919, 1.
15. *Newport News Daily Press*, April 13, 1919, 1, 10. A photograph taken by the pilot appeared in an undated clipping from *Charlottesville Daily Progress*. Virginia War Memorial Archives, Accession no. W.M.002.027.AR, box 158, folder 2. The caption concludes that "to obtain an aerial picture from such a low altitude would be impossible today by reason of safety regulations."
16. "Gift Honors Dead and Living Today at Victory Arch," *Newport News Daily Press*, September 17, 1919, 1.
17. "Victory Arch Built to Welcome," *Charlottesville Daily Progress*, April 1962, 1.
18. War History Commission Series X, Scrapbook 34, section 14, p. 43, Library of Virginia, Accession no. 37219, box 142.
19. *Newport News Daily Press*, April 13, 1919, 1, 10.
20. Braddan, *Under Fire with the 370th Infantry*.
21. *Richmond Planet*, March 22, 1919, 1.
22. Emmett J. Scott Papers, Morgan State Library, Baltimore, cited in Barbeau and Henri, *The Unknown Soldiers*, 100–101.
23. *Newport News Daily Press*, 1919, 1.
24. War History Commission Scrapbook 33, Library of Virginia, possibly an excerpt from *Newport News Times-Herald*, "For Colored Soldiers," August 13, 1919.
25. Cartoon by George H. Ben Johnson, *Richmond Planet*, June 21, 1919.
26. Stoner, "The Crutches' Tune," 90.

27. *Alexandria Gazette*, December 12, 1921, 2.
28. "Local Hospital Made Big Record," *Newport News Daily Press*, August 6, 1919, 1.
29. "United States Public Health Service," *Alexandria Gazette*, September 1, 1921, 6.
30. "Red Cross Assists Disabled Veterans," *Big Stone (VA) Gap Post*, October 20, 1920, 2.
31. Cholmeley-Jones, "American Legion War Risk Insurance," 188.
32. *Alexandria Gazette*, "Aid for the Ex-Soldier," September 1, 1921, 6.
33. Linker, *War's Waste*, 58–62.
34. *Ibid.*, 91, 96, 99.
35. Full-page advertisement for the British Star Company and its copyrighted artificial limb products, *Richmond Times-Dispatch*, June 16, 1918.
36. Undated newspaper clipping, Scrapbook 47, VHS, Mss 3Un328a1.
37. Looney, "'I Really Never Thought War Was So Cruel,'" Veterans' Questionnaires of the Virginia War History Commission, 131.
38. Viets, *Shell-Shock, A Digest of the English Literature* pamphlet reprinted from article in *Journal of the American Medical Association* 69 (November 24, 1917): 1779–86.
39. *Ibid.*, 4.
40. *Ibid.*, 18.
41. *Richmond Times-Dispatch*, May 21, 1919.
42. Viets, *Shell-Shock*, 24.
43. "Seeking Federal Aid to Care for Patients," *Richmond Times-Dispatch*, January 15, 1919, 14.
44. Letter to the editor, *Alexandria Gazette*, January 5, 1922, 4; Miller, "A Brief History of Southwestern Virginia Mental Health Institute."
45. Walter S. Buchanan, letter to the editor, *Alexandria Gazette*, January 5, 1922, 4.
46. Death certificate, Commonwealth of Virginia, Charles Leslie Fletcher, August 13, 1931.
47. "Lieutenant Ends Life," *Alexandria Gazette*, November 6, 1919, 1.
48. "Samuel Hunt Staples," Find a Grave, http://www.findagrave.com/cgi-bin/fg.cgi?page=pv&GRid=55882406&Plpi=31507856.
49. War Commission Questionnaire, W. G. Lucas, May 27, 1919, Library of Virginia, http://image.lva.virginia.gov/WWI/pages/004/0240.html.
50. "For Distribution: Questionnaires for Virginia War History Arrive," *Alexandria Gazette*, September 4, 1920, 1.
51. *Richmond Times-Dispatch*, "War History Commission Is to Distribute Questionnaires," March 6, 1921, 15.
52. "About the World War I History Commission Questionnaires Collection," Library of Virginia, http://www.lva.virginia.gov/public/guides/opac/wwiqabout.htm.
53. Looney, "I Really Never Thought War Was So Cruel," Veterans' Questionnaires of the Virginia War History Commission," 125–33.
54. *Ibid.*, 131.
55. Editorial in the West Virginia Labor journal *Majority*, January 23, 1919, cited in Jessup, "Public Attitudes toward Ex-Servicemen after World War I," 1064.
56. A. K. Davis, "Clifton Forge," *Virginia Communities in War Time*, 6:67–68.
57. Jessup, "Public Attitudes toward Ex-Servicemen after World War I," 1064.
58. "W. H. Magee in Richmond to Aid Maimed Soldiers," *Richmond Times-Dispatch*, March 9, 1919, 11.
59. Thurber, "Veterans in District No. 12," 68.
60. *Ibid.*, 69.
61. Jessup, "Public Attitudes Toward Ex-Servicemen after World War I," 1071.
62. *Richmond Times-Dispatch*, February 9, 1919, 46.
63. "Employment Situation Is Improving in Virginia," *Richmond Times-Dispatch*, April 10, 1919, 14.
64. "High-Power Rifles on Mountain Guard Entrances to Mine," *Richmond Times-Dispatch*, November 24, 1919, 1.
65. *Richmond Times-Dispatch*, December 1, 1919, 4.
66. *Alexandria Gazette*, "For Ex-Servicemen," April 1, 1921, 2.
67. "Veterans of the Great War," *Washington Evening Star*, October 10, 1920, 8.
68. "Enlisted Men Will Be Seen Armistice Day," *Richmond Times-Dispatch*, October 20, 1920, 12.
69. "Richmond Legion Will Observe Armistice Day," *Richmond Times-Dispatch*, October 18, 1920, 10.
70. Ortiz, *Beyond the Bonus March and GI Bill*, 14.
71. *Ibid.*, 14–15.
72. *Ibid.*, 22.
73. "Patriotism of Our Soldiers Can Not Be Bought for Cash," *Big Stone Gap (VA) Post*, July 12, 1922, 6.
74. *Ibid.*
75. Adjusted Compensation Act, March 25–29, 1924.

76. Ortiz, *Beyond the Bonus March*, 27–8.
77. "All Stock Sales Records Broken on Market Today," *Charlottesville Daily Progress*, October 29, 1929, 1.
78. Ortiz, *Beyond the Bonus March*, 34–5.
79. Schultz, "'Carry Me Back to Old Virginny,'" 20–24.
80. Ortiz, *Beyond the Bonus March*, 44–47.
81. "Veterans Swarm into Washington Demanding Bonus," *Charlottesville Daily Progress*, April 8, 1932, 1.
82. "Opponents of Bonus Fight to the Last," *Charlottesville Daily Progress*, January 27, 1936, 7.
83. "Moonshining Reputation Built on Long History," *Franklin News-Post*, October 9, 2007.
84. Kennedy, *Over Here*, 185.
85. Debbie Robinson, "Purcellville Bush Meeting Auditorium Now Purcellville Roller Rink, Purcellville, VA, Built 1903," Northern Virginia History Notes, December 12, 2009, http://www.novahistory.org/Purcellville_Rink/Purcellville_Roller_Rink.html.
86. "Appeals for Boys in Camps," *Richmond Times-Dispatch*, November 7, 1917, 7.
87. "W.C.T.U," *Clinch Valley News*, July 13, 1917, 4.
88. "Peters Lauds His Liquor Squad and Scores Opponents," *Richmond Times-Dispatch*, June 4, 1919, 1.
89. "Troops Leave for Woodstock," *Charlottesville Daily Progress*, April 1, 1919, 1.
90. "Dry Agents Are Protected by Troops," *Charlottesville Daily Progress*, April 1, 1919, 2.
91. "Employs Attorneys," *Charlottesville Daily Progress*, April 1, 1919, 2.
92. "Deputies Wounded in Moonshine Raid," *Big Stone Gap (VA) Post*, May 28, 1919, 1.
93. "Likeable Young Man Pays the Freight," *Big Stone Gap (VA) Post*, November 29, 1922, 1.
94. Obituary, *Richmond Times-Dispatch*, December 2, 1939.
95. Hugh A. White, Lexington, to *Richmond Times-Dispatch*, August 28, 1919, 10, part of a series of letters to the paper under the headline "Virginians Opposing President's Appeal That Assembly Approve Equal Suffrage."
96. "House Defeats Woman Suffrage by 75 to 13 Vote," *Richmond Times-Dispatch*, March 12, 1914, 1.
97. Thanks to Dr. Terry Sharrer for the lead about "Mrs. Louis Powell."
98. "Convention City," *Lynchburg News*, May 7, 1913.
99. *Richmond Times-Dispatch*, September 3, 1919, 10.
100. Editorial by labor and civil rights activist Lucy Randolph Mason, *Richmond Times-Dispatch*, September 8, 1919, 3.
101. Debbie Robison, "Women's Suffrage Movement Led to Occoquan Workhouse Imprisonment," Northern Virginia History Notes, http://www.novahistory.org/Lorton_Womens_Suffrage.htm.
102. *Richmond Times-Dispatch*, November 18, 1917, 1, 9.
103. *Alexandria Gazette*, November 19, 1917, 1.
104. Woodrow Wilson, "A Moral Partnership Legitimized," September 30, 1918. In, Gottheimer, *Ripples of Hope*, 151.
105. *Richmond Times-Dispatch*, August 19, 1920, 1–2.
106. "Virginians Lynch Negro after Breaking in Jail," *Alexandria Gazette*, November 16, 1920, 8; *Clinch Valley News*, November 19, 1920, 2.
107. "Negro Educators Appeals for Racial Good Will," *Richmond Times-Dispatch*, February 17, 1919, 2.
108. McWhirter, *Red Summer*, 11.
109. "Riot in Hopewell Quelled by Troops; Three Shot," *Richmond Planet*, October 12, 1918, 1.
110. "Altercation between Spaniard and Colored Men Causes Serious Race Trouble," *Richmond Planet*, October 12, 1918, 6.
111. "Riot in Hopewell Quelled by Troops," *Richmond Times-Dispatch*, October 5, 1918, 1.
112. A. K. Davis, "Petersburg," in *Virginia Communities in War Time*, 7:182.
113. *Richmond Planet*, August 16, 1919, 2.
114. A. K. Davis, "Hopewell and City Point," *Virginia Communities in War Time*, 6:227.
115. *Richmond Planet*, August 16, 1919, 2.
116. National Register of Historic Places Inventory—Nomination Form, "Truxtun Historic District," 3.
117. Portsmouth Library Exhibition, Mirrored Communities, "Truxtun, Virginia," http://www.racetimeplace.com/mirror/truxtun/PICTURES/plan2.htm.
118. National Register of Historic Places Inventory—Nomination Form, "Truxtun Historic District," 8.

119. A. K. Davis, "Portsmouth," in *Virginia Communities in War Time*, 7:217.

Chapter 6

1. "Armistice Day Imposes Duty," *Washington Herald*, November 11, 1922, 1.
2. Quoted in "History of Veterans Day," U.S. Department of Veterans Affairs, Office of Public and Governmental Affairs, http://www.va.gov/opa/vetsday/vetdayhistory.asp.
3. *Ibid.*
4. 52 Stat. 351; 5 U.S. Code, Sec. 87a.
5. "Proclamation 3071," issued by Dwight D. Eisenhower. F.R. Doc. 54–8050, filed October 11, 1954.
6. "Armistice Society Circus," *Richmond Times-Dispatch*, November 9, 1919, 10.
7. *Richmond Times-Dispatch* November 2, 1919, 11.
8. *Richmond Times-Dispatch* November 7, 1919, 7.
9. *Richmond Times-Dispatch* November 8, 1919,12.
10. *Richmond Times-Dispatch* November 9, 1919, 1.
11. *Ibid.*
12. *Richmond Times-Dispatch* November 11, 1919, 1.
13. *Richmond Times-Dispatch* November 9, 1919, 1.
14. *Ibid.*
15. *Ibid.*, 6.
16. *Richmond Times-Dispatch*, November 11, 1919, 1.
17. *Ibid.*, 2.
18. *Richmond Times-Dispatch* November 9, 1919, 1.
19. Dickon, *The Foreign Burial of American War Dead*, 57.
20. "This Is World's Independence Day Says Pershing," *Richmond Times-Dispatch*, November 11, 1920, 2.
21. "Richmond Pays Tribute Today to War Heroes," *Richmond Times-Dispatch*, November 11, 1920, 1.
22. *Ibid.*
23. *Ibid.*, 1, 8.
24. *Ibid.*, 3.
25. *Alexandria Gazette*, November 11, 1920, 1.
26. *Richmond Times-Dispatch*, November 11, 1922, 13.
27. *Charlottesville Daily Progress*, November 11, 1929, 1.
28. *Charlottesville Daily Progress*, November 11, 1939, 1.
29. *Charlottesville Daily Progress*, November, 11, 1949, 9.
30. *Ibid.*
31. *Ibid.*, 10.
32. *Charlottesville Daily Progress*, November, 11, 1959, 5.
33. Rev. Frank Hampton Fox, "Most Glorious 'Fourth,'" *Richmond Times-Dispatch*, July 1, 1919, 6.
34. A. K. Davis, "Washington County," in *Virginia Communities in War Time*, 6:592.
35. *Big Stone Gap (VA) Post*, May 28, 1919, 1.
36. *Richmond Times-Dispatch*, June 6, 1919, 3.
37. *Clinch Valley News*, June 13, 1919, 1.
38. "Fourth Celebration Picnic Suggestions," *Richmond Times-Dispatch*, July 3, 1919, 5.
39. Miller & Rhoads advertisement, *Richmond Times-Dispatch*, July 4, 1919, 10.
40. "Raid on a Still," *Richmond Times-Dispatch*, July 3, 1919, 3.
41. *Big Stone Gap (VA) Post*, "Good Roads Day," July 2, 1919, 1.
42. Woodrow Wilson, "Proclamation 1335—Flag Day."
43. "The Great Seal of the United States," Publications.USA.gov, https://publications.usa.gov/epublications/ourflag/greatseal.htm.
44. "Buy a Flag To-Day," *Richmond Times-Dispatch*, April 4, 1917, 1.
45. A. K. Davis, "Roanoke City History," in *Virginia Communities in War Time*, 6:467.
46. "Line of March Jammed with Hot Humanity," June 5, 1919, Library of Virginia Scrapbook, 11.
47. "The American Flag," *Richmond Times-Dispatch*, June 14, 1919, 6.
48. "Thanksgiving Day Is Generally Observed," *Richmond Times-Dispatch*, November 26, 1915, 5.
49. "Day of Thanksgiving," *Newport News Daily Press*, November 30, 1905, 2.
50. Advertisement for H. W. Pobst, Jeweler, *Tazewell Republican*, November 23, 1905, 1.
51. *Big Stone Gap (VA) Post*, November 24, 1915, 2. Thanksgiving was changed to the fourth Thursday in November in 1941.
52. *Ibid.*
53. "Needlework Guild," *Alexandria Gazette*, November 26, 1915, 2.
54. Woodrow Wilson, "Proclamation 1316—Thanksgiving Day, 1915."
55. Woodrow Wilson: "Proclamation 1405—Thanksgiving Day, 1917."
56. "Richmond College S.A.T.C. Guests

of Westhampton," *Richmond Times-Dispatch*, November 28, 1918, 7.
57. *Ibid.*
58. *Alexandria Gazette*, November 26, 1919, 1.
59. *Alexandria Gazette*, November 22, 1919, 1.
60. *Lest We Forget*, 7.
61. "Christmas Stockings Being Filled for Blues," *Richmond Times-Dispatch*, December 10, 1917, 10.
62. For example, the communities of Williamsburg, Roanoke, Radford, Goochland, Loudoun, Warren, and Wise. A. K. Davis *Virginia Communities in War Time*.
63. A. K. Davis, "Goochland County," in *Virginia Communities in War Time*, 6:188.
64. A. K. Davis, "Williamsburg and James City County," in *Virginia Communities in War Time*, 6:602.
65. Base Hospital No. 45, Scrapbook History, vol. 1, VHS, Mss3Un328a.
66. Newspaper clipping in a VHS Scrapbook titled "Letter from France," February 15, 1919 (describing events from December 1918).
67. Equal Suffrage League (Richmond City), Records 1909–1935, Accession 22002. Referenced in McDaid, "Virginia Women and the First World War."
68. Anne Lee Lewis, "Christmas at the Base Hospital," Base Hospital No. 45 Scrapbook History 1, Mss3Un328a, 278–82.
69. "Christmas Dinner," VHS, Mss1.H7185h106.
70. "Camp Lee Permeated by Holiday Spirit," *Richmond Times-Dispatch*, December 24, 1918.
71. *Lest We Forget*, 71.
72. "American Legion Auxiliary to Give Veterans Xmas Cheer," *Alexandria Gazette*, December 12, 1921, 2.
73. *Lest We Forget*, 70.
74. Quoted in "Memorial Day of 1919," *Alexandria Gazette*, May, 30, 1919, 2.
75. "Gray and Khaki Men: Both Will Be Honored," *Richmond Times-Dispatch*, May 28, 1919, 16.
76. Janney, *Burying the Dead but Not the Past*.
77. "Our War Sacrifice Still Greatest," *Alexandria Gazette*, June 20, 1916, 3.
78. Kennedy, *Over Here*, 178.
79. Henry F. May, *The End of American Innocence*, 363, quoted in Kennedy, *Over Here*, 179.
80. *Richmond Times-Dispatch*, June 4, 1917, 1, 7.

81. A. K. Davis, "Goochland County," in *Virginia Communities in War Time*, 6:185.
82. J. Albert Hill, commander, to "comrades" from the Base Hospital 45 Veterans Association, undated 1974 correspondence, VHS, Mss 3Un328 B2.
83. Crews, "A Virginia Hospital Abroad," 190.
84. Geisinger, *History of U.S. Army Base Hospital No. 45 in the Great War*, 352.
85. *Ibid.*, 321.
86. William B. Elwang, commentary in Geisinger, *U.S. Army Base Hospital No. 45 in The Great War*, 323.
87. Samuel M. Bemiss, "Address Before Base Hospital 45, February 25, 1956," 1–8, VHS, call no. F226.5 B46 A227.
88. Scrapbook, VHS, Mss 3 Lin 328b2–17, box 2.
89. "80th Division History Synopsis," 80th Infantry Division website, http://www.80thdivision.com/80thHistory.htm.
90. Organizational chart provided by Alexander F. Barnes, "80th Infantry Division," World War I Memorials in Virginia, http://www.lynnrainville.org/ww1-memorials/80-regiment_chart.php.
91. Vance, *Death So Noble*, 3.
92. Public Law 112–272, 112th Congress, H.R. 6364, passed January 14, 2013.
93. "The Weight of Sacrifice," United States World War One Centennial Commission, http://www.worldwar1centennial.org/stage-ii-design-development/the-weight-of-sacrifice.html.
94. Virginia General Assembly, House Joint Resolution No. 71, March 8, 2014.
95. In 2015 I relinquished this project, and the site was redesigned and migrated to the World War I and World War II Commemoration Commission's website, www.virginiawwiandwwii.org.
96. "Virginia Tattoo to Honor U.S. Entry into World War I," *Newport News Daily Press* January 27, 2017.
97. "WWI Signature Event," Virginia Arts Festival website, https://www.vafest.org/tattoo/wwi-signature-event/.
98. "Carillon Event to Commemorate 100th Anniversary of World War I," *Richmond Free Press*, March 31, 2017.
99. "New Event Tells the Story of Alumni Who Fought in World War I," Virginia Tech website, http://vtnews.vt.edu/articles/2017/03/clahs-stories-from-great-war.html.
100. VPI in World War I Project, http://vpiworldwarone.lib.vt.edu/.

101. "Norfolk, VA, 1917," World War I in Norfolk, VA: A Norfolk State University Project, https://norfolk1917.com/.

102. Amy Alonzo, "Winchester Man Works to Reveal History of City's WWI Markers," *Washington Times*, July 17, 2016, http://www.washingtontimes.com/news/2016/jul/17/winchester-man-works-to-reveal-history-of-citys-ww/.

103. Order of Battle of the United States Land Forces in the World War, *American Expeditionary Forces: Divisions* 2, 2:439–40.

104. Alonzo, "Winchester Man Works to Reveal History of City's WWI Markers," Gene Shultz, personal communication with author, August 27, 2016.

105. Email, Alexander F. Barnes to Lynn Rainville, August 26, 2016.

106. "Over Here, Over There: America Enters the Great War," http://www.macarthurmemorial.org/DocumentCenter/View/1733.

107. Fabiansson, "The Internet and the Great War," 166.

108. "Standards of Learning (SOL) and Testing," Virginia Department of Education, http://www.doe.virginia.gov/testing/.

109. "The Standards & SOL-Based Instructional Resources," VUS.9, Virginia Department of Education, http://www.doe.virginia.gov/testing/sol/standards_docs/.

110. *Ibid.*, USII.5.

111. *Ibid.*, WHII.10. The updated SOLs for history and social science, adopted in 2015, can be found at http://www.doe.virginia.gov/testing/sol/standards_docs/history_socialscience/index.shtml.

112. *Alexandria Gazette*, November 10, 1920, 1.

113. "Lack of Proper Maps Felt in Schools Here," *Richmond Times-Dispatch*, September 2, 1919, 2.

114. Rob Hedelt, "Book's Setting, Lesson in Respect Make Northern Neck Proud," *Fredericksburg Free Lance-Star*, November 16, 1999, C1, C4.

115. "Arlington May Re-think Implications of War Memorial," InsideNova, http://www.insidenova.com/news/arlington/arlington-may-re-think-racial-implications-of-war-memorial/article_a62afae2-4385-11e6-9569-2b42579a8ecf.html#user-comment-area

116. Virginia statute §15.2–1812, "Memorials for War Veterans," http://law.lis.virginia.gov/vacode/15.2–1812/.

117. House Joint Resolution no. 71, passed March 8, 2014.

118. This informal group sponsored a Facebook page, "Virginia in the Great War," and met periodically in 2017 and 2018 to share their expertise and feedback on commemorative events throughout the commonwealth.

119. "The Great War," American Experience, http://www.pbs.org/wgbh/americanexperience/films/great-war/.

Epilogue

1. Loose papers associated with the Virginia War Commission, Library of Virginia, Accession no. 37219, box 160, 1.

2. *Ibid.*, 3.

Bibliography

Archival Research and Unpublished Documents

American Battle Monuments Commission Annual Report, Memorandum to Commission, "Suggestions of Members Regarding Plans of the Commission." November 20, 1914, 4. Military Records Group 117, National Archives.
Barnes, Alexander F. "Draft." Unpublished MS, 2016.
Braddan, William S. *Under Fire with the 370th Infantry (8th I.N.G.) A.E.F. Memoirs of the World War*. Ca. 1920s. Published by William S. Braddan.
Cooper, Joe. Correspondence. Butler Center for Arkansas Studies, Central Arkansas Library System, BC.MSS.99.31.
"A Medieval Virginia Town, 1914–1918."
National Register of Historic Places Inventory—Nomination Form, "Hilton Village," 1969. Also on Virginia Historic Register, 121–0009.
National Register of Historic Places Inventory—Nomination Form, "Truxtun Historic District," 1982. Also on Virginia Historic Register, 124–0047.
National Register of Historic Places Inventory—Nomination Form, "Virginia War Memorial Carillon," 1984. Also on Virginia Historic Register, 127–387.
Palmer, Elijah. "Christ and St. Luke's Episcopal Church." Unpublished MS, 2016. Prepared for a final project in an Independent Study at Old Dominion University.
Sharrer, Terry. "Let's Celebrate the Plowed Fields: Loudoun's Farmers during the Great War." Unpublished MS, 2015.
_____. "Loudoun Chronology." Unpublished MS, 2015.

Documenting the American South

James R. McConnell (James Rogers), 1887–1917 Collection. http://docsouth.unc.edu/wwi/mcconnell/bio.html.

Library of Virginia, Richmond

Equal Suffrage League of Virginia. Papers, 1909–1938. Organization records collection. Accession 22022.
Joannes, Francis Y. "Homes for the Newport News Shipbuilding and Dry Dock Company, Newport News, 1918." Business Records Collection 42229.
Virginia War History Commission. Record Group 66, Scrapbook 34, section 14. Accession no. 37219, box 142.
_____. Record Group 66. Series 11, Office Files, 94 boxes. Accession no. 37219.
_____. Record Group 66. Series 14, Second Virginia Council of Defense. 39 boxes.

———. Unpublished source materials. Record Group 66, series 11, 1917–1927. Accesion no. 37219. State government records collection.
Virginia War Memorial Archives.
Vogt, George. "To whom it may concern." Broadside 191–.T6FF. Luray Print Co., ca. 1917–1918. Accession no. 001453_02.
War History Commission Archives.

National Archives

American Battle Monuments Commission Annual Report (Military Records Group 117 at the National Archives), Memorandum to Commission, Suggestions of Members Regarding Plans of the Commission, 20 November 1914.
Miller, Phyllis. "A Brief History of Southwestern Virginia Mental Health Institute." Compiled for the 125th anniversary of the institute, 2012.
Schultz, Steven Patrick. "'Carry Me Back to Old Virginny': Virginia and the Bonus March of 1932," MA thesis, University of Richmond.

Special Collections and University Archives, University of Massachusetts Amherst Libraries

Return of the 807th Pioneer Regiment, ca. 1919. W. E. B. Du Bois Papers (MS 312).

University of Virginia

James Rogers McConnell Collections, https://explore.lib.virginia.edu/exhibits/show/mcconnell.

Virginia Historical Society

Bean, Paul. "Profile of the USS Virginia." Virginia Historical Society website. 2016.
Faulkner Papers. Mss 1 F2735 b, section 3, folder 8, files 101–12.
Geisinger, Joseph Francis. *History of U.S. Army Base Hospital No. 45 in the Great War.* Richmond: William Byrd, 1924. D 807 U72 no.45, General Collection.
Holladay Diary. Mss1 H7185h105, section 5.
Holladay Family Papers. Mss1 H7185h 9–16; MS1 H7185 h 45–104.
Lake, Robert L. "The Epidemic." Mss 7:3 RC150 L 1488.
Lest We Forget: Base Hospital, Camp Lee, Virginia. Privately printed. D 629.U6 U55, 1919 General Collection.
March, Gen. Peyton C., and P. C. Harris, acting adjutant general. *Students' Army Training Corps Regulations*. Special Regulations no. 103. Washington: Government Printing Office, 1918. UA 43 V81 General Collection.
Quartermaster log. Mss 3M 4435a1 (Maui).
Sheet music collection.
U.S. Army, Base Hospital No. 45. Records, 1917–1952. Mss 3 Un328a-b (includes scrapbooks).
U.S. Army, Base Hospital No. 45. Veterans Association. UH 474.5 R6, General Collection.
Ware Family Papers. Mss1W22960 4472–4481, section 27.
Warrenton Garden Club Receipts. Accesion no. TX 715 W26.

Virginia War Museum

Newspaper clipping. W.M.084.000.AR, box 29, folder 4, September 18, 1919.

President Woodrow Wilson Speeches

"Address of President Wilson Delivered at Mount Vernon, July 4, 1918." Washington, D.C.: Government Printing Office, 1918.
"An Address to the Senate." September 30, 1918. In *Ripples of Hope: Great American Civil Rights Speeches*, edited by Josh Gottheimer, 151–53. New York: Perseus Books.
"Proclamation 1335—Flag Day." May 30, 1916. Gerhard Peters and John T. Woolley, *The American Presidency Project*. http://www.presidency.ucsb.edu/ws/?pid=62991.
"Proclamation 1316—Thanksgiving Day, 1915." October 20, 1915. Gerhard Peters and John T. Woolley, *The American Presidency Project*. http://www.presidency.ucsb.edu/ws/?pid=72441.
"Proclamation 1405—Thanksgiving Day, 1917." November 7, 1917. Gerhard Peters and John T. Woolley, *The American Presidency Project*. http://www.presidency.ucsb.edu/ws/?pid=72443.

Contemporary Periodicals

Alexandria Gazette
Big Stone Gap (VA) *Post* (Wise County)
Clinch Valley News (Southwestern Virginia)
Charlottesville Daily Progress
El Paso Herald
Express (United Kingdom)
Franklin News-Post (Rocky Mount, Virginia)
Fredericksburg Free Lance-Star
Hamilton Enterprise (Loudoun County)
Hampton Roads Virginian-Pilot
Indianapolis Journal
Lexington Gazette
Loudoun Mirror (Loudoun County)
Lynchburg News
Monroe (NC) *Journal*
Nashville Globe
Newport News Daily Press
Newport News Times-Herald
New York Evening World
New York Times
New York Tribune
Ocala (FL) *Evening Star*
Ogden Standard
Petersburg Progress-Index
Richmond News-Leader
Richmond Planet
Richmond Times
Richmond Times-Dispatch
Richmonder Anzeiger
St. Martinsville (LA) *Weekly Messenger*
Tazewell Republican
University of Virginia Alumni News
Washington Evening Star
Washington Herald
Washington Sunday Star
Washington Times
Wilmington (DE) *Starline News*

Published Books and Articles

Abousnnouga, Gill, and David Machin. *The Language of War Monuments*. New York: Bloomsbury Academic, 2013.
Andre, Nick J. *Draft Environmental Impact Statement: Fort Eustis, Va Ongoing Mission*. Fort Eustis, VA: United States Army Transportation Center, 1979.
Ayres, Leonard P. *The War with Germany: A Statistical Summary*. Washington, D.C.: Government Printing Office 1918.
Barbeau, Arthur E., and Florette Henri. *The Unknown Soldiers: Black American Troops in World War I*. Philadelphia: Temple University Press, 1974.
Barnes, Alexander F., with Tim Williams and Chris Calkins. *Let's Go! The History of the 29th Infantry Division, 1917–2001*. Atglen, PA: Schiffer, 2014.
Bate, T. R. F. "Buying British Remounts in America." In *The Horse and the War*, by Captain Sidney Galtrey, 27–35. London: Country Life, and Chicago: Percheron [Horse] Society of America, 1918.

Bekers, Willem, Ronald De Meyer, and Tiemen Strobbe. "Shape Recognition for Ships: World War I Naval Camouflage under the Magnifying Glass." *WIT Transactions on the Built Environment* 158 (2016): 1–12.

Bellware, Daniel, and Richard Gardiner. *The Genesis of the Memorial Day Holiday in America*. Columbus, GA: Columbus State University, 2014.

Bennett, Merrill K. "Wheat and War, 1914–18 and Now." *Wheat Studies of the Food Research Institute* 16, no. 3 (November 1939): 67–112.

Bostridge, Mark. *Vera Brittain and the First World War: The Story of Testament of Youth*. London: Bloomsbury, 2014.

Bowen, Albert S. *The Medical Department of the United States Army in the World War*. Washington, D.C.: U.S. Government Printing Office, 1928.

Bristow, Nancy. *American Pandemic: The Lost Worlds of the 1918 Influenza Epidemic*. Oxford: Oxford University Press, 2012.

Brittain, Vera. *Testament of Youth*. New York: Macmillan, 1933.

Budreau, Lisa M. *Bodies of War: World War I and the Politics of Commemoration in America, 1919–1933*. New York: New York University Press, 2011.

Capozzola, Christopher. *Uncle Sam Wants You: World War I and the Making of the Modern American Citizen*. Oxford: Oxford University Press, 2008.

Carroll, Betty B. *First Ladies: From Martha Washington to Michelle Obama*. Oxford: Oxford University Press, 2010.

Chambers, John Whiteclay. *To Raise an Army: The Draft Comes to Modern America*. New York: Free Press, 1987.

Cholmeley-Jones, R. G. "American Legion War Risk Insurance." Paper presented at American Legion War Risk Insurance Conference, Washington, D.C., December 15–17, 1919.

Clapp, Frederick M. *A History of the Aero Squadron*. Self-published, 1920. Reprint, Nashville: Battery, 1990.

Cramer, C. H. *Newton Baker: A Biography*. Cleveland: World, 1961.

Crews, Edward R. "A Virginia Hospital Abroad: U.S. Army Base Hospital No. 45 in the Great War." *Virginia Cavalcade* 42, no. 4 (Spring 1993): 178–91.

Crosby, Alfred W. *America's Forgotten Pandemic: The Influenza of 1918*. Cambridge: Cambridge University Press, 2003.

Crouch, Tom D. *First Flight: The Wright Brothers and the Invention of the Airplane*. Harpers Ferry Center, WV: National Park Service Handbook, 2002.

Crowder, Enoch H. *Second Report of the Provost Marshal General to the Secretary of War on the Operations of the Selective Service System to December 20, 1918*. Washington, D.C.: Government Printing Office, 1919.

Crowell, Thomas Irving. *A History of the 313th Field Artillery, U.S.A.* New York: Crowell, 1920.

Davis, Arthur Kyle, ed. *Virginia War History in Newspaper Clippings*. Source vol. 2. Richmond: Virginia War History Commission, 1924.

_____, ed. *Virginia War Letters, Diaries, and Editorials*. Source vol. 3. Richmond: Virginia War History Commission, 1925.

_____, ed. *Virginia War Agencies, Selective Service and Volunteer*. Source vol. 4. Richmond: Virginia War History Commission, 1926.

_____, ed. *Virginia Military Organizations in the World War, with Supplements of Distinguished Service*. Source vol. 5. Richmond: Virginia War History Commission, 1927.

_____, ed. *Virginia Communities in War Time* (First Series). Source vol. 6. Richmond: Virginia War History Commission, Source Volume VI, 1926.

_____, ed. *Virginia Communities in War Time* (Second Series). Source vol. 7. Richmond: Virginia War History Commission, Source Volume VII, 1927.

_____, ed. *Virginians of Distinguished Service in the World War*. Source vol. 1. Richmond: Virginia War History Commission, 1923.

Davis, David John. "Bacteriology and the War." *Scientific Monthly* 5 (November 1917): 385–99.
Davis, Westmoreland. *Address of Governor Westmoreland Davis.* Delivered before the General Assembly of Virginia, January 14, 1920. Richmond: Davis Bottom.
DeBruyne, Nese F. and Anne Leland. *American War and Military Operations Casualties: Lists and Statistics.* Congressional Research Service, 2015.
Dickon, Chris. *The Foreign Burial of American War Dead: A History.* Jefferson, NC: McFarland, 2011.
Dodge, George W. *Arlington National Cemetery.* Charleston, SC: Arcadia, 2006.
Elson, James M. *Lynchburg, Virginia: The First Two Hundred Years, 1787–1986.* Lynchburg, VA: Warwick House, 2004.
Engelbrecht, H. C., and F. C. Hanighen. *Merchants of Death: A Study of the International Armament Industry.* New York: Dodd, Mead, 1934.
Eggleston, Joseph D. "Supplement to Food Administration Papers," addendum to Carl L. Lokke, "The Food Administration Papers for the State of Virginia in the National Archives," *Virginia Magazine of History and Biography* 50, no. 3 (July 1942): 227–29.
Fabiansson, Nils. "The Internet and the Great War: The Impact on the Making and Meaning of Great War History." In *Matters of Conflict: Material Culture, Memory, and the First World War*, edited by Nicholas J. Saunders, 166–78. London: Routledge, 2004.
Faust, Drew Gilpin. *This Republic of Suffering: Death and the American Civil War.* New York: Vintage, 2009.
Ferrell, Robert H. *Collapse at Meuse-Argonne: The Failure of the Missouri-Kansas Division.* Columbia: University of Missouri Press, 2004.
Ferro, Marc. *The Great War, 1914–1918.* Translated by Nicole Stone. London: Routledge and Kegan Paul, 1973.
Fisher, W. Douglas, and Joann H. Buckley. *African American Doctors of World War I: The Lives of 104 Volunteers.* Jefferson, NC: McFarland, 2015.
Ford, Joseph H. *Details of Military Medical Administration.* General Order no. 204, December 20, 1906. Superseded by General Orders no. 80, June 30, 1917. Philadelphia: P. Blakiston's Son, 1918.
Förster, Stig, and Jörg Nagler, eds. *On The Road to Total War: The American Civil War and the German Wars of Unification, 1861–1871.* Cambridge: Cambridge University Press, 1997.
Foxwell, Elizabeth, ed. *In Their Own Words: American Women in World War I.* Waverly, TN: Oconee Spirit Press, 2015.
Galtrey, Sidney. *The Horse and the War.* Chicago: Percheron Society of America, 1918.
Gammage, Bill. *The Broken Years: Australian Soldiers in the Great War.* Canberra: Australian National University Press, 1974.
Gorrell, Edgar S. *History of the American Expeditionary Forces Air Service, 1917–1919.* National Archives. Record group 120.5.1.
Graham, John W. *The Gold Star Mother Pilgrimages of the 1930s: Overseas Grave Visitations by Mothers and Widows of World War I Soldiers.* Jefferson, NC: McFarland, 2005.
Hall, Phyllis A. "The German Village at the Portsmouth Naval Shipyard." *Olde Times* 2, no. 2 (1987): 5–7.
Harter, Dale F. "A Soldier of Song in World War I: William Howe Ruebush, Virginia National Guard." *Virginia Cavalcade* 50, no. 3 (Summer 2001): 102–113.
Hazeltine, Mary E. *Anniversaries and Holidays: A Calendar of Days and How to Observe Them.* Chicago: American Library Association, 1928.
Healy, Maureen. *Vienna and the Fall of the Habsburg Empire: Total War and Everyday Life in World War I.* Cambridge: Cambridge University Press, 2004.
Hennessy, Juliette A. "Men and Planes of World War I and History of Lafayette Escadrille." *Air Power History* (Summer 2014): 15–27.

Hewitt, Linda J. *Women Marines in World War I*. Washington, D.C.: U.S. Marine Corps, History and Museums Division Headquarters, 1974.

Hodgkinson, Peter E. "Clearing the Dead." WWI Resource Centre, http://www.vlib.us/wwi/resources/clearingthedead.html.

Hubbard, Henry V., and Francis Y. Joannes. "The First War Emergency Government Towns II: Hilton, Virginia." *Journal of the American Institute of Architects* 6, no. 7 (July 1918): 333–45.

Imlay, Talbot. "Total War." *Journal of Strategic Studies* 30, no. 3 (June 2007): 547–570.

Ireland, Maj. Gen. M. W. *The Medical Department of the United States Army in the World War: Administration American Expeditionary Forces* 2. Washington, D.C.: United States Government Printing Office, 1927.

Jackson, Henry E. *Community Building as Soldiers' Memorials*. Community circular no. 2. Department of the Interior, Bureau of Education, January 1919.

Janney, Caroline E. *Burying the Dead but Not the Past: Ladies' Memorial Associations and the Lost Cause*. Chapel Hill: University of North Carolina Press, 2012.

Janney, Asa, and Werner Janney. *A Medieval Virginia Town, 1914–1918*. Lincoln, VA: self-published, 1986.

Jessup, Mary Frost. "Public Attitudes toward Ex-Servicemen after World War I." *Monthly Labor Review* 57, no. 6 (December 1943): 1063–73.

Journal of the American Society of Naval Engineers 11 (1899). Advertisement.

Kennedy, David M. *Over Here: The First World War and American Society*. Oxford: Oxford University Press, 2004.

Kern, Susan A. "Virginia's World War I Memorial: Government versus Public Opinion." MA thesis, University of Virginia, 1990.

Koenig, Robert, *The Fourth Horseman: One Man's Mission to Wage The Great War in America*. New York: Public Affairs, 2006.

Lee, Lauranett. "Giles B. Jackson (1853–1924)." *Encyclopedia Virginia*. Virginia Foundation for the Humanities, March 23, 2014.

Lengel, Edward. *To Conquer Hell: The Battle of Meuse-Argonne, 1918*. New York: Henry Holt, 2009.

Lentz-Smith, Adriane. *Freedom Struggles: African Americans and World War I*. Cambridge: Harvard University Press, 2011.

Levinson, Sanford. *Written in Stone: Public Monuments in Changing Societies*. Durham: Duke University Press, 1998.

Linker, Beth. *War's Waste: Rehabilitation in World War I America*. Chicago: University of Chicago Press, 2011.

Lokke, Carl L. "The Food Administration Papers for the State of Virginia in the National Archives." *Virginia Magazine of History and Biography* 50, no. 3 (July 1942): 221–29.

Looney, J. Jefferson. "'I Really Never Thought War Was So Cruel': The Veterans' Questionnaires of the Virginia War History Commission." *Virginia Cavalcade* 50, no. 3 (Summer 2001): 124–33.

MacDonald, George W. "The Discovery of Nitroglycerine." *Arms & Explosives* 16, no. 184 (January 1908) 5–6.

_____. "Guncotton in France." *Arms & Explosives* 16, no. 191 (August 1908) 106–107.

McConnell, James R. *Flying for France with the American Escadrille at Verdun*. Garden City, NY: Doubleday, Page, 1917.

McConnell, Stuart. "Reading the Flag: A Reconsideration of the Patriotic Cults of the 1890s." In *Bonds of Affection: American Define Their Patriotism*, edited by John Bodnar, 102–19. Princeton: Princeton: University Press, 1996.

McCrae, John. *In Flanders Field*. 1915. https://www.poetryfoundation.org/poems-and-poets/poems/detail/47380.

McDaid, Jennifer Davis. "'Our Share in the War Is No Small One': Virginia Women and World War I." *Virginia Cavalcade* 50, no. 3 (Summer 2001): 114–23.

McHenry, Kathy. *U.S. World War I Naval Deaths, 1917–1919* [database online]. Provo, UT: Ancestry.com.
McWhirter, Cameron. *Red Summer: The Summer of 1919 and the Awakening of Black America.* New York: Henry Holt, 2011.
Molineux, Will. "Penniman and the Powder Plant Boom: Williamsburg in World War I." *Colonial Williamsburg Magazine* 22, no. 2 (2000): 63–68.
Moore, Charles. "New Plans for Arlington National Cemetery." *American Institute of Architects Journal* 52 (1917): 491–96.
Mosse, George. "National Cemeteries and National Revival: The Cult of the Fallen Soldiers in Germany." *Journal of Contemporary History* 14, no. 1 (January 1979): 1–20.
_____. *Fallen Soldiers: Reshaping the Memory of the World Wars.* Oxford: Oxford University Press, 1991.
O'Gorman, Tim, and Steve Anders. *Fort Lee: Birthplace of the Motion Picture Industry.* Charleston, SC: Arcadia, 2003.
Order of Battle of the United States Land Forces in the World War. *American Expeditionary Forces: Divisions* 2. United States Army. Washington, D.C.: Center of Military History, 1988. First printed 1931—CMH Pub 23–2.
_____. *American Expeditionary Forces: General Headquarters, Armies, Army Corps, Service of Supply, Separate Forces* 1. United States Army. Washington, D.C.: Center of Military History, 1988. First printed 1937—CMH Pub 23–1.
_____. *Zone of the Interior: Organization and Activities of the War Department* 3, part 1. 1931–1941. Reprint, Washington, D.C.: Center of Military History, 1988.
_____. *Zone of the Interior: Territorial Departments, Tactical Divisions Organized in 1918, Posts, Camps, and Stations* 3, part 2. 1931–1949. Reprint, Washington, D.C.: Center of Military History, 1988.
Ortiz, Stephen R. *Beyond the Bonus March and GI Bill: How Veteran Politics Shaped the New Deal Era.* New York: New York University Press, 2009.
Orwig, Marcy Leasum. "Persuading the Home Front: The Communication Surrounding the World War I Campaign to 'Knit' Patriotism." *Journal of Communication Inquiry* 41, no. 1 (2016): 60–82.
Parker, Earl. "U.S. Cavalry Remount Program: The Centennial Year for Front Royal Depot Then and Now." *Cavalry Journal* 36, no. 2 (2011): 7–11.
Quarstein, John V. *World War I on the Virginia Peninsula.* Charleston, SC: Arcadia, 1999.
Rainville, Lynn. "Memorials to the Fallen: World War I Monuments in Virginia." *Journal of America's Military Past* 41, no. 2 (2016): 51–62.
_____. "Memorials from the Great War: Symbolism and Meaning in Gravestones and Statues from World War I." *Markers* 31 (2015): 6–29.
Ramsay, David. *Lusitania: Saga and Myth.* New York: W. W. Norton, 2001.
Reed, Otis Lowell, and George Roland. *The Camel Drivers: The 17th Aero Squadron in World War I.* Atglen, PA: Schiffer, 1996.
Rountree, Helen. *Pocahontas's People: The Powhatan Indians of Virginia through Four Centuries.* Norman: University of Oklahoma Press, 1990.
Schwarzkopf, Olaf. "The Changed Status of the Horse in War." *American Journal of Veterinary Medicine* 11 (February 1916): 59–70.
Shepherd, Samuel C., Jr. "No 'Summer Holiday': The Chaplaincy of Richmond's Walter Russell Bowie in World War I." *Virginia Magazine of History and Biography* 112, no. 3 (2004): 266–302.
Sterba, Christopher M. *Good Americans: Italian and Jewish Immigrants during the First World War.* Oxford: Oxford University Press, 2003.
Stoner, Elizabeth R. "The Crutches' Tune." *Everybody's Magazine* 40, no. 4 (April 1919): 90.
Thornton, Marilyn Elizabeth. *Letters from Edgar's Trunk: Tell Them All to Write.* Washington, D.C.: Politics & Prose, 2016.
Thornton, Rosemary. *The Houses That Sears Built: Everything You Ever Wanted to Know about Sears Catalog Homes.* Alton, IL: Gentle Beam, 2004.

Thurber, Evangeline. "Rehabilitation of World War I Veterans in District No. 12." *Pacific Historical Review* 15, no. 1 (1946): 68–76.
Traylor, Waverly. *The Great Dismal Swamp in Myth and Legend*. Rosedog Books, 2010.
U.S. Senate. *Adjusted Compensation Act. Hearings before the Committee on Finance*. 68th Congress, 1st sess., on H.R. 7959, An Act to Provide Adjusted Compensation for Veterans of the World War, and for Other Purposes. Printed for the use of the Committee on Finance, March 25–29, 1924.
———. *Naval Investigation: Hearings before the Subcommittee of the Committee on Naval Affairs*. Vol. 1. 66th Congress, 2nd Sess. Washington, D.C.: Government Printing Office, 1921.
U.S. Department of Agriculture. *Usual Planting and Harvesting Dates for U.S. Field Crops*. Agricultural Handbook no. 628, December 1997.
U.S. Congress. *Official Congressional Directory*. 65th Congress, first sess., 1917.
Vance, Jonathan L. *Death So Noble: Memory, Meaning, and the First World War*. Vancouver: University of British Columbia Press, 1997.
Viets, Henry. "Shell-Shock, A Digest of the English Literature." Reprinted as a pamphlet from the original article in *Journal of the American Medical Association* 69 (November 24, 1917): 1779–86.
Virginia Foundation for the Humanities and the Fayette Area Historical Initiative. *Fayette Street: A Hundred-Year History of African American Life in Martinsville, Virginia, 1905–2005*. Charlottesville: Virginia Foundation for the Humanities, 2006.
Walters, John Bennett. "General William T. Sherman and Total War." *Journal of Southern History* 14, no. 4 (November 1948): 447–80.
War Memorials: Suggestions as to the Forms of Memorials and the Methods of Obtaining Designers. Washington, D.C.: National Commission of Fine Arts, 1919.
"War Memorials—Suggestions for Their Treatment." *American City* 20 (1919): 307.
Wayland, John W. *Men of Mark and Representative Citizens of Harrisonburg and Rockingham County, Virginia: Portraits and Biographies of Men and Women*. Genealogical Publishing Company. Staunton, VA: McClure, 1943.
William and Mary Quarterly. Review of "Publications of the Virginia War History Commission," by Arthur Kyle Davis. *William and Mary Quarterly*, 2nd ser., 6, no. 3 (July 1926): 265–68.
Williams, Chad L. *Torchbearers of Democracy: African American Soldiers in the World War I Era*. Chapel Hill: University of North Carolina Press, 2013.
Williams, William B. *History of the Manufacture of Explosives for the World War, 1917–1918*. Chicago: University of Chicago Press, 1920.
Wilson, Ross J. *New York and the First World War: Shaping an American City*. Farmham: Ashgate, 2014.
Yarsinske, Amy Waters. *Lost Norfolk*. Charleston, SC: History, 2009.
Zieger, Robert H. *America's Great War: World War I and the American Experience*. Lanham, MD: Rowman and Littlefield, 2000.

Index

Numbers in **_bold italics_** indicate pages with illustrations

Abbot (ship) 37
Abingdon (Virginia): Fourth of July celebrations in 185; historical significance of 110; Sinking Spring Cemetery in 112–113; tourist attractions in 109; war memorials in 113; wartime contributions of 111–114
ABMC (American Battle Monuments Commission) 129–131
Abousnnouga, Gill 144
Adams, Ralph Cram 139
Adjusted Compensation Act of 1924 166–167
advertisements: Armistice Day 183; for food conservation 12; Fourth of July 185; for homes 26–27, 102; for liberty bonds 73, 74; for munitions factories **_25_**; "welcome home" 153; *see also* propaganda posters
AEF *see* American Expeditionary Force
Aerial Experiment Association 31
African Americans: Armistice Day celebrations for 180; casualties in World War I 55, 219*n*70; in centennial celebrations 207–208; as gravediggers 50, 127, 128; homecoming celebrations for 156–157; in labor battalions 49–50, 55, 127, 156; lynching of 55, 156, 173–174; in medical field 57; military training for 54–55; in overseas combat 55–56; in race riots 175; in war memorials 143–144; women 76; *see also* segregation
agriculture: cotton 23; peanuts 104; technological advancements in 5–6; tobacco 23; transport systems for 8; women in 61–63
Agriculture Department, U.S. 12
airplanes 29–31
Aisne-Marne American Cemetery 131

Aisne-Marne offensive (1918) 46
alcohol, bans on 168–170
Alderman, Edwin A. 50
Alexander, John Hanks 55
All Quiet on the Western Front (film) 209
American Battle Monuments Commission (ABMC) 129–131
American Bible Society 80, 122
American Expeditionary Force (AEF): African Americans in 56; deaths in 124; dismantling of 152; draft registration for 41, 43; immigrants in 70–71; in Meuse Argonne offensive 87; morale of 164; in overseas combat 56; women in 69
American Federation of Arts 147
American flag: adoption of 186; readoption in Confederate states 44; symbolism of 141; *see also* Flag Day
American Graves Registration Service 126, 127
American Indians, military service of 70
American Legion 97, 105, 147, 164–167, 182–183, 192
American Library Association 122
American Revolution *see* Revolutionary War
American Social Hygiene Association 121
ancestry research 211
Anti-Saloon League 168
Areizaga-Soto, Jaime 200
Arlington National Cemetery 68, 106, 132–134, **_133_**, 144, 183
Armistice Day 164, 176–183, **_178_**
Army, U.S.: balloons utilized by 31; enlistment poster **_42_**; identification tags for soldiers in 128; integration of 54; Medical Service Corps of 159, 160; Quartermaster Corps 18; railside canteens

recognized by 16; remount depots 22; segregation in 55, 57, 100, 206–207; troop strength 41; *see also* soldiers
artificial limbs 159
artillery shells 26, 27, 67
Ashby, Isaiah 43
Atlantic Coast Aeronautical Station 30–31
Aviation Experimental Station and Proving Grounds 31
The Aviator (Borglum) 84, **85**, 148

Baden-Powell, Robert 71–72
Baker, Newton D. 39, 41, 128, 139, 192
Baker, W. E. 106
Baldwin, Dana Olden 57
Ballinger, Isaac 5–6
balloons 31
Band of Brothers (television series) 209
banking industry 8
Barnes, Alexander F. 202–204
Barton, Clara 53
Base Hospital 45: Christmas celebrations at 191; memorials to 90; organization of 89–90; staff of 59; Veterans' Association established by 196–197
Bass, Urbane Francis 57, **58**
battles *see* specific battles
beaux-arts method 129–130
Bell, Alexander Graham 31
Beth Ahabah Synagogue 92, **92**, 190
Bickford, Robert G. 154
The Big Parade (film) 209
Binswanger, H. S. 92
USS *Birmingham* (ship) 29
Blackford, W. W. 112
blacks *see* African Americans
Boggs, John Campbell 181
bonds *see* war bonds
Bonus Army 166–168
Boone, Daniel 110
bootlegging 169
Borglum, Gutzon 84, **85**, 148
Bowie, Walter Russell 79
Boy Scouts 71–74, 182, 184
Boyce, William 72
breeding programs 6–7, 20
Breedlove, Jesse Mack 34
Brees, Anton 139
Bright, John Fulmer 89
Brittain, Vera 115
Brown, Andrew Davidson 80
Brown, John Lenwood 175
Buckles, Frank 197
Bulla, Thomas McNeill 80, **81**
burials 125–137; and chaplains 127–128; equine 21; erection of gravestones 134–137; and gravediggers 50, 127, 128; mass graves 106, 125–128; military headstones 88, 130, 134; overseas 3, 106, 128–132; repatriation of deceased soldiers for 126, **126**, 128–129, 132–134; temporary 106, 127; *see also* specific names of cemeteries
Burke, David Duncan 135
Burke, John Woolfolk 162
Burns, Lucy **172**

Camilla Rickners (ship) 34
Camp Lee (Virginia): artillery regiments at 28; Christmas celebrations at 192; construction of 95; daily life at 96; history of 94–95; influenza epidemic at 118–119; provisions sent to 7, 65; as training site 49, 60, 71, 75, 95; YWCA hostess house at 61
canning 7, **7**, 54, 62
Cannon, James, III 80
cannons 28
canteens, railside 15–17, **15**
casualties of World War I 55, 90, 115–117, 219n70
Caton, Blanche Stansbury 68
cemeteries *see* burials; specific names of cemeteries
censorship of mail 122–123
census statistics 34, 69–70, 101, 116, 221n136
centennial celebrations 198–209; African Americans in 207–208; at colleges and universities 200–201; commissions created for 198, 208–209; exhibitions 199–200, 203–204; social media promotion of 205, 232n118; student participation in 205–206; by Virginia National Guard 202–203
Chambrun, Charles de 111
chaplains 78–81, **81**, 127–128
Charlottesville (Virginia): Armistice Day celebrations in 182; canning factory in 7; propaganda posters in 9; war memorials in 83–85, **85**
Chateau-Thierry, Battle of (1918) 131
Chesapeake Dry Dock and Construction Company 32
Chesser, Hurshel Tilson 197
children: in Armistice Day celebrations 182; food conservation by 14; fund-raising by 74–75; gardening by 11; social organizations for 71–75; war assemblies for 73; *see also* students
Christ and St. Luke's Church memorial **145**, 145–146
Christmas celebrations 190–192, **191**
civil rights movement 106
Civil War (1861–1865): American flag readoption in after 44; burials in 125–

126, 128; celebrations in honor of 149–150, 181, 194–195; draft during 43; Lost Cause of Confederacy in 44, 194; preservation of sites from 28; remount stations during 18; siege of Petersburg during 94; socioeconomic divide following 44; vestiges of 88
Clark, Kanin *199*
Clarke, Harris 124
Clemenceau, Georges 77
Clements, Hobart 86, 223n5
coal mine strike (1919) 163–164
colleges and universities: centennial celebrations at 200–201; fund-raising by 50, 53; military training at 50–55, *51*; war colleges 51; Women's Land Army at 61–62; *see also* specific institutions; students
commemorations 177–209; Armistice Day 164, 176–183, *178*; Christmas 190–192, *191*; Flag Day 141, 186–188; Fourth of July 105, 181, 184–185; Memorial Day 149–150, 176, 192–195, *193*; reunions for veterans 196–197; Thanksgiving Day 188–190; Veterans Day 177–179, 183; *see also* centennial celebrations; war memorials
Committee on Public Information 9
communication in wartime 121–124
Confederacy, Lost Cause of 44, 194; *see also* Civil War
Conrad, Holmes 130
Conrad, Robert Y. 130, 132
conscientious objectors 52, 64
conscription *see* draft
conservation of food 7, 12–14, *13*, 76
Cooke, John 113
Cooperative Extension Service 6
cotton production 23–24
Council of National Defense 63, 76
Cox, James M. 173
Cox, Kirk 200
Cradock development 176
Crater, Battle of the (1864) 94
Creel, George 9
Cret, Paul P. 129, 137–139
Crockett, Bill 104
Cronkhite, Adelbert 96, 150–151
Crowder, Enoch H. 43
"The Crutches' Tune" (Stoner) 157
Cult of Domesticity 67
cult of the fallen soldier 144, 150
Curtiss, Glenn Hammond 31
Curtiss Flying School 30
Cutchins, John Abram 89

Daughters of the American Revolution (DAR) 142, 147

Davis, Arthur Kyle: casualties documented by 115–116; on Shenandoah Valley 106; as Southern Female College president 82, 97; on War History Commission 82, 110, 161, 208, 210; on women's wartime efforts 64–65
Davis, Gordan R. 96
Davis, Jefferson 88, 92, 195
Davis, Marguerite Inman 63
Davis, Westmoreland 63, 77, 82, 163, 170, 185
Dawson, Charles, and Henrietta 121
Dawson, Franklin L. 121, 125, 132
daylight saving time 11, 168
decommissioning of soldiers 152–153
USS *Delaware* (ship) 33
Dilger, Anton 22, 23
dirigibles 31
disabled veterans 158, 164, 165
discrimination *see* segregation
diseases: equine 21; pneumonia 35, 60, 89, 116, 119, 124; sabotage campaigns involving 23; thyroid 120; of troops 59; venereal 59, 121; *see also* influenza epidemic
doctors *see* medical personnel
Dodson, Wilson Brown 132
dog tags 128
Doughboy at Rest (Pollia) 105
draft: domestic support for 9; exemptions from 43, 50; geographical quotas for 41–43; immigrants in 70, 104; labor shortages following 26; registration for 39, 41, 43; resistance to 43; student participation in 50
dreadnoughts 33
Driscoll, T. L. 120
dry docks 32, 33
DuPont, E. I. 23–26
dynamite 24–26

eagle, symbolism of 141, 146
education *see* colleges and universities; students
Eighteenth Amendment 169
Eisenhower, Dwight 167, 178, 183
Eitel Wilhelm settlement 35, *36*
employment: strikes 163–164; for veterans 104, 162–163; for women 26, 67–69, 162
Entente Alliance of 1907 1
Epes, Charles C. 155
Epes, Mattie Walton 181
epidemics *see* influenza epidemic
Equal Suffrage League. 171, 173, 192
Equestrian Statue of General Thomas "Stonewall" Jackson (Pollia) 105
espionage 23
Ewing, E. Thomas 201

244 Index

Facebook 205, 232*n*118
family tree research 211
farmerettes 17, 61–63, *212*, 213
farming *see* agriculture
Farnsworth, Charles S. 49
Faulkner, Lucy Ashton 10, 12, 14
Federal Aid Road Act of 1916 8
Federal Farm Loan Act of 1917 8
Federation of Mothers Clubs 180
females *see* women
Ferdinand, Franz 1–2
Ferguson, Homer L. 38, 101
First World War *see* World War I
Flag Day 141, 186–188, *187*; *see also* American flag
Flanders Field American Cemetery 131
Fletcher, Charles L. 160
Floyd, John B. 112
flu *see* influenza epidemic
Food Administration, U.S. 9, 11, *13*, 76
food conservation 7, 12–14, *13*, 76
food production: canning 7, *7*, 54, 62; propaganda 9; technological advancements in 5–6; transport systems for 8; victory gardens 9, *10*
food rationing 8–9, 11–12
Forms of Memorials and Methods of Obtaining Designers (National Commission of Fine Arts) 147
four-minute men 74, 120
Fourth of July 105, 181, 184–185
Franz Joseph I (Austrian emperor) 1
Fred, Edwin Broun 6
Freeman, Ben 106
Front Royal Remount Station 18–22, 216*n*49
fund-raising efforts: by children 74–75; by colleges and universities 50, 53; for Red Cross 53, 54, 66; war bonds 17, 73–74, 78, 221*n*153; war-relief funds 87; by women 50, 53, 66
Furniss, Otha Lennox 161

Garcia, Leon C. 157–158
gardening 9–12, *10*, 14
Gary, Julian Vaughan 89
gas masks 63, 220*n*97
German immigrants 106–108
Girl Scouts 71, 73, 74, 182, 184
Girls' Protective Association 75
Glenn, George Preston 131–132
Gold Star Mothers 122, 139
Good Roads Day 185
Grant, Ulysses S. 20, 65
gravediggers 50, 127, 128
graves *see* burials
Graves, Harvey C. 124
Great Dismal Swamp 103, 104

Great War *see* World War I
The Great War (television series) 209
Great White Fleet 33–34
Great Wilderness Road 110
guncotton 23–24

Hagy, Hubert Ray 112, 135, 199
Hall, "Black Jack" 112
Hamilton, Norman 35
Hampton Institute 54, 56
Hampton Roads (Virginia): housing projects in 101–103, *102*; military base at 32; port area of 29, 32, 35, 99–100; racism in 156; soldier-civilian relations in 100–101; strategic importance of 31–33, 97–98; as transport hub 98–99; wartime ships launched from 37; welcome home festivities in 153
Haraden (ship) 37
Harding, Warren G. 129, 133, 173
Haskett, Walter L. 46
Hawkins, Pitt 176
Hays, Bessie 69
Hedskin, Charles A. 119
Henderson, E. H. 160
Henderson, John Jesse 111–112
Herron, Charles D. 28
highway systems 8
Hill, Charles T. 38
Hill, J. Albert 196
Hilton Village project 101–103, *102*, 175–176
Hirschberg, John 159
Hoban, Katie Mercedes 69
Hofstra, Warren 201
holidays *see* specific holidays
Holladay, Aphelia "Affie" Yerby 121–122, 124
Holladay, Mary Caroline *123*
Holladay, Percy 49, 122–124, *123*
Holladay, Phillip 122–124
Holliday, Henry L. 135–136
Holloman, Herbert R. 106
Hollywood Cemetery 88, 150, 195
Home Beautiful movement 27
homecoming celebrations 105, 153, 155–157, 184–185, 188
Hoover, Herbert 11, 76, 165, 167
Hopewell guncotton plant 23–24, *25*, 107
Hopkins, Albert L. 37–38
horses: agricultural uses for 6; breeding 6, 20; burial grounds for 21; diseases of 21; poisoning plot 22–23; remount depots for 17–23; taxonomic family of 216*n*41; transport of 18, *19*, 21–22, 98–99
hot-bedding 101
housing projects 101–103, *102*, 175–176

Index

Howitzers' Association 66, 112, 150, 190
Hubbard, Henry V. 102
Hudson, Lawrence 169
Hudson, McKnight Tingle 46
Hughes, Robert 112
Hunt, Dave 173
Hunter, Sarah Ethel 69
Huntington, Collis P. 31–32, 103
Huntington Ingalls Industries 100

immigrants 69–71, 104–108
"In Flanders Field" (McCrae) 125, 131
Independence Day *see* Fourth of July
Indian Citizenship Act of 1924 70
influenza epidemic (1918) 59–61, 115–120, *117*
injured soldiers 157–159, *158*
integration of armed forces 54
Isdell, George Grover Cleveland 44, 45, 218n25

Jackson, Giles B. 54–55
Jackson, Thomas "Stonewall" 89, 211
Jad and Old Ananias (Howard-Douglas) 206
Jaffe, Mohammed 71
Jamerson, George Hairston 197
Janney, Asa, and Werner 8
Jefferson, Thomas 170, 171
Jewish Girls' Service Club 75
Jewish Welfare Board 180, 192
Jim Crow policies 100, 103, 157, 175
jitney buses 101
Joannes, Francis Y. 102
jobs *see* employment
Johnson, Solomon 202
Jones, Anna Lewis 69
Jones, W. L. 27

Kearns, Hal 127–128
Kearsarge (ship) 32
Keck, Charles 142, *212*
Keneally, Thomas 209
Kentucky (ship) 32
Khaki Clubs 66
Kiefer, Anna *212*
kit homes 26–27
Knights of Columbus 119, 122, 164, 180
knitting 17, 53, 65, 73, 190
Kronprinz Wilhelm (ship) 35–36, *36*
Ku Klux Klan (KKK) 173, 174

labor battalions 49–50, 55, 127, 156
Lafayette Escadrille 30, 148
Lafayette Flying Corps 30
Lake, Robert L. 60–61
Langley Field 31
Laycock, Fanny E. 69

Lee, L. Valentine 79
Lee, Robert E. 18, 65, 92
Lewis, Frank Nelson 134
Liberty (Keck) 142, *212*, 213
liberty bonds 73–74, 78, 221n153
The Listening Post (Keck) *151*
litter bearers 47
living memorials 140–141
Lost Cause of Confederacy 44, 194
Loudoun County War memorial 8, 60
Lusitania sinking (1915) 37–38, 40
lynchings 55, 156, 173–174
Lyon, John 135

MacArthur, Douglas 167
Machin, David 144
Magee, W. H. 163
mail, censorship of 122–123
mallein test 23
Mapp Prohibition Act of 1916 168
Marne, Second Battle of the (1918) 46
mass graves 106, 125–128
USS *Maui* (ship) 34–35
May, Henry 194
McAuliffe, Terry 200
McCleave, Robert P. 125
McConnell, James Rogers 29, 30, 84, *85*, 148–149
McCrae, John 125, 131
McFadden, Anna Elizabeth 59
McGuire, Hunter 89, 90
McGuire, Stuart 59, 89–91, 191, 193–194, 196
mechanization of agriculture 6
Medical College of Virginia (MCV) 59, 89–91
medical personnel 57–59, 89, 158–160
Memorial Day 149–150, 176, 192–195, *193*
memorials *see* war memorials
Meuse Argonne American Cemetery 130, *131*
Meuse Argonne offensive (1918): chaplains in 80; deaths during 119, 127, 132, 135; labor battalions in 49; litter bearers in 47; participants of 45, 46, 87, 124, 125, 197
Michaux, Kathleen Virginia Venable 68
military *see* Army, U.S.; Navy, U.S
military chaplains 78–81, *81*, 127–128
military training: for African Americans 54–55; in aviation 30–31; at Camp Lee 49, 60, 71, 75, 95; for chaplains 79–80; at colleges and universities 50–55, *51*
Minenwerfer (mine thrower) 202–203, *203*
Mitchell, Rossel Edward 176
Mitchell, William 30

moonshine 168, 169
Moore, Charles 129
Munford, Mary Cooke Branch 76
munitions *see* weaponry
music and musicians 47–49, **48**

USS *Nashville* (ship) 33
National Association for the Advancement of Colored People (NAACP) 208
National Commission of Fine Arts 129, 137, 146, 147
National Emergency Food Garden Commission 11
National Guard 41, 47, 84; *see also* Virginia National Guard
National Home for Disabled Volunteer Soldiers 136, 165
National League for Woman's Service 63
National War Garden Commission 9, **10**, 11
National Woman's Trade League 63
nationalism 141, 184
Native Americans, military service of 70
Naval Station Norfolk 31, 36, 200
Navy, U.S.: preparation for war by 39; role during World War I 32–33; seizure of ships by 35–36; women in 68, 146; *see also* ships
Nelson, Clifton A. 202
Nelson, Ronald 202
Newport News Shipyard and Dry Dock Construction Company 33, 37
Newport News Victory Arch 154–156, ***154***
Nichols, E. W. 5
Nichols, Edward M. 52
Nichols, J. V. 6
Nineteenth Amendment 170, 171, 173, 185
Nobel, Alfred 24
Noland, Charlotte Haxall 63
Noland, Rosalie 63
Norfolk State University (NSU) 201
nurses 57–59, 89

Obama, Barack 198
Obici, Amedeo 104
observation balloons 31
Occoquan Workhouse 172–173
Ogden, Graham 153
Old Dominion Land Company 32, 102, 103, 176
Overmountain Men 110

parachutes 31
participants of World War I 39–81; chaplains 78–81, ***81***, 127–128; children 11, 14, 71–75, **72**; Council of Defense 75–77; draftees 39, 41–43; homecoming celebrations for 105, 153, 155–157, 184–185, 188; immigrants 69–71; medical personnel 57–59, 89; musicians 47–49; Native Americans 70; overseas troops 44–50; Red Cross 53–54, 64–66; State Guard 77–78; students 50–55, 61; *see also* African Americans; soldiers; veterans; women
Passamaneck, Isadore 77
Patterson, Juanita Massie 61
Patterson, Malvern C. 63
Patton, George S., Jr. 167
peanut production 104
Peck, Myron, and Mary 134
Penniman, Russell Sylvanus 24
Penniman explosives plant 24–28, ***25***, 67
pensions 165
Pershing, John J. 20, 21, 45, 129, 198
Peters, J. Sidney 168
Petersburg, siege of (1864) 94
physicians *see* medical personnel
pilots 29–31
Pinterest 205
pioneer infantry regiments 49, 127
Planters Nut and Chocolate Company 104
pneumonia 35, 60, 89, 116, 119, 124
Pollia, Joseph P. 105
post-traumatic stress disorder 160
Powell, Jane Lee 171
USS *Powhatan* (ship) 155
Preston, Francis 109
Price, Lawrence T. 120
Princip, Gavrilo 1
Prinz Eitel (ship) 35
Prohibition 168–170
propaganda posters: anti-suffrage 171; army enlistment **42**; canning 7; Flag Day 187, ***187***; food conservation 12–14, ***13***; food production 9; from religious associations 80; victory gardens 9, **10**; Women's Land Army ***62***; *see also* advertisements
provisions for war 5–38; airplanes 29–31; conservation efforts 7, 12–14, ***13***; food production 5–7, **7**, 9; from railside canteens ***15***, 15–17; rationing 8–9, 11–12; remount depots 17–23; from victory gardens 9–12, **10**, 14; weaponry 23–28; *see also* ships
public education campaigns 119
Public Health Service, U.S. 120, 158
Pullman, George 103
Puritan (ship) 32

Queisser, Robert L. 122

Index

race riots 175
racism 55, 56, 156, 173; *see also* African Americans; segregation
Ragland, Eugene W. 49–50, 127, 225–226*n*45
railroads: horse transport by 18, *19*, 21, 98–99; in Richmond 94; transcontinental 32; wartime materials transported by 86
railside canteens *15*, 15–17
Randolph-Macon Woman's College 61–62
rationing of food 8–9, 11–12
recipes 14
Red Cross: in American Legion celebrations 164; in Armistice Day celebrations 180, 182; establishment of 53; foreign battalions hosted by 97; functions of 53–54, 65–66; fund-raising for 53, 54, 66; gas masks made by 220*n*97; Home Service Section of 158; influenza epidemic 120; railside canteens sponsored by 16; supply drives by 83; wartime communication funded by 124; in welcome home celebrations 184
Red Summer 174
religious associations 80
remount depots 17–23
repatriation of deceased soldiers 126, *126*, 128–129, 132–134
Reserve Officers' Training Corps (ROTC) 54, 111
resources *see* provisions for war
Revolutionary War (1775–1783) 107, 110, 185, 186
Richmond (Virginia): balloon supply depot in 31; base hospitals in 89–90, *91*; as Confederate capital 27; draft agencies in 41; Hollywood Cemetery in 88–89; immigrants in 70; influenza epidemic in 119–120; Memorial Day celebrations in 192–195; racism in 156; railway hubs in 94; Thrift Day Parade held in 75; war memorials in 87–93, *91–93*, 137–139, *138*
Richmond, Stephanie 201
Richmond Times-Dispatch (newspaper): on American flag 44, 187–188; on Armistice Day celebrations 181; on Camp Lee conversion 94; on children's wartime efforts 71; on draft quotas 41–42; on Ferdinand assassination 1; on food restrictions 14; on Hampton Roads 97–98; on *Lusitania* victims 38; on Memorial Day celebrations 149; Roll of Honor in 124; on student participation in war efforts 50; on Thanksgiving Day celebrations 188; on Virginia

Council of Defense 75; on war-relief funds 87; on women's suffrage 170, 171; on women's wartime efforts 66, 67
Richthofen, Manfred Albrecht Freiherr von 29
riots, race 175
Riticor, Charles 46
road systems 8, 185
Roanoke Memorial Bridge 211–212
Robertson, John Dill 119
Robertson, Ruth 59, 89, 196
Robinson, Frank 112–113
Rockwell, Kiffin Yates 29–30
Roosevelt, Franklin 182
Roosevelt, Theodore 33–34
ROTC (Reserve Officers' Training Corps) 54, 111
Ruebush, William Howe 47–49

Saint-Mihiel, Battle of (1918) 45, 46, 80, 197
St. Paul's Episcopal Church 92–93, *93*
Sale, Anne E. 7
Salvation Army 53, 164, 182
SATC *see* Student Army Training Corps
Schindler's Ark (Keneally) 209
Schönbein, Christian F. 23
schools *see* colleges and universities; students
Schultz, Charles 29
Schultz, Gene 201–202
Scouting for Boys (Baden-Powell) 72
Sears & Roebuck 26, 27
segregation: of armed forces 55, 57, 100, 206–207; of homecoming celebrations 156–157, 188; in housing 103, 175–176; Jim Crow policies 100, 103, 157, 175; in war memorials 105, 144, 207–208; *see also* African Americans
Selective Service Act of 1917 41, 70, 95
Selfridge, Thomas 29
Seneca Falls convention (1848) 170
Serene, James H. 86
Sgt. Stubby: An American Hero (film) 209
Sergeant York (film) 209
Shackelford, Raymond 169
Shelka, Ramchandra 70–71
shell shock 117, 159–161
Shenandoah Valley (Virginia): landscape of 47; remount depot in 19–20; vestiges of World War I in 106–108
Shepherd, John 170
Sherman, William Tecumseh 76–77, 161
ships 31–38; camouflage for 68; daily life on 34–35; dreadnoughts 33; dry docks for 32, 33; *Lusitania* sinking (1915) 37–38, 40; naming conventions for 33; neutrality laws for 35; seizure of 34–36;

soldiers transported by 45; submarines 34, 37–38, 40, 68, 99, 107; *see also* specific ships
Sinking Spring Cemetery 112–113
Smith, John 104
Smith, Sarah Haines 170
Smith-Lever Act of 1914 6
Smith-Sears Vocational Education Bill of 1918 163
Snyder, Russell 135, **136**
soapstone production 86
social media 205, 232*n*118
Social Security 168
soldiers: civilian relations with 100–101; cult of the fallen soldier 144, 150; decommissioning of 152–153; draftees 39, 41–43; homecoming celebrations for 105, 153, 155–157, 184–185, 188; identification tags for 128; overseas troops 44–50; repatriation of remains 126, **126**, 128–129, 132–134; shell shock experienced by 117, 159–161; transportation for 45; wounded 157–159, **158**; *see also* veterans
SOLs (Standards of Learning) 205–206, 211
"Somewhere in France Is My Daddy" (song) 47, **48**
Somme offensive (1918) 197
Spanish American War (1898) 18, 33, 77, 79, 181
Spanish Flu *see* influenza epidemic
speakeasies 169
The Spirit of the American Doughboy (Viquesney) 97, **98**
Standards of Learning (SOLs) 205–206, 211
Staples, Samuel H. 160–161
State Guard 77–78
Steinmetz, Francis, and Mary 145
Stern, Joseph Lane 169
Stoner, Elizabeth R. 157
strikes 163–164
Stuart, Elizabeth Litchfield 110–111
Student Army Training Corps (SATC) **51**, 51–52, 54, 111, 119
students: centennial celebration participation by 205–206; in draft 50; fundraising by 50, 53; military training for 50–55, **51**; Standards of Learning for 205–206, 211; war memorials for 146; women as 53, 61; *see also* colleges and universities
Stump, Joseph 130–131
submarines 34, 37–38, 40, 68, 99, 107
Suffolk (Virginia), vestiges of World War I in 103–106
suffrage for women 170–173, 185

supplies *see* provisions for war
symbolism on war memorials 141, 146

Take a Soldier Home program 101
Tapscott, Hunter Hilton 87, 223*n*10
telegrams 124
temperance movement 168–170
Thanksgiving Day 188–190
Thomas (ship) 37
Thompson, George Parker 144–145
Thompson, Willie 206
Thornton, Margaret 117–118
Thrift, Lula May McDonough 68
Thrift Day Parade 75
Thurston, Sandy 56
thyroid disease 120
USS *Ticonderoga* (ship) 34
TNT poisoning 67
tobacco production 23
Tomb of the Unknown Soldier 132–133, **133**, 183
total war concept 3, 77
training *see* military training
trains *see* railroads
transcontinental railroad 32
transportation: of food 8; for horses 18, **19**, 21–22, 98–99; roads and highways 8, 185; for soldiers 45; *see also* railroads; ships
Treaty of Versailles (1919) 177, 205
trench warfare 18, 45, 94, 96
Truxtun, Thomas 176

U-boats *see* submarines
"Under Many Flags" (cartoon) **174**
Underground Railroad 104
United Daughters of the Confederacy (UDC) 66, 195
United States: census statistics 34, 69–70, 101, 116, 221*n*136; entrance into World War I 2, 9, 32, 40–41; influenza epidemic in 59–61, 115–120, **117**; neutrality policy of 2, 35
United States School Garden Army 11
universities *see* colleges and universities
University of Richmond 53, 201
University of Virginia (UVA): farmerette training at 63; Memorial Gymnasium at 84, 140; military training at **51**, 51–52; war memorials erected by 84, **85**, 148; Women's Land Army training at **62**, 68

Vance, Jonathan L. 198
venereal diseases 59, 121
Versailles, Treaty of (1919) 177, 205
vestiges of World War I 82–114; in Abingdon 109–114; in Albemarle County 86–87; at Camp Lee 94–96; in

Index

Charlottesville 83–85, **85**; documentation efforts 82–83; in Hampton Roads 97–103; in Petersburg 96–97, **98**; in Richmond 87–94, **91–93**; in Shenandoah Valley 106–108; in Suffolk and Great Dismal Swamp 103–106; *see also* commemorations; war memorials
veterans: American Legion for 164–167; bonuses for 166–168; disabled 158, 164, 165; employment for 104, 162–163; pensions for 165; reunions for 196–197; war questionnaire given to 46, 56, 82, 161–162; *see also* commemorations; war memorials
Veterans Administration 165
Veterans Day 177–179, 183
Veterans of Foreign Wars (VFW) 147, 165–167
victory bread 11–12
victory gardens 9–12, **10**, 14
Viets, Henry 159
Viquesney, Ernest Moore 97, **98**
Virginia: agricultural production in 5–6, 8; aviation training stations in 30–31; casualties of war from 115–117; draft quotas in 41–43; homecoming celebrations in 105, 153, 155–157, 184–185, 188; immigrant populations in 69–70, 104–108; influenza epidemic in 60–61, 116–120, **117**; mobilization efforts in 2, 3; Prohibition in 168–170; regional distribution of sites and communities **109**; road systems in 8; soapstone production in 86; Standards of Learning in 205–206, 211; troop contributions by 116, 225n4; women's suffrage movement in 171–173; *see also* commemorations; participants of World War I; provisions for war; specific locations; vestiges of World War I
USS *Virginia* (ship) 33–34, 153
Virginia Commonwealth University 90, 91, 200
Virginia Council of Defense 11, 14, 52, 76–78
Virginia Defense Force 78
Virginia International Tattoo 200
Virginia League of Women Voters 173
Virginia Military Institute (VMI) 29, 50, 52
Virginia National Guard: in Armistice Day celebrations 164; assistance forces to 78; centennial celebrations by 202–203; at dedication events 139; mobilization efforts 41–42; Richmond Light Infantry Blues unit 39; wartime replacement of 77
Virginia Union University 54

Virginia War History Commission: casualties documented by 115–116; questionnaires from 46, 161; volumes published by 82–83, 208, 210; on women's wartime efforts 66
Virginia World War Memorial Carillon 87–88, **138**, 139, 200
Virginia's Military Dead database 116, 219n70
VMI (Virginia Military Institute) 29, 50, 52
Vocational Rehabilitation Act of 1918 163
Vogt, George 107
voting rights for women 170–173, 185

Walters, Edward B. 106
war bonds 17, 73–74, 78, 221n153
War Camp Community Service 180
war colleges 51
war gardens *see* victory gardens
war memorials 139–149; in Abingdon 113; African Americans in 143–144; in Albemarle County 86; to all-black units 55; in Charlottesville 83–85, **85**; dedication of 137–139; design and construction of 140–141, 146–149; interpretation of 139–146; living memorials 140–141; in Loudoun County 8, 60; objectives of 150; in Petersburg 97, **98**; prevalence of 3; in Richmond 87–93, **91–93**, 137–139, **138**; segregation in 105, 144, 207–208; for students 146; in Suffolk 105; symbolism on 141, 146; in Washington, D.C. 198; women in 141–143, **143**, 146; word choice in 144–145, 150; *see also* commemorations
war-relief funds 87
War Risk Insurance Bureau 158, 165
war savings stamps 17, 73–75, 78
Warrior (ship) 99
wartime provisions *see* provisions for war
Washington, Booker T. 55
Washington, George 104
Washington, Martha 109
Washington and Lee University 18, 29–30, 39, 52
WCTU (Women's Christian Temperance Union) 162, 168–170, 184–185
weaponry 23–28; artillery shells 26, 27, 67; cannons 28; dynamite 24–26; guncotton 23–24; mine throwers 202–203, **203**
Webster, George Washington 49
welcome home festivities *see* homecoming celebrations
West, Bernice Ruth 113
Wheatley, Eugene 29

White, Oliver M. 35
Whitesell, William E. 47
Whitmore, Floyd H. 124
Whittaker, W. H. 173
Williams, Charles Holston 56
Williams, Harry Clay 111
Williams, Lloyd W. 45–46
Williams, Timothy P. 200
USS *Wilmington* (ship) 33
Wilson, Edith 113–114, 206, ***207***
Wilson, Woodrow: alcohol ban supported by 168, 169; on Armistice Day 177; Flag Day created by 141, 186; on gardening efforts 11; on immigrants 69, 71; seizure of ships authorized by 35; Thanksgiving Day address by 189; on U.S. entrance into World War I 2, 9, 40–41; on women's suffrage 171, 173
Withers, Arthur Speece 113
women: African American 76; in agriculture 61–63; in Armistice Day celebrations 180, 182; canning by 7, *7*, 54, 62; and Cult of Domesticity 67; employment for 26, 67–69, 162; as farmerettes 17, 61–63, ***212***, 213; flags provided by 187–188; food conservation efforts by 7, 14, 76; fund-raising by 50, 53, 66; gardening by 11; Gold Star Mothers 122; knitting by 17, 53, 65, 73, 190; in medical field 58–59; as physiotherapy aides 158; in prohibition 168–170; at railside canteens *15*, 15–16; as students 53, 61; voting rights for 170–173, 185; in war memorials 141–143, *143*, 146; workhouses for 172–173
Women's Christian Temperance Union (WCTU) 162, 168–170, 184–185

Women's Land Army 61–64, ***62***, ***64***, 68
Women's Patriotic League 97
women's suffrage movement 170–173, 185
Wonder Woman (film) 209
Woodbury, Charles H. 124
Woodson, James Lewis 86–87
workhouses 172–173
Works Progress Administration 168
World War I (1914–1918): airborne combat during 29–31; beginnings of 1–2; casualties of 55, 90, 115–117, 219*n*70; communication during 121–124; conscientious objectors to 52, 64; domestic support for 9; espionage during 23; in film and television 209; societal changes during 168; U.S. entrance into 2, 9, 32, 40–41; *see also* burials; commemorations; participants of World War I; provisions for war; specific battles; vestiges of World War I
World War II (1939–1945) 11, 69, 78, 176, 183
wounded soldiers 157–159, ***158***
Wray, Desmond 74
Wright, Arthur D. 54
Wright, Orville 29

York, Alvin 183
Young Men's Christian Association (YMCA) 26, 50, 119, 122, 164, 181–182
Young Women's Christian Association (YWCA) 26, 50, 111, 120, 164, 182
Younger, Edward F. 132

zeppelins 31
Zimmerman telegram 40

www.ingramcontent.com/pod-product-compliance
Lightning Source LLC
Chambersburg PA
CBHW051216300426
44116CB00006B/597